CW01373182

# NY AT ITS CORE

# NY AT ITS CORE

## 400 Years of New York City History

Based on the award-winning exhibition at the **Museum of the City of New York**

**MUSEUM OF THE CITY OF NEW YORK**

This volume is published as a companion to the exhibition *New York at Its Core* organized by and presented at the Museum of the City of New York beginning on November 18, 2016.

First published in the United States of America in 2017 by

Museum of the City of New York
1220 Fifth Avenue
New York, NY 10029
www.mcny.org

Ronay Menschel Director and President: Whitney W. Donhauser
Chief Curator: Sarah M. Henry
Contributing Curators: Steven H. Jaffe and Lilly Tuttle
Curator, *Future City Lab*: Hilary Ballon
Project Director, *Future City Lab*: Kubi Ackerman
Director of Publications: Susan Gail Johnson

Book Design and Typography:
Michael Bierut, Katie Rominger, and Britt Cobb, Pentagram

© Museum of the City of New York

All rights reserved. No part of this publication may be reproduced, stored in a retrieval system, or transmitted in any form or by any means, electronic, mechanical, photocopying, recording, or otherwise, without prior consent of the publisher.

Cover Image:
New York City, 1932
Photograph by Samuel H. Gottscho
Museum of the City of New York, gift of Samuel H. Gottscho, 39.20.2

ISBN: 978-0-692-98202-0

# Table of Contents

| | | | | | |
|---|---|---|---|---|---|
| 7 | Chairman and Director's Note | 93 | **1898–1914** <br> The World's Port | 188 | Acknowledgments |
| 9 | Introducing *New York at Its Core* | | | 189 | Funders |
| | | | | 190 | Image credits |

13 **1609–1664**
Dutch Trading Colony

21 **1664–1775**
English Imperial Port

29 **1776–1827**
Rebirth

41 **1810–1865**
Confronting Density

51 **1830–1865**
The New Diversity

61 **1865–1898**
The Gilded Age

73 **1880–1898**
Ethnic New York

83 **1880–1898**
Making Greater New York

93 **1898–1914**
The World's Port

105 **1914–1929**
New York Roars into
The Twenties

115 **1929–1941**
New York's New Deal

125 **1941–1960**
Capital of the World

137 **1960–1970**
What Is the City For?

147 **1970–1980**
On the Brink

159 **1980–2001**
New York Comes Back

173 **2001–2012**
Debating the City

181 **Into the Future**

188 Acknowledgments
189 Funders
190 Image credits

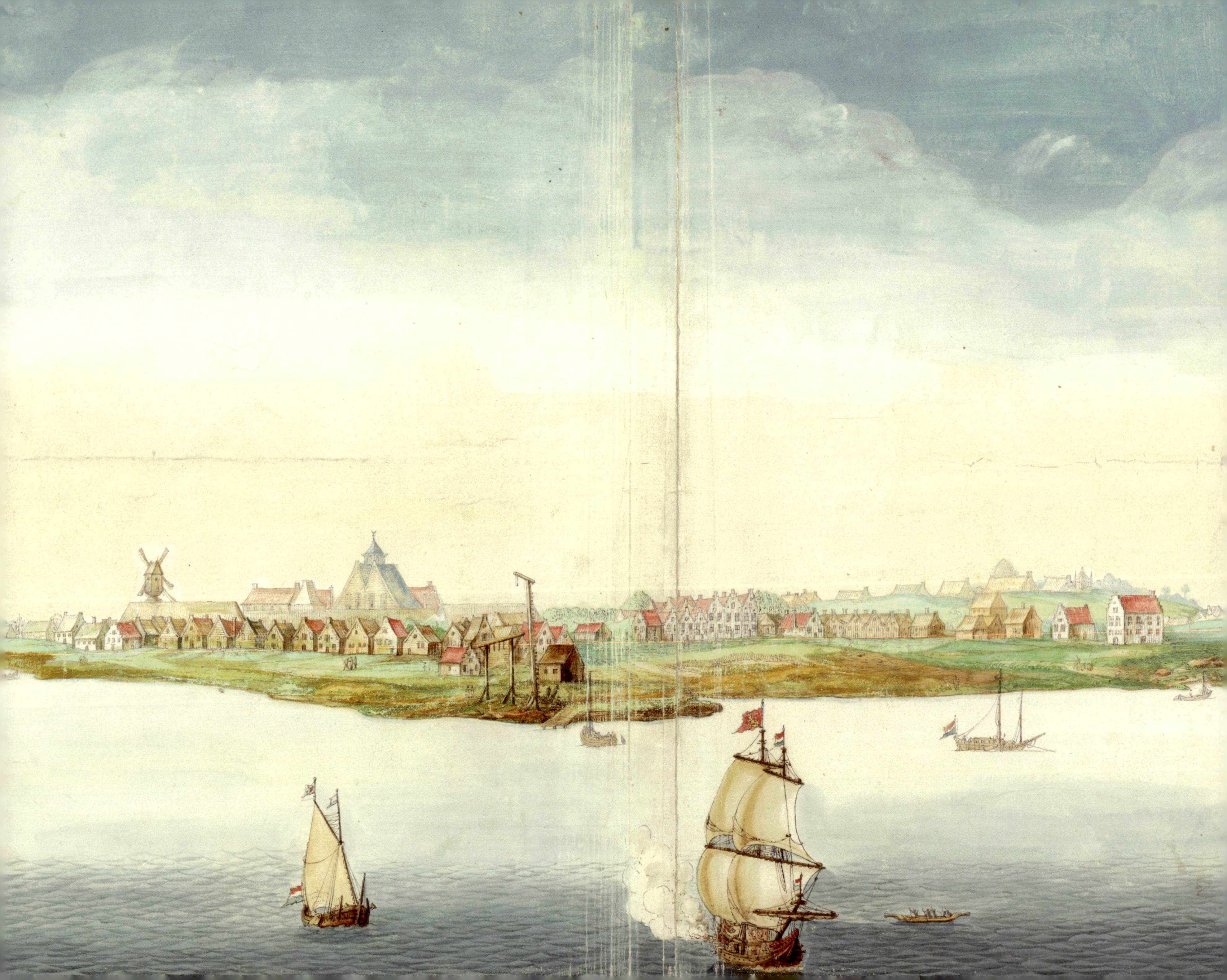

# Chairman and Director's Note

In November, 2016, the Museum of the City of New York unveiled the biggest and most important project in its history: the award-winning, three-gallery, cutting-edge exhibition called *New York at Its Core*. *New York at Its Core* gives this city what it has never had before: an exhibition about itself, a place where New Yorkers, visitors, schoolchildren of all ages—indeed anyone who loves and is fascinated by this complex, challenging, and altogether extraordinary city—can come to discover its past, investigate its present, and help imagine its future.

*New York at Its Core* probes the qualities that define New York through two historical galleries that highlight rare artifacts drawn from the Museum's own collection and beyond in dialogue with innovative uses of technology to provide depth, context, and a profoundly moving experience. The exhibition also features a first-of-its-kind gallery entirely dedicated to where New York is now and where it may be headed in the future: the hands-on *Future City Lab*. This book gives you a sampling of some of the riches that *New York at Its Core* deploys to weave a rich story about the character of New York City.

We are deeply thankful for the generous funders who made this enormous and important effort possible—foundations, individuals, corporations, and government agencies. You can find all of them listed on page 189, but we are particularly grateful to our lead sponsors: James Dinan and Elizabeth Miller, Pierre DeMenasce, The Thompson Family Foundation, the Jerome L. Greene Foundation in honor of Susan Henshaw Jones, Heather and Bill Vrattos, the Charina Endowment Fund, the National Endowment for the Humanities, Citi, Zegar Family Foundation, Tracey A. and Kenneth A. Pontarelli, Hilary Ballon and Orin Kramer, Jill and John Chalsty, Dyson Foundation, The Robert A. and Elizabeth R. Jeffe Foundation, Valerie and Jack Rowe, and Mary Ann and Bruno A. Quinson. We also have a host of associated educational programs that enlighten tens of thousands of schoolchildren and teachers, made possible by The Thompson Family Foundation Fund and Institute of Museum and Library Services.

*New York at Its Core*, five years in the making, was launched under the visionary leadership of Susan Henshaw Jones, the former Ronay Menschel Director of the Museum. The creation of this unprecedented exhibition was the product of many hands: in addition to Susan's, they included those of our Deputy Director and Chief Curator Sarah M. Henry, with colleagues Kubi Ackerman, Steven H. Jaffe, Susan Gail Johnson, Lilly Tuttle, and the late Hilary Ballon, whose untimely passing in the spring of 2017 left this museum and this city mourning one of its greatest interpreters. They were assisted by literally hundreds of others, including scholarly advisors whose names you will find listed at the back of the book. And the beautiful exhibition design by Studio Joseph, experience design by Local Projects, and graphic design by Pentagram, made it all come to life.

The volume you hold in your hands enables you to explore the city's history through some of the rotating cast of more than 400 historic objects and images that make up the exhibition, but it can only begin to convey the content and excitement of the exhibition. In our galleries you can be brought through the dramatic sweep of New York's 400+ year history in the film *Timescapes*, watch the city's history unfold in animated maps, "meet" New Yorkers from the past—famous and infamous, known and undiscovered, human and animal—through dozens of interactive stories, lose yourself in immersive historic images and footage, and try your hand at creating a new city and digitally enter it in the *Future City Lab*. Add to this public programs, lectures, tours, concerts, and learning opportunities for all ages, and we know that you will be enlightened about all of the factors that make New York New York!

**James Dinan**
Chairman

**Whitney Donhauser**
Ronay Menschel Director and President

OPPOSITE
**View of New Amsterdam (*Nieuw Amsterdam ofte Nue New Iorx opt't. Eylant Man*)** 1665
Watercolor by Johannes Vingboons

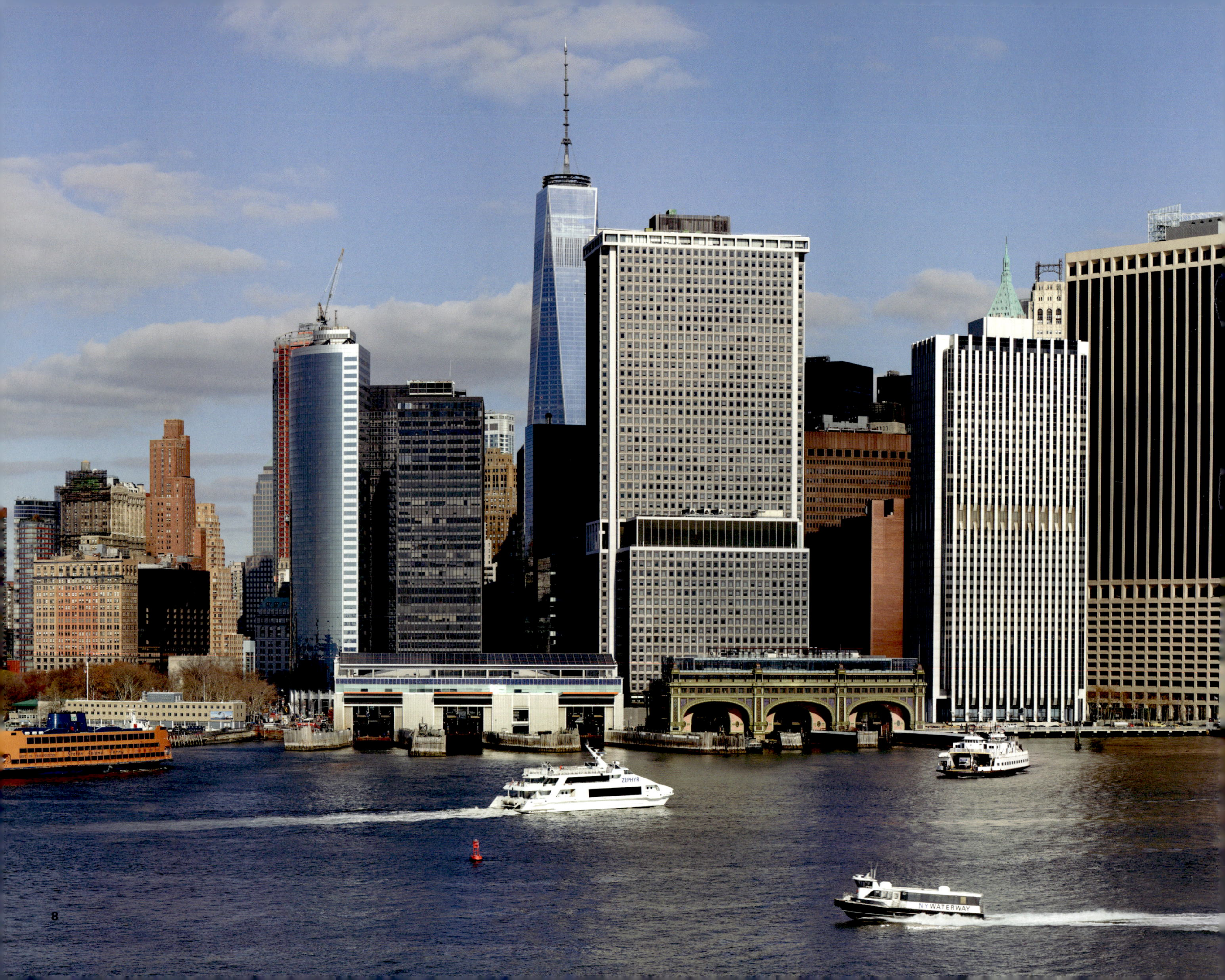
ZEPHYR
NY WATERWAY

# Introducing *New York at Its Core*

What makes New York New York? *New York at Its Core* argues that the city's identity has been shaped by four defining themes: money, diversity, density, and creativity. Indeed, these four words embody a dynamic that runs through New York's history from the founding of the Dutch settlement into the 21st century. Together, they reflect the struggles and triumphs of the city's residents and the potent blend of people, ambition, and place that give rise to the ineffable creative energy of this astonishing metropolis.

This book—like the exhibition it accompanies at the Museum of the City of New York—invites you to explore how these elements changed and interacted as they influenced life in the city over its 400-year history. It tells the story of how New York City evolved from a small outpost for trade between the Native people and the Dutch into the largest, most densely populated, most diverse, and most influential city in the United States.

Money shaped that dynamic from the beginning. Indeed, the saga began in a search for profit, when the Dutch created New Amsterdam as an anchor for their international fur trade. Location was key: they chose the best natural deep-water harbor on the Atlantic coast for their trading enterprise, and the town soon grew into a thriving seaport that the English renamed "New-York." Over the centuries that followed, the port remained the heart of the economic life of the region, an area that encompassed the cities of New York and Brooklyn and adjoining communities in the Bronx, Queens, and Staten Island. But it was human ambition, conflict, and ingenuity that transformed this promising location into a great, growing, and perpetually changing metropolis.

In the 19th century, the merchant city mushroomed into America's economic and cultural capital, attracting people, money, and ideas from all over the globe. But New York was also full of contradictions—freedom and slavery, opportunity and struggle, openness and exclusion were all woven into the fabric of the city. By the 1890s, when New York was well on its way to becoming the world's second largest metropolis after London, visitor Paul Bourget wrote that the city "is so colossal, it encloses so formidable an accumulation of human efforts, as to surpass the bounds of imagination."

As the 20th century opened, New York was a five-borough city with almost three and a half million people, a modern metropolis poised to challenge the supremacy of the great European capitals. It was a whirlwind of ambitious enterprise, daring entertainment, new political ideas, and unprecedented immigration and urban crowding. New York was, in the words of essayist Hamilton Wright Mabie, "a city of a new type" whose "very diversities are creating here a kind of city which men have not seen before." And indeed, over the decades that followed, the pace of change was staggering. Skyscrapers rose, subways snaked beneath and above the city's streets, and old neighborhoods fell to make way for modern developments. Factories proliferated and then moved away in droves, leaving the city challenged to remake itself for a postindustrial, suburbanizing age. In less than a century, New York changed from a city principally of European immigrants and their descendants into a multiracial, multicultural city whose residents reflected the world.

Yet the 20th century was also a roller-coaster ride: a series of daunting crises that led to periods of remarkable reinvention. Moments of systemic challenges—notably the Great Depression of the 1930s and the urban and fiscal crises of the 1960s and '70s—caused some to wonder whether the city itself could survive. The story of how it did survive, and repeatedly reshaped its own fate, continued to unfold in the early 21st century, when New York was tested by both terrorism and climate change. These are the stories told in the pages that follow, brought to life by some of the objects, images, and people from the galleries of *New York at Its Core*.

OPPOSITE
*Manhattan* 2015
Photograph by Jeff Chien-Hsing Liao

# What makes New York New York?

New York has always been a **money** town—a fierce marketplace and global financial engine. A place of both great opportunity and inequality, the city has also pioneered reforms to temper the hardships created by its competitive economy.

The power of New York's economy has drawn people from around the world. The resulting **diversity** has caused social conflict, but New York has also been a model of cross-cultural interaction and tolerance.

**Density**, a defining feature of New York, is both an asset and a challenge. The concentration of people fuels commerce and culture, while the stresses of the crowded city have spurred innovations to make New York more livable.

New York's potent blend of money, diversity, and density has sparked creativity across all spheres of life. **Creativity** drives New York's relentless change and energy, attracting yet more money, diversity, and density, and continually redefining the urban condition.

REDRAFT of THE CASTELLO PLAN NEW AMSTERDAM in 1660

JOHN WOLCOTT ADAMS
I.N. PHELPS STOKES
1916

# 1609–1664

## Dutch Trading Colony

The town that became New York City was born as a commercial enterprise. In 1609 explorer Henry Hudson sailed into New York Bay and found the homeland of the Lenape. Hudson was seeking a route to the spice markets of Asia, but recognizing the natural resources of the area, a land rich with furs, fish, and plants, he immediately laid claim to the territory for his Dutch employers. In 1624 a new firm, the Dutch West India Company, sent European traders and settlers to cash in on the colony's potential. The new arrivals traded European goods to the local people—also known as the Munsee—for beaver pelts to ship back to Europe.

By 1628, 270 European colonists and enslaved Africans had built the town of New Amsterdam at the southern tip of Manhattan. It was the capital of New Netherland, which stretched as far north as today's Albany, with farms and villages scattered across today's Bronx, Brooklyn, upper Manhattan, Queens, Staten Island, and northern New Jersey. They also transformed its bay—one of the world's finest natural harbors—into a commercial seaport embedded in a global Dutch trading empire. By 1664 New Amsterdam was a settlement of 1,500 people who reportedly spoke at least 18 languages, making it one of the world's most diverse places.

OPPOSITE
**New Amsterdam in 1660** 1916
**John Wolcott Adams**

In 1916 John Wolcott Adams redrafted the original 1660 map of New Amsterdam (known as the Castello Plan) for I.N. Phelps Stokes's *Iconography of Manhattan Island*.

## 1609–1664
# Land of the Lenape

The Lenape of the 17th century lived where their predecessors had for at least 6,000 years before Hudson arrived. Their matrilineal society was based on hunting, fishing, and planting, and they moved seasonally among networks of local villages located along the region's many waterways. Although their farming and hunting were fairly localized, the Lenape were part of a vast trading network, acquiring goods like corn seed from the southwest and copper from the west.

The natural resources of the Hudson River estuary provided materials for daily life. The plentiful oysters and clams were not just food: their shells could be turned into tools and ornaments. Clay and stone were useful for making containers, and stone also provided materials for axe heads and arrowheads. The Lenape also left their mark on the landscape, setting careful fires to clear underbrush for planting and hunting grounds.

By the 1660s their presence in New Netherland had diminished dramatically as the population was decimated by disease, warfare, and migration. By 1700 only small groups remained in settlements scattered across the Bronx, Brooklyn, Queens, and Staten Island.

CLOCKWISE FROM TOP LEFT
**Ceremonial Native American wood and shell club collected by Johan Printz** early 1600s

This club depicts a man or spirit and was acquired by European settlers in the New Sweden colony in the Delaware Valley. It survives because it was shipped back to Sweden in the mid-17th century, possibly through the port of New Amsterdam.

***An American from Virginia** (Unus Americanus ex Virginia)* 1645
Etching by Wenceslaus Hollar

This illustration likely depicts Jacques, a Native warrior who was taken prisoner in New Netherland and displayed in Amsterdam in 1664.

**Grooved stone axe** no date

**Carved stone paint cups** no date

These small cups were used to hold pigments, perhaps for painting the face or body.

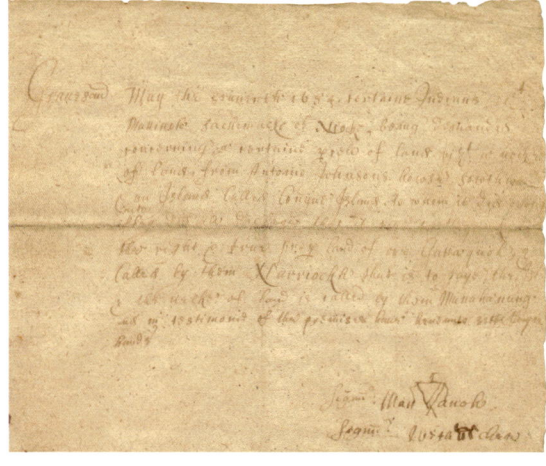

## 1609–1664

# Encounter

Henry Hudson and his crew had been at sea for five months when they came upon New York Bay in September 1609. Over several days they traded knives and beads for local tobacco offered by Native people who came aboard clothed in "good furs." But there was also bloodshed, leaving several Lenape and one European sailor dead.

Native inhabitants forged a complex relationship with settlers who followed. They traded furs; and colonists also secured territory from the Lenape—including the famous "purchase" of Manhattan Island in 1626. Although the Native people probably initially viewed such transactions as agreements to share land, as time went by they strategically used "sales" to improve their own security. The exchanges also brought them manufactured goods that helped them face the upheavals of disease and war.

The growing European population brought new struggles and shifting balances of power. In Kieft's War (1643–45) Dutch soldiers massacred Native people across the region and Native warriors burned European farms and killed settlers, including preacher Anne Hutchinson. By 1664 three more wars and European diseases had broken Lenape power and reduced the region's Native population from about 2,000 to a few hundred.

CLOCKWISE FROM TOP LEFT
**Model of *Half Moon* (*Halve Maen*)** c. 1929
By Joseph Wheeler Appleton

**The Purchase of Meadow & Upland (detail)**
May 7, 1654

**Native American-made wood comb in Dutch style** c. 17th century

As the Native people interacted and traded with the Dutch, they also adapted European goods and materials for their own uses, turning European brass kettles into arrowheads and tools and making their own versions of Dutch objects.

## 1609–1664

# Cultural Crossroads of Trade

The fur trade sparked other exchanges between the Dutch and Native peoples. One Norwegian immigrant, Sara Kierstede, capitalized on the freedom available to women in New Amsterdam and became an interpreter for Dutch Governor Petrus Stuyvesant in negotiations with the Lenape. By the 1650s an open-air market stood near her house and artifacts found there reveal the mix of cultures that came together in New Amsterdam.

Other colonists, lacking sufficient gold or silver coins, paid the Lenape to mass-produce beads (wampum) out of carved seashells. In the 17th century most wampum was carved out of local whelk or quahog shells, using stone, bone, and wooden tools, as well as points made from Dutch metal objects. Dutch (or later English) trade with the Caribbean also seems to have provided conch shells for making wampum. This practice transformed wampum, which had rich ceremonial meanings for the Lenape, into a local money supply for daily use by settlers in a colony where European currency was scarce.

CLOCKWISE FROM TOP LEFT
**Native American ceramic sherds**
14th–17th century

**Delft tile fragment** c. 17th century

**Cut conch shell** 17th century

**Boring tool** 17th century

**Chinese porcelain dish sherd** 17th century

**Gaming pieces made from a redware vessel**
c. 17th century

The Native American ceramic, Delft tile, and Chinese porcelain fragments and redware gaming pieces above were found in and around Sara Kierstede's home in lower Manhattan. The cut conch shell (found in lower Manhattan) and boring tool (found in Seapack, New Jersey) are evidence of wampum making operations.

LEFT
**Proposed Coat of Arms for New Amsterdam, New Netherland** c. 1630
Ink, wash, watercolor, chalk, and gouache on paper

## 1609–1664

# Religious Pluralism

Dutch Calvinism was the official religion of New Netherland, but the need for more settlers to people the colony reinforced the Dutch West India Company's policy of admitting other Europeans (with the exception of Catholics) who wanted to settle here. Although colonial governor Petrus Stuyvesant and the town's Calvinist clergymen wanted to exclude "heretics," the company directors in Amsterdam ordered them to "allow everyone to have his own belief, as long as he behaves quietly and legally."

In 1654 the Dutch West India Company allowed 23 Jewish refugees from Brazil to stay, over Governor Stuyvesant's objections, creating the beginnings of what would become the first Jewish community in North America. They joined a growing town that included slaves and semi-free Africans, Lutherans, and at least one settler known to be Muslim. Quakers, whose religion was considered a threat to civic order, managed to worship outside the town limits, and they eventually successfully petitioned for the right to stay.

**ABOVE**
**Deed by which Asser Levy purchased property from Jacob Young** 1667

Asser Levy, one of the first Jewish settlers in the colony, was also one of the town's first Jewish landowners.

**LEFT**
**Stained glass window from the First Dutch Reformed Church in Albany, New York** c. 1656
Made by Evert Duyckinck

# New Yorkers

## 1609–1664

*The Fort of New Amsterdam on Manhattan* (*T'Fort nieuw Amsterdam op de Manhatans*) (detail) 1651

*An American from Virginia* (*Unus Americanus ex Virginia*) (detail) 1645
Etching by Wenceslaus Hollar

### Penhawitz
(Early 17th century)
Sachem in a Time of Change

The sachem Penhawitz was leader of the Keschaechquereren in what is now Canarsie, Brooklyn. Lenape communities like Keschaechquereren participated in trade networks that spanned the northeast and beyond. As sachem, Penhawitz played an important role in trade and diplomacy—a role that would expand to include relations with Dutch and English colonists.

Keschaechquereren was one of the first Lenape communities on Long Island to disappear from Dutch records, probably as a result of violent conflicts like Kieft's War and diseases brought by Europeans. As a Canarsie Sachem said in 1643: "When you first came upon our coast, you sometimes had no food... We helped you with oysters and fish to eat, and now for a reward you have killed our people."

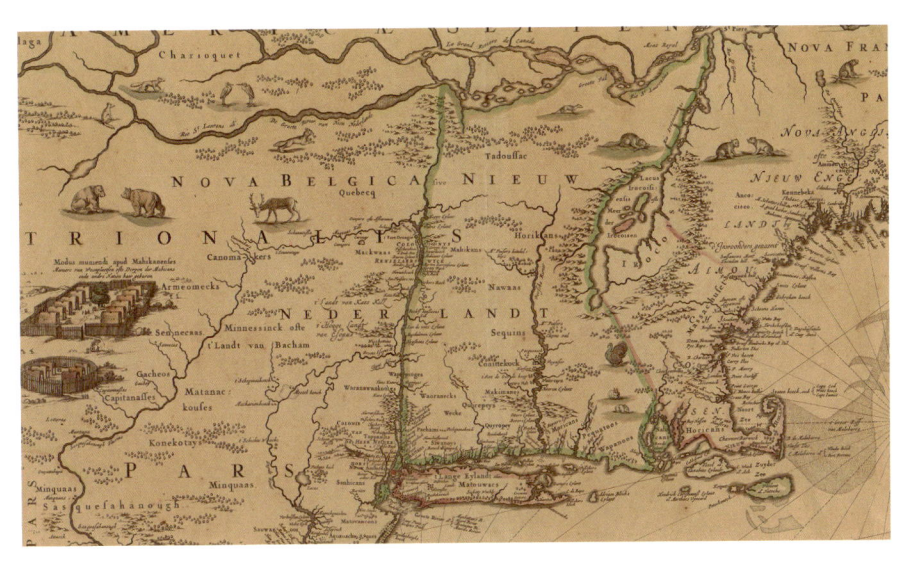

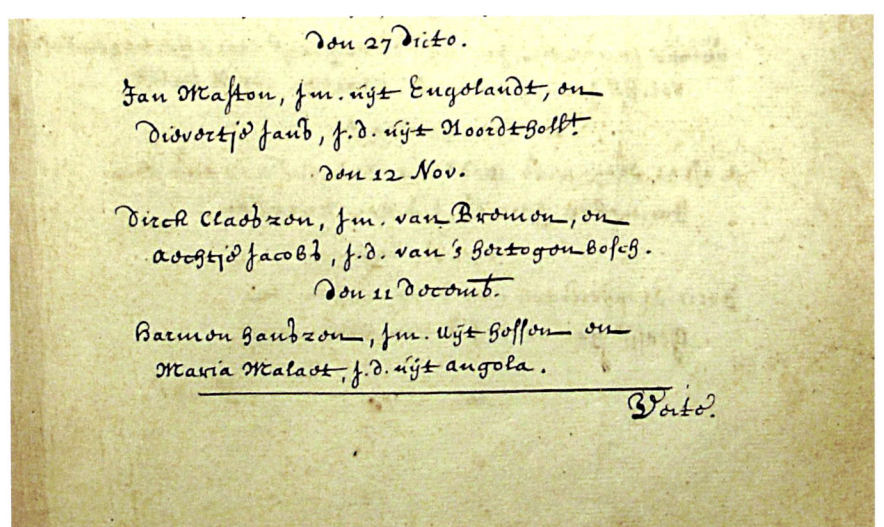

## Henry Hudson
### (c. 1565–1611)
### Exploring for Profit

Henry Hudson, an English captain sailing for the Dutch, was supposed to be seeking a passage to Asia by sailing northeast around Europe, but he made an unauthorized turn west. He and his crew aboard the 85-foot Dutch East India ship *Halve Maen* (*Half Moon*) reached the coast of North America in July of 1609.

Believing they had found their route, Hudson sailed up the river now named after him. Although he later realized the river was too narrow to lead to the Far East, he claimed the territory he found for the Dutch. The animal skins he brought back convinced Dutch merchants to set up a rudimentary trading outpost on Manhattan Island—New Amsterdam. The island was, in the words of Hudson's first mate Robert Juet, "a very good Land…and a pleasant land to see."

**Portrait of Henry Hudson**

ABOVE
**Eastern North America (detail)**
c. 1651–53
Published by Nicolaes Visscher

## Maria Van Angola
### (Mid-17th century)
### Free Black Colonist

Almost from the beginning, slavery was part of life in the settlement: by 1650, about a quarter of the people in New Amsterdam were slaves. But for some, there was a route out: the Dutch system enabled some slaves to own property, get married, and even petition for freedom.

Maria Van Angola was one of them. Records suggest that she and her husband Anthony were among those who received their freedom and a small plot of land north of the wall on today's Wall Street. Although the English imposed harsher rules after they took over in 1664, Maria and her children retained their freedom and made their way as free people in the colony of New-York.

**Portrait of a young black woman with lacy head cap and matching collar (detail)** 1645
Etching by Wenceslaus Hollar

ABOVE
**Liber A (Common Register of the Dutch Reformed Church in New York), recording an interracial marriage between Harman Hanzen, a German, and Maria Malaet from Angola in southwest Africa (detail)**
December 11, 1650

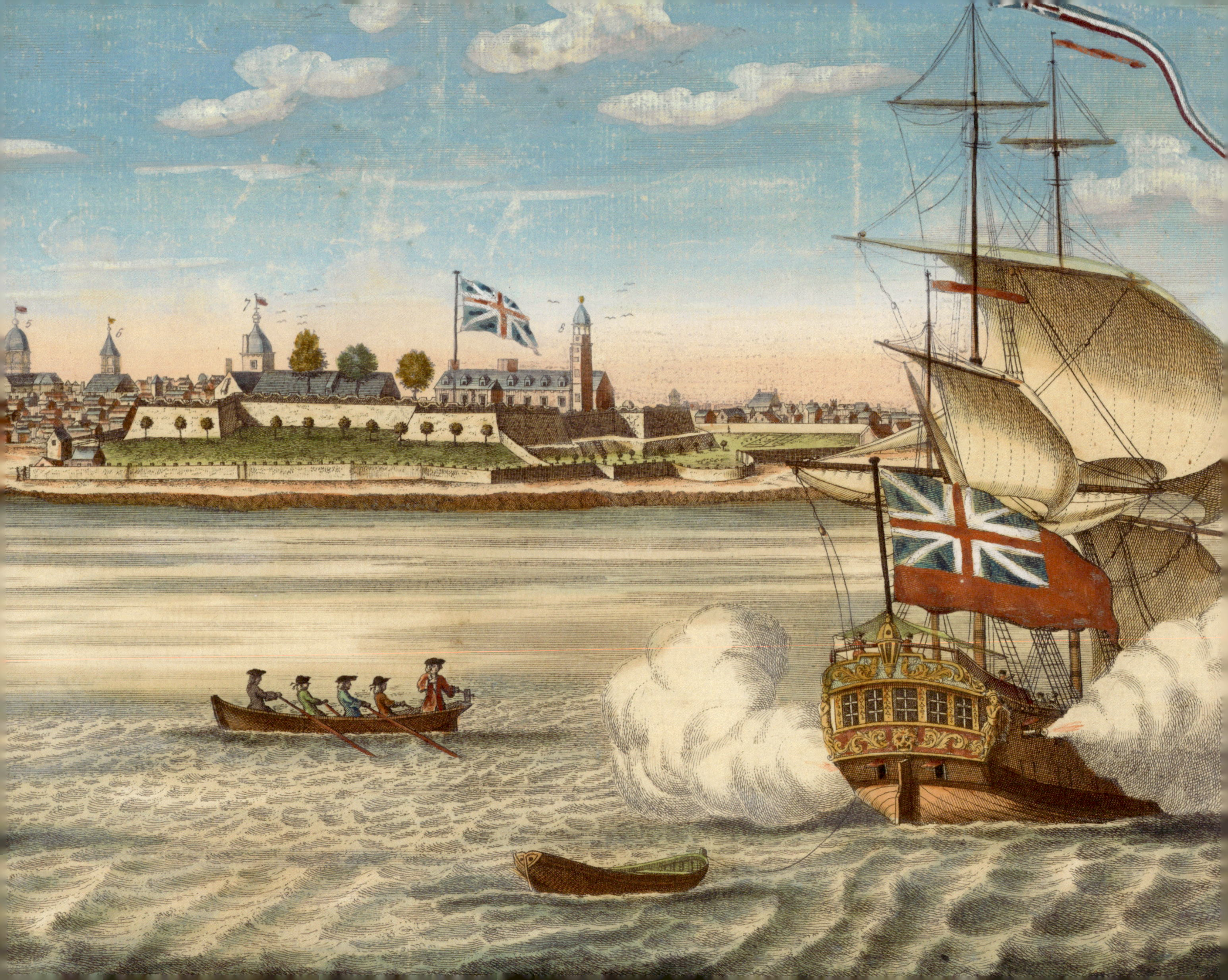
5
6
7
8

# 1664–1775

## English Imperial Port

In 1664 an English fleet sailed into the harbor and seized the Dutch colony. The English renamed it for King Charles II's brother, the Duke of York, and "New Amsterdam" became "New-York." Most Dutch residents stayed on and adjusted quickly, maintaining their language and customs while their businesses expanded along with England's trading empire. New York merchants shipped wheat and flour to Caribbean ports in exchange for sugar, molasses, and rum. They also sent ships across the Atlantic to sell fur, fish, and lumber and bring back European wares and enslaved Africans for sale in New York and other colonies.

Under English rule, New York became home to an even wider variety of people. English settlers mingled with French Protestants, Jews, Africans, and German, Scottish, and Irish servants. The English removed most restrictions on the public practice of religion and, by 1744, the city had eight different Protestant churches and one synagogue (although not a single Catholic church, as a ban on Catholicism continued). But limits on the privacy and free movement of the growing black population increased as the slave system became more violent and routes to freedom more difficult.

By the eve of the American Revolution in 1775, New York was the continent's second most important city after Philadelphia, with maritime trade still its driving engine.

OPPOSITE
*A View of Fort George with the City of New York from the Southwest* c. 1740
Hand colored engraving, J. Carwitham for Carington Bowles Map & Printseller

# 1664–1775

# Law and (Dis)order in the Seaport City

English officials presided over a small but cosmopolitan port, a place awash with merchants speaking multiple languages and using a dozen different European currencies. The East River waterfront's taverns and coffeehouses were settings for buying and selling Hudson Valley flour, English woolens, Portuguese lemons, Jamaican rum, and scores of other wares, as well as enslaved Africans. Weekly newspapers like *The New-York Chronicle* and *The New-York Gazette* (New York's first, appearing in 1725) allowed merchants to track international trading conditions and scan advertisements of Manhattan sales and auctions.

English New York was a busy, chaotic, sometimes violent place. Colonial governors tried to control trade for the British Empire's benefit, while Manhattan merchants and ship captains often sidestepped the rules in pursuit of profit. Magistrates sought to punish the port's pirates and smugglers (when not collaborating with them for a share of the spoils). They also exerted increasingly harsh authority over the growing slave population, amidst a white community living in fear of revolt.

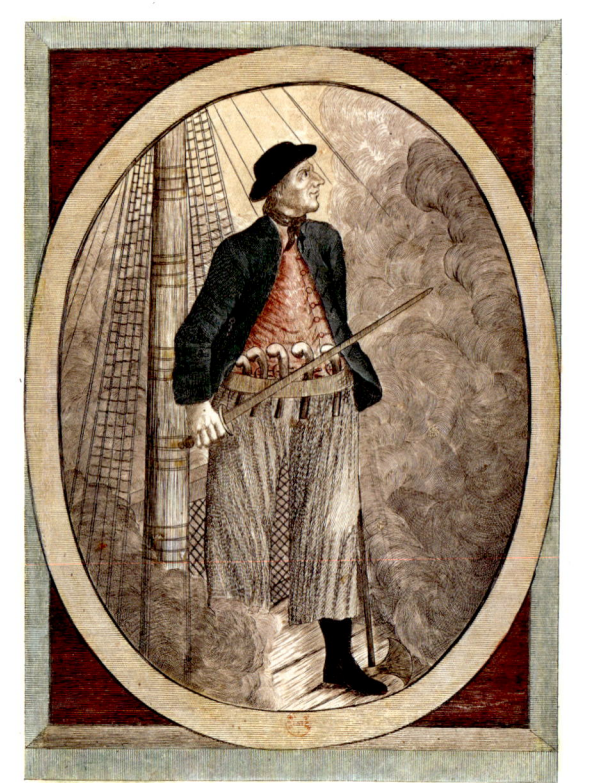

CLOCKWISE FROM TOP

**Silver mace of the Court of Vice Admiralty, a symbol of English power in the colonial port** c. 1725
Made by Charles Le Roux

**Account book of Petrus Elting, a Dutch-American shopkeeper who regularly traveled to New York City to purchase goods for his Hudson Valley store** 1762–74

**Portrait of Augustatus Kuningam, an American pirate** c. 1780
Engraving

## 1664-1775

# African New Yorkers

By 1740 one in every five New Yorkers was an enslaved African or African American, making New York the second largest slaveholding city in the colonies, after Charleston. Some had come via the torturous transatlantic "Middle Passage" on slave ships, others were transported from the Caribbean, and still others were born in the American colonies. Some managed to sustain West African spiritual traditions even as they joined the city's Protestant churches. A small population of freed people struggled to hold on to their land granted under the Dutch.

But conflicts also boiled over. As the English tightened regulations on slave behavior, anger rose. In 1712 dozens of enslaved New Yorkers staged a rebellion. In 1741 local officials blamed a series of fires on a supposed slave plot. In both cases white New Yorkers punished slaves brutally. Other enslaved people resisted by running away from their owners temporarily or permanently in pursuit of freedom. And during the American Revolution, when the city served as the main British military headquarters, New York would attract untold numbers of black men and women, fleeing American masters for freedom, paid work, and army service under English commanders on Manhattan Island.

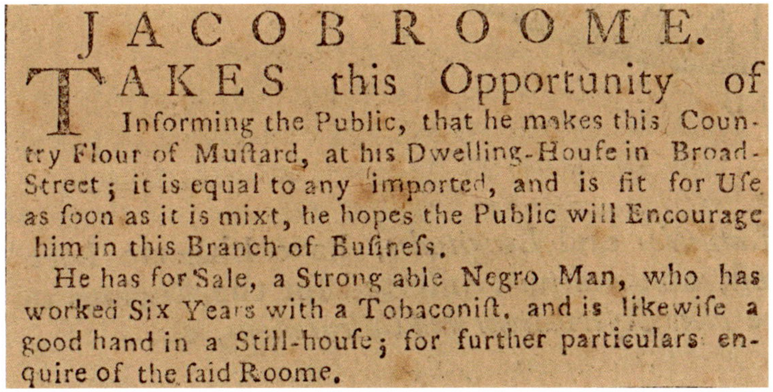

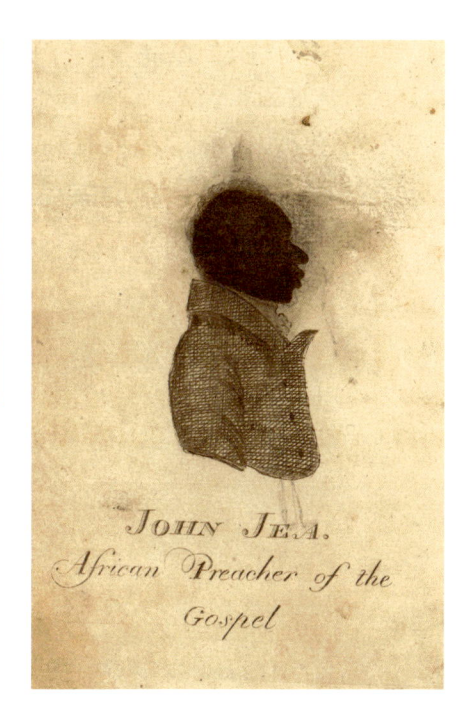

CLOCKWISE FROM TOP LEFT
***The New-York Chronicle*, advertising the sale of "a Strong able Negro Man"** June 15, 1769

**John Jea, a free evangelical preacher originally from West Africa, who was enslaved in New York in the 1770s (frontispiece to *The Life, History, and Unparalleled Sufferings of John Jea*)** 1811

**Wrought iron ankle cuff, possibly used to restrain newly imported or uncooperative slave, excavated near Hanover Square, Manhattan** 18th Century

**Baby's shoe** late 18th-early 19th century
Archaeologists found this baby's shoe along with corncobs, a leather pouch fragment, a sheep or goat pelvis, and an oyster shell arranged beneath the attic floorboards of the Lott House in Marine Park, Brooklyn. Archaeologists suspect that these items represent African traditions hidden by household slaves or servants from white eyes.

# 1664-1775
# Diverse Craftsmen

New York's artisans, who created objects for the city's merchants and consumers, embodied its mix of European peoples. The city's silversmiths were a case in point: they included Dutch New Yorker John Brevoort, Englishman Benjamin Halsted, French Protestant Peter Quintard, and Jewish New Yorker Myer Myers.

New York's relatively open environment notably let Myer Myers straddle two worlds. He became the chairman of the city's Gold and Silver Smith's Society and designed tableware for elite Protestant families. He also created Jewish ritual objects and was a leading member of Shearith Israel (New York's only synagogue until 1825).

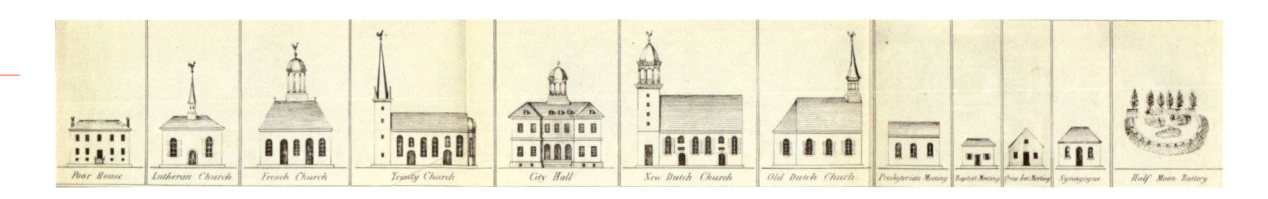

ABOVE
**Religious Buildings of New York, including Shearith Israel (second from right), detail from *A Plan of the City and Environs of New York...*** c. 1743
Lithograph by George Hayward from a drawing by David Grim

CLOCKWISE FROM LEFT
**Silver cup with anti-Catholic verses** c. 1750
Made by Hugues Lossieux, engraved by Joseph Leddel

Anti-Catholicism continued under the Protestant English, who outlawed priests in the colony.

**Silver sugar tongs** 1787–98
Made by Jeronimus Alstyne

**Silver sugar tongs,** c. 1783
Made by Daniel Van Voorhis

**Silver sugar scissors** 1750–70
Made by John Brevoort

**Silver sugar scissors** 1730–60
Made by George Fielding

**Silver and wood coffee pot** c. 1765
Made by Myer Myers

## 1664–1775

# Urban Dangers

New York City grew from 5,000 people in 1700 to over 21,000 by 1771, but most residents remained concentrated within the city limits in lower Manhattan. Urban crowding in the largely wooden settlement brought the risks of fire and epidemic disease like yellow fever and smallpox (causing those who could afford to do so to flee temporarily to healthier rural retreats such as Greenwich Village, Harlem, or the Bronx).

Fearing invasion by French or Spanish enemies and uprisings by their own slaves, many white New Yorkers viewed arson as a real threat. Eighteenth-century New Yorkers had to rely on volunteer fire companies to fight fires (the city did not get a professional fire department until 1865). Watchmen used rattles to alert New Yorkers of a blaze, and each household was required by law to own a bucket, which would be filled at wells and pumps and poured into hand-pumped fire engines.

Such measures were no match for major blazes, like the Great Fire that struck Manhattan in September 1776, devastating one-quarter of the city's buildings.

CLOCKWISE FROM TOP LEFT
**Leather fire bucket** 18th century

**Watchman's rattle used to warn New Yorkers of fire** early 19th century

**Certificate of appointment as a New York City fireman** July 5, 1787

## New Yorkers 1664–1775

RUN away from PHILIP LIVINGSON, of New-York, on the 28th October laſt; A Negro Man, lately imported from Africa, his Hair or Wool is curled in Locks, in a very remarkable Manner; he is a very likely luſty Fellow, and cannot ſpeak a Word of Engliſh, or Dutch, or any other Language but that of his own Country. He was ſeen laſt Monday on New-York Iſland, and is ſuppoſed now to be in the Woods near Harlem. Whoever takes up the ſaid Fellow, and delivers him to his ſaid Maſter ſhall receive THREE POUNDS as a Reward, from PHILIP LIVINGSTON.

**Illustration (detail) from *Anti-slavery record*, published in New York for the American Anti-Slavery Society by R.G. Williams** 1837

### Livingston's Runaway
(Mid-18th century)
Resisting Slavery

In late 1752, a young African man slipped away from the estate of his master, Philip Livingston, and vanished into the woods. His story, like that of millions of enslaved people, is largely undocumented, but we can piece together some of his story through hints in the historical record.

The man had been carried to the New World in the belly of a slave ship, possibly Livingston's ship *Wolf*. Though slaves were subjected to brutal conditions and harsh treatment in New York, they did all they could to preserve their own humanity; their resistance took many forms, from refusing to work to open and violent rebellion. Many, like Livingston's fugitive, resisted by running away; this man's fate is not known.

ABOVE
**Advertisement for a runaway slave from *New-York Gazette*** November 11, 1752

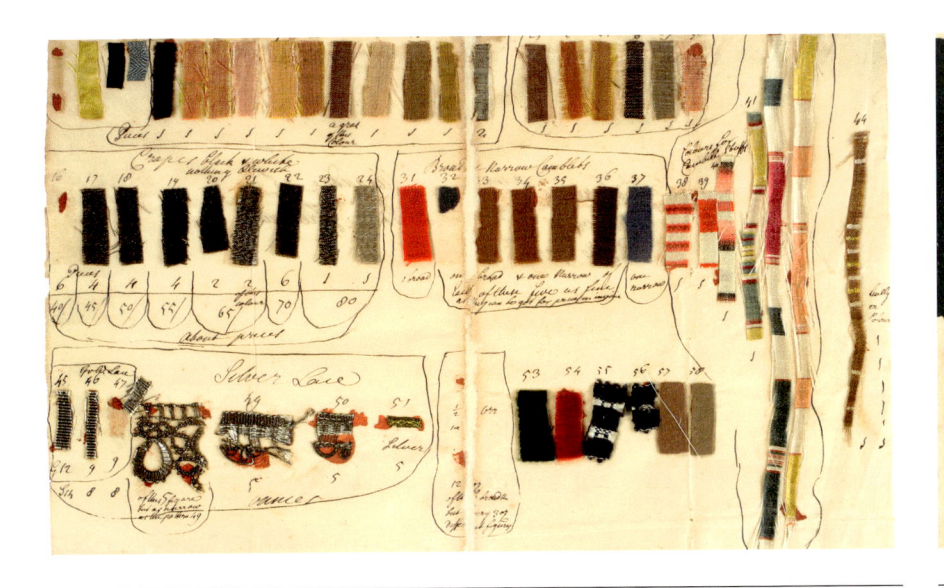

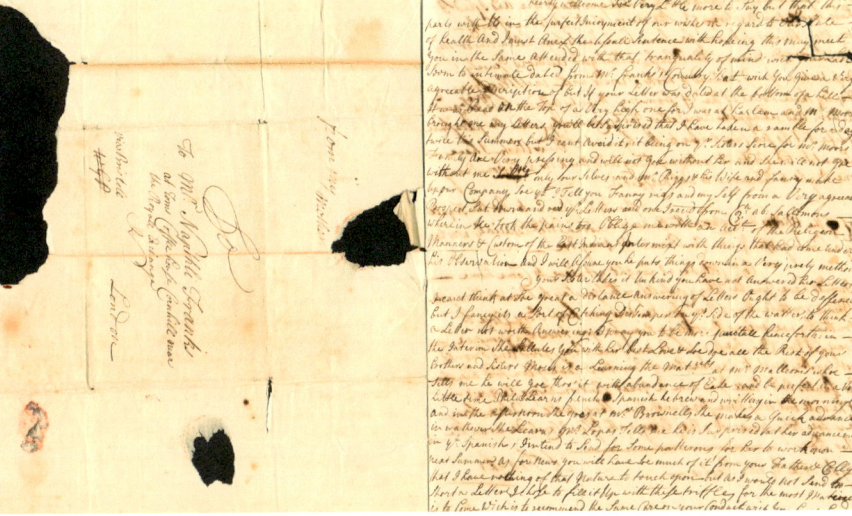

## Mary Alexander
### (1693–1760)
### Trading on Empire

Mary Alexander ran one of colonial New York's most successful import businesses, which sold textiles, porcelain, tools, and other dry goods. After her first husband's death, Alexander took over his firm. She ran the business for the next 40 years, placing orders, negotiating contracts, and generally operating autonomously in a male-dominated world.

Alexander ordered fabric like crepe, silk, and lace by sending fabric swatches to London. Ships could take 60-80 days to travel between New York and London. She was a shrewd businesswoman, warning one associate to come and pay his debt, "or otherwise you may Expect Trouble."

*Mary Spratt Provoost Alexander* (detail) c. 1750
Oil on canvas by John Wollaston

ABOVE
**Fabric order from Mary Alexander** 1730

## Abigail Franks
### (c. 1695–1756)
### A Jewish Mother in the New World

Abigail Levy Franks was one of colonial New York's Jewish elite, a small group that was working to carve out a place in the New World. Her letters show that, although she did her best to maintain her family's religious identity even as they integrated into New York society, this proved to be a struggle. In fact, two Franks childen married outside of the faith: after her daughter Phila wed Oliver De Lancey, Abigail and Phila never spoke again.

In the end, social acceptance proved a double-edged sword, leaving Abigail and others in a struggle to sustain tradition while embracing inclusion—a drama that would be repeated by subsequent generations of immigrants.

*Mrs. Jacob Franks* (Abigail Levy) (detail) c. 1735
Oil on canvas attributed to Gerardus Duyckinck

ABOVE
**Letter from Abigail Levy Franks to her son, nicknamed "Heartsy"** 1733

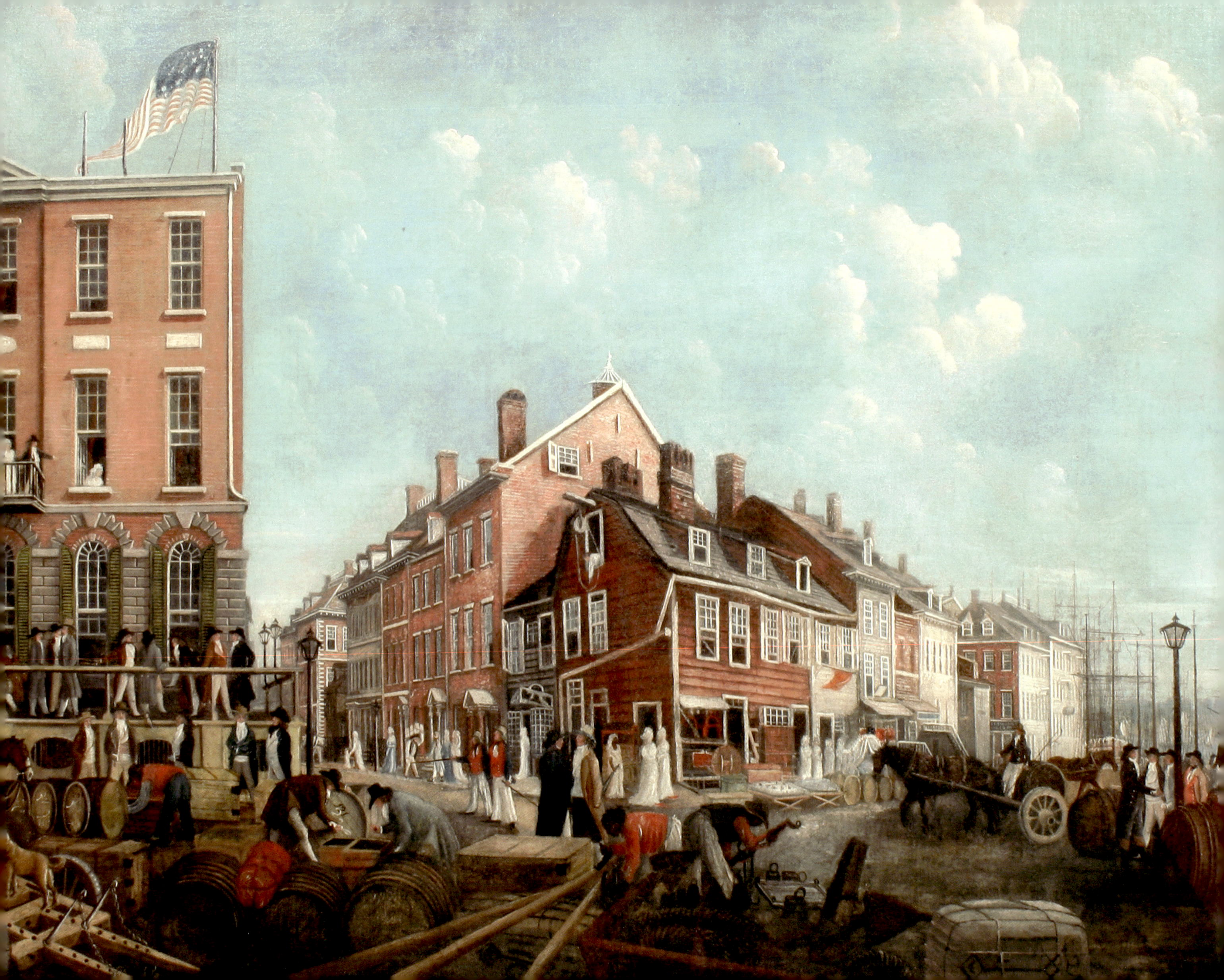

# 1776–1827

## Rebirth

The American Revolution was a turning point for New York City. When British forces sailed away in 1783 after occupying the wartime city for seven years, Manhattan's population had plummeted, money was scarce, and a quarter of the city's buildings lay in ruins. The question for New Yorkers was how the city could regain its momentum as an independent seaport. Although New York was only briefly (1789–90) the nation's capital, merchants and politicians strove to secure New York's preeminence, envisioning it as the new nation's "Empire City."

They made bold gambles and innovations in banking and overseas trade that fueled the city's economy. Their success was remarkable. With its population almost tripling from 33,000 in 1790 to 96,000 in 1810, New York surpassed Philadelphia to become the nation's most populous city and busiest seaport. Soon regularly scheduled packet ships, steamboats, and the completion of the Erie Canal (1825) further enhanced the city's primacy. Yet, while white New Yorkers enjoyed new opportunities to expand trade and earn profits, they did not officially end slavery for all African Americans until 1827, some 50 years after the Revolution proclaimed the ideals of liberty and independence.

## 1776–1827

# Devastation and Recovery

In 1776, following a major victory in the Battle of Brooklyn, British troops drove George Washington's Continental Army out of New York City. As the British army, with its redcoat soldiers, moved in, a vast fire—possibly accidental—destroyed 493 buildings in the city's heart. For the next seven years Manhattan served as Britain's headquarters for fighting the war.

Over the course of the Revolutionary War, at least 11,000 American patriots died from disease, neglect, or beatings in makeshift jails set up in warehouses, churches, and infamous prison ships. The city's population plunged from 25,000 in 1775 to 12,000 in 1783, as many New Yorkers moved away. When the British evacuated in November 1783 they left behind a half-deserted city; much of lower Manhattan, consumed by fire in 1776, remained in ruins.

The returning revolutionaries tackled the task of rebuilding and erasing the vestiges of royal rule. By early 1785, the nation's Congress had made the city its home, and in 1789 New York became the site of the inauguration of George Washington as the young nation's first president.

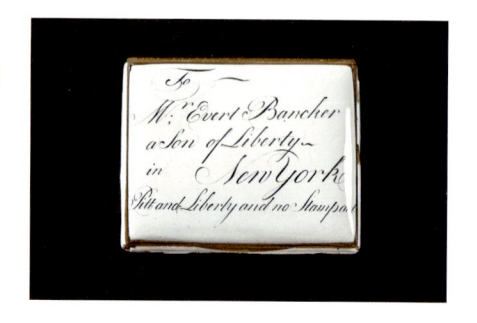

CLOCKWISE FROM TOP LEFT
**Document certifying the freedom of former slave George Elliga Moore** July 18, 1783

After the British offered liberty to slaves fleeing "rebel" owners, African-American runaways flocked to New York City. Many others enlisted to fight against a revolution that, ironically, promised them no freedom. Over 3,000 former slaves sailed away with the British in late 1783, while returning Americans resumed slave ownership in the city.

**Enamel snuffbox owned by a member of the "Sons of Liberty"** 1765

**"Evacuation Day" salt-glazed stoneware jug** c. 1800
Attributed to John Crolius and Clarkson Crolius

Evacuation Day (November 25, 1783), when the British finally sailed away, was celebrated for generations as a New York holiday. This jug depicts a key moment: the attempt by departing English soldiers to grease a flagpole so that patriots could not tear down the British flag. One figure says, "Damn the rebels, I will give them some trouble," while the other says, "Slush [grease] it well, Johnny."

**Key to a warehouse prison** late 18th century

OPPOSITE
**Shoes worn to George Washington's inaugural ball, held in New York City** 1789
Spitalfields silk, linen, and kid

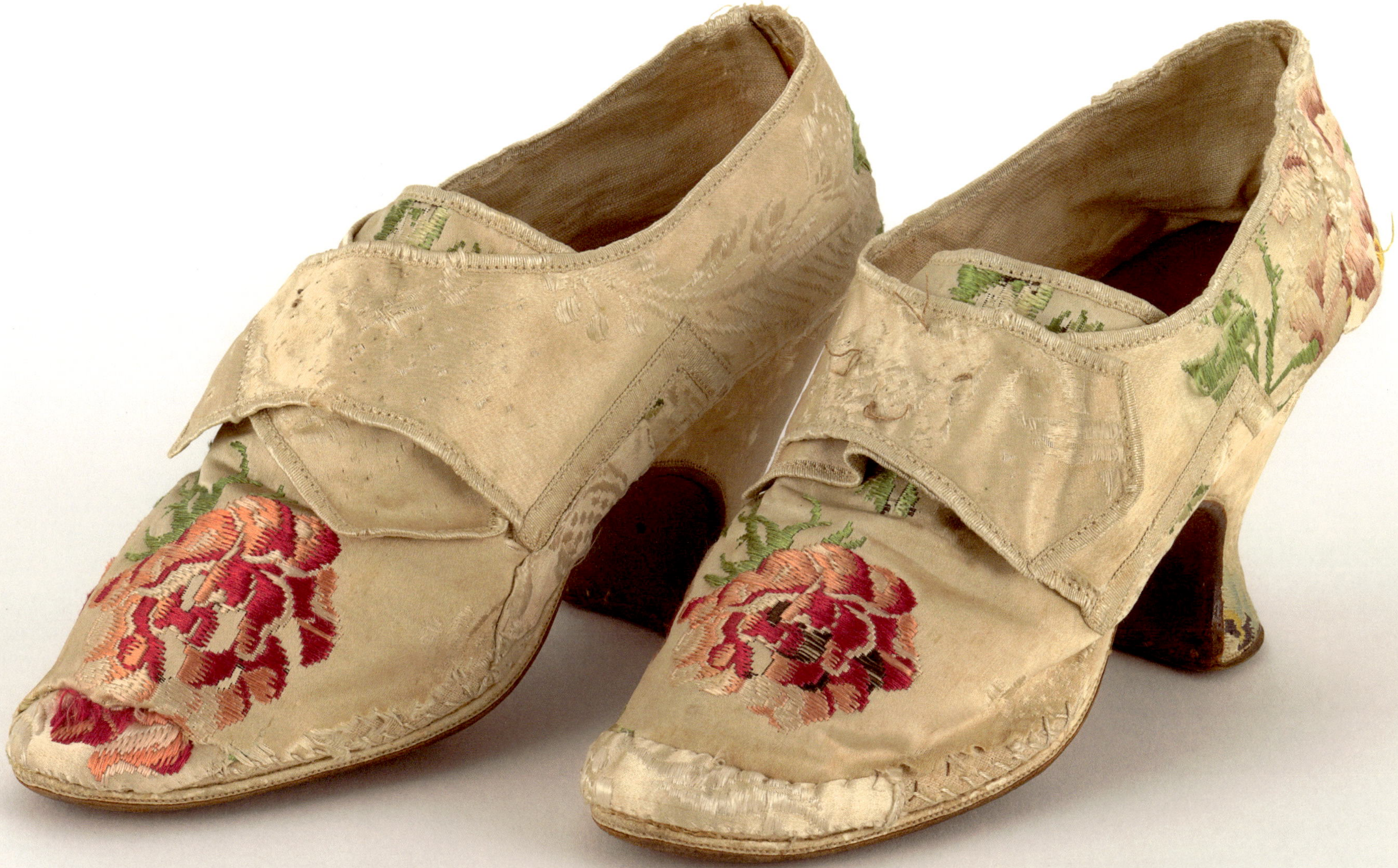

## 1776–1827

# Creating New York Finance

New York merchants were eager to jumpstart the city's postwar economy. Just months after the peace treaty was signed, Caribbean immigrant and lawyer Alexander Hamilton helped found the Bank of New-York (1784). It was the city's first bank and only the second in the nation. Among its investors were recent enemies who had fought on the British side; Hamilton strategically brought them back into the fold as a way to advance the city's business sector.

By offering loans and by issuing notes that served as a money supply, the bank helped New York merchants reenter foreign trade. Bank credit also helped fuel a market in stocks and bonds, leading brokers to sign the Buttonwood Agreement (1792), which gave rise to the New York Stock Exchange. By 1825 Wall Street was lined with 11 banks, 29 insurance companies, and numerous brokers' offices.

CLOCKWISE FROM TOP
**Wall St., depicting building numbers 30 to 46**
c. 1854
Engraving by Alfred Tallis

**City Trust & Banking Company note** 1839

***Alexander Hamilton*** c. 1804
Oil on canvas by John Trumbull

## 1776–1827

# On the Road to Freedom

In 1799 and 1817, New York State enacted gradual emancipation laws that promised to end slavery in 1827, and many slave owners began to free their remaining slaves before then. By 1820, 2,600 slaves remained, while the free black population of the New York City area had grown to over 15,000.

Black labor contributed to the economy of the region, especially in heavily agricultural Kings' County (Brooklyn), where enslaved and free African-American laborers were central to the farm economy that fed the growing port. Meanwhile, the number of middle-class black New Yorkers was expanding, as they established their own institutions, including churches, schools, and the nation's first black newspaper. Some held property, but they found themselves barred from equal access to the ballot, jobs, and public amenities.

CLOCKWISE FROM TOP

**Winter Scene in Brooklyn New York** 1817–20
Oil on canvas by Louisa Coleman after Francis Guy

This painting includes rare depictions of black Brooklynites, who numbered 1,761 in 1820.

**Hatchel and flax from Brooklyn** 19th century

Linen-making was an important task on Brooklyn farms, where enslaved people worked alongside their female owners. They used hatchels to comb flax fibers, enabling them to be spun and woven into linen.

**"Manumission for the release of slave Cato"** 1812

Nicholas Wyckoff of the farming village of Jamaica, Queens freed his slave Cato in 1812.

THIS BOX
was made out of a piece
of wood, brought from Erie
in the first Canal Boat
THE SENECA CHIEF.
PRESENTED
CITY OF NEW YORK
UNION OF ERIE WITH THE ATLANTIC

## 1776–1827

# "Clinton's Ditch"

Could New York beat Boston and Philadelphia to the agricultural riches of the American west? New York Governor DeWitt Clinton clinched the answer with the Erie Canal, a 364-mile waterway stretching from the Hudson River to the Great Lakes. Finished in 1825, "Clinton's Ditch" enabled New York merchants to ship manufactured goods to western farmers in exchange for flour, grain, and lumber.

New Yorkers welcomed the Erie Canal's completion with citywide celebrations, including a ceremony in which Governor Clinton poured Lake Erie water into the Atlantic. Two thousand boats towed by mules worked on the canal; by 1826 they hauled over 300,000 tons of wheat, flour, and other goods eastward annually, much of it bound for packet ships sailing from New York City to European and Caribbean ports.

The canal was only one arm of New York's expanding trade. Transatlantic packets, Pacific clipper ships, coastal steamboats, and steam-powered ferries all put cargo and people in motion. The city's first railroad, the New York & Harlem line (1832), soon ushered in a new era: by 1860 the value of freight carried by New York's railways exceeded that of the Erie Canal.

CLOCKWISE FROM ABOVE
**The Charcoal Cart, from the series "Cries of New York"** 1840–44
Watercolor by Nicolino Calyo

In a series of watercolors painted during the 1840s, Italian immigrant Nicolino Calyo depicted New York's cart drivers as they hawked wares or moved cargo between wharves and warehouses. By then, white cartmen were joined by a few black drivers who sold goods from carts in the streets.

**Silver handcartman's license for George Hurst**
1825
Made by George Smith and Jabez C. Lord

By 1812 over 1,300 cartmen moved cargo through the city's streets.

**Wood model of the canal barge Empire of Troy**
no date

OPPOSITE
**Silver Erie Canal commemorative medal and wood box** 1826
Designed by Archibald Robertson, engraved by Charles C. Wright

Leading furniture maker Duncan Phyfe carved the box for this medal out of wood brought from western forests by Seneca Chief, the first canal boat to arrive in New York City.

## 1776–1827

# New Trade

To piece the postwar economy back together New York merchants had to strike out on their own, looking for markets outside the network of British trade relations. Just months after the war's end, New York and Philadelphia merchants sent a ship, *Empress of China*, to inaugurate the new nation's trade with China. Others on the East River waterfront expanded their networks to the Caribbean, South America, Africa, and Europe, while New York packet ships carried slave-produced southern cotton to Britain and returned with European immigrants.

**Chinese-made porcelain teapot and sugar bowl adorned with New York State's coat of arms**
c. 1800

Canton and Hong Kong exporters sought to attract American customers with "Yankee" emblems. These pieces were adorned in coastal China with New York State's coat of arms.

OPPOSITE
**View of South Street, from Maiden Lane** 1827
Watercolor by William James Bennett

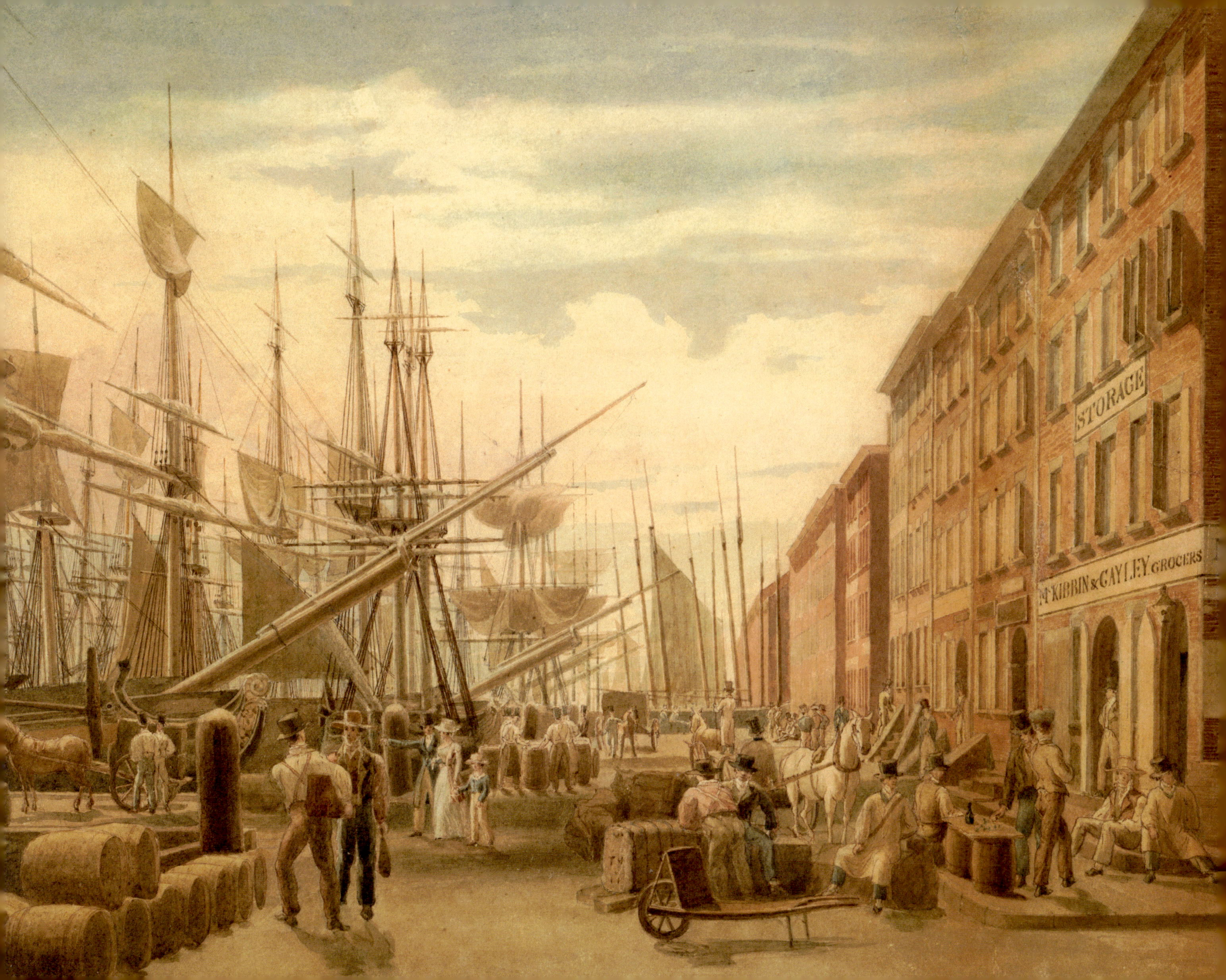
STORAGE
McKIBBIN & GAYLEY GROCERS

# New Yorkers
## 1776–1827

ABOVE
**The Bank of New-York (detail)** 1798
Engraving by Samuel M. Spedon and W. H. McCully

### Alexander Hamilton
(1755/57–1804)
Father of New York Finance

After serving in the Revolution, Alexander Hamilton returned to New York ready to promote his vision for the nation's urban future. He found the city in disarray: wealthy loyalists were fleeing and the recovery from seven years of occupation was slow. Hamilton proposed jumpstarting the economy by creating the city's first bank to offer credit and protect investments.

Hamilton's experience making the Bank of New-York informed his plan for the American economy as its first secretary of the treasury under President Washington. That plan included a national bank, taxes on imports to protect American industry, a regulated economy to protect merchants, and a strong central government to protect it all.

*Alexander Hamilton* **(detail)**
c. 1804
Oil on canvas by John Trumbull

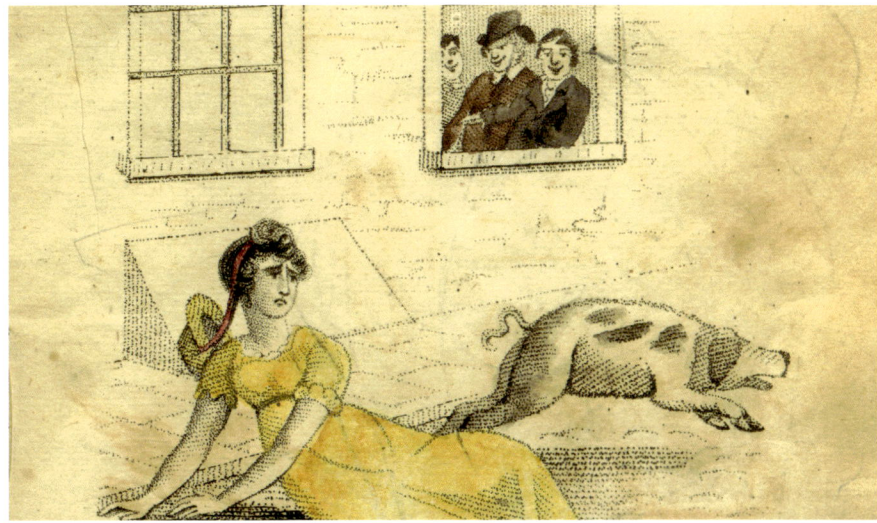

## Felix Varela
### (1788–1853)
### Fighting for Catholic New York

Father Felix Varela began as a Cuban freedom fighter and ended up ministering to poor Irish immigrants in Manhattan's infamous Five Points district. By 1823, when Varela arrived in New York, the city where Catholicism had been illegal just a generation before was becoming home to Catholics from Ireland as well as Germany, Italy, and southern Europe, most struggling to overcome poverty and prejudice to make a home for themselves in the city.

They were aided in this effort by the Cuban priest who, during his 27-year service, laid the foundations of the Catholic Church in New York, founded two new congregations, published several newspapers, wrote hundreds of articles, and served thousands of the most vulnerable parishioners in the city—all while continuing the Cuban freedom struggle from afar.

**The V. Rev. Felix Varela, D.D. (detail)** c. 1853
Print by Nagel and Weingartner, N.Y.

ABOVE
**"The Propagation Society. More free than welcome," an anti-Catholic cartoon** 1855
Print by N. Currier

## The Pig
### Putting the Urban Hog on Trial

In 1818 pigs became the subject of a lawsuit in Manhattan. Prosecutors claimed that pigs running free in the streets created a public nuisance. The defense countered that New Yorkers depended on hogs—some 20,000 of them—to feed their families. The fight was in many ways a struggle between wealthier New Yorkers pushing for their vision of a modern city and poorer residents struggling to maintain the freedom to use public space.

The jury decided for the prosecution and fined the pig owner. But it took several decades for the law to become a reality on the ground: hogs remained common in the streets until the 1850s and '60s, when increasingly determined city officials finally pushed the animals to the periphery of the developed city.

ABOVE
**Plate from *Some very gentle touches to some very gentle men*, a children's book lampooning New Yorkers for allowing pigs in the street (detail)** c. 1800

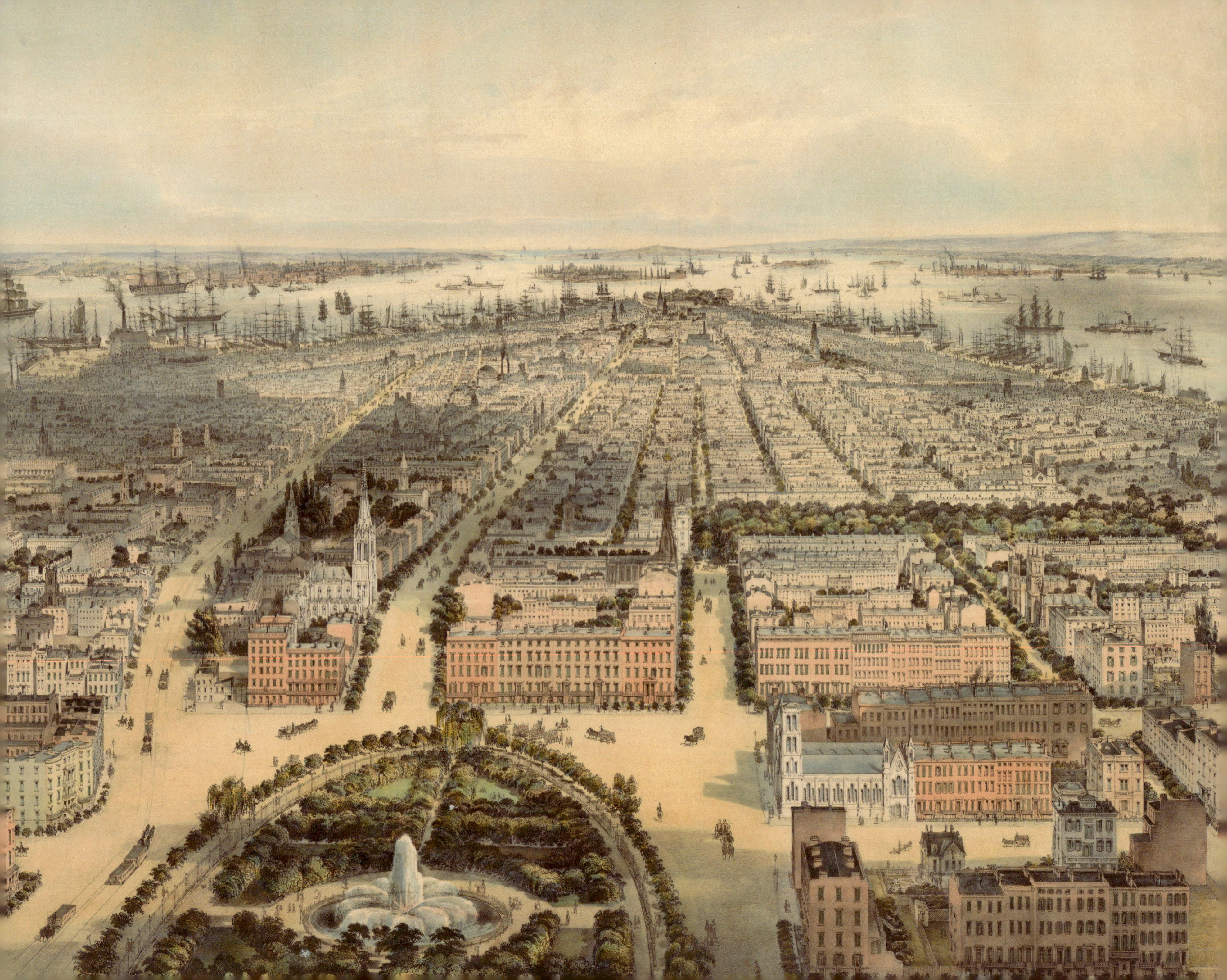

# 1810–1865

## Confronting Density

The city's success after the Revolution—its growing economy and population—came with a price. By 1810 New York City, still clustered below today's Houston Street, was becoming a very crowded place, with a population of 96,000 and growing. The limited and polluted water supply increased the risks of fire and epidemic. Yellow fever and smallpox regularly swept through neighborhoods filled with new arrivals and old residents alike. Fearful observers blamed immigrants, African Americans, and the poor, suggesting that New York might be headed for the same urban ills that plagued Europe's great cities.

How to cope with such conditions? An ambitious program of public works aimed to support the expanding population. In 1811 a state commission planned a grid of numbered streets and avenues that laid out the rest of Manhattan for development; across the East River in Brooklyn, civic leaders drafted their own plans for expansion during the 1830s. Angling to match European cities of the era, officials planned roads, parks, and a massive aqueduct system that brought fresh water from Westchester County's Croton River to Manhattan. These efforts to make growth sustainable also fostered a real estate boom and prompted New Yorkers to move to new neighborhoods, even as new immigrants continued to settle in the older areas of the city.

OPPOSITE
*New York* 1849
Lithography by John Bachmann

## 1810–1865

# The Grid Plan

Manhattan's 1811 street plan offered a sweeping vision for the city's urban future: a template of numbered streets and avenues stretching eight miles up the island, laid out over the existing acres of wooded country estates, farms, and other rural properties that filled the landscape north of the developed city.

Surveyor John Randel Jr. carefully mapped the entire island north of today's Houston Street in order to prepare the way for building out the street grid. He made 92 maps between 1818 and 1820, capturing both existing conditions and the urban future of the island. The Randel maps showed Manhattan's terrain of scattered buildings, property lines, roads, creeks, ponds, marshlands, and hills, while overlaying the planned new system of regularly gridded streets and avenues on the landscape.

Over the years that followed, city officials oversaw a massive public construction project that leveled and filled Manhattan's high and low ground to enable development.

ABOVE
**View of 2d Ave. Looking up from 42nd St.** 1861
Lithograph by Sarony, Major & Knapp for D.T. Valentine's Manual

The creation of Second Avenue in the 1850s left existing farmhouses and "suburban" homes above street level until they were demolished and the hills were flattened.

OPPOSITE
**Randel Farm Map no. 54 showing 101st to 109th Streets, Third to Sixth Avenues, vol. 2 p. 13 (detail)**
1820
Pen, ink, and watercolor on paper by John Randel Jr.

108th ST.

107th ST.

106th STREET

105th ST.

104th ST.

103rd ST.

102nd ST.

Old Haerlem
McGowans Pafs
Haerlem creek
Andrew McGowan
Kingsbr
Lawrence Benson
FIFTH AVENUE
Helen Van A...
Benjamin P. Benson
Sampson Benson
Haerlem bridge Road
AVENUE
Benson
Benjamin
Sampson

## 1810–1865

# Disease

The growing density of New York's built and human environment could become dangerous: yellow fever and other contagious diseases took thousands of lives. During regular summer outbreaks, the wealthy left New York for the countryside, leaving poorer New Yorkers behind.

When cholera struck for the first time in 1832, terrified residents turned to everything from herbs to fasting and demands for quarantine; and doctors carried medicine cases filled with remedies like laudanum, a powerfully addictive and dangerous opiate prescribed for cholera. The outbreak killed almost two percent of the population and helped to spur the movement for a new water system.

ABOVE
**Traveling medicine case owned by Rufus King**
c. 1814

LEFT
**Cholera Health Reporter** 1832

City officials published daily newssheets tallying the deaths and new cases, street by street.

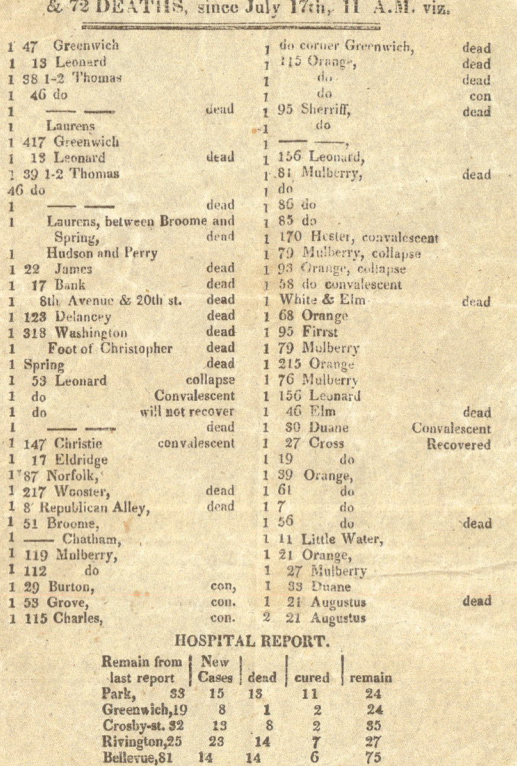

CLOCKWISE FROM ABOVE
**Croton Aqueduct at Harlem River** 1842
Ink on paper by Fayette B. Tower

**Soda water bottle found under 474 Pearl Street**
1847–55

**Manhattan Company wooden water pipe section**
late 18th century

## 1810–1865
# Water

New York's first water system had been a private venture, built by Aaron Burr's Manhattan Company in 1799. But Burr, Alexander Hamilton's rival, was actually more interested in using his state-granted company charter to create a new bank (the forerunner of Chase Bank) than in providing the city with clean water. Few New Yorkers paid to use the service, which drew from a well that was fed by the polluted Collect Pond and used pine logs to transport water beneath the city's streets. Fearing polluted water, some New Yorkers drank mineral or soda water, and others bought water carted in barrels from unpolluted springs in rural northern Manhattan.

In 1835 residents voted to build a system of masonry aqueducts and reservoirs to bring clean water from the Croton River, 41 miles north of the city. The Croton Aqueduct's completion in 1842 was marked with clean, fresh water piped into homes and businesses and spouting from a fountain in City Hall Park.

## 1810–1865

# Parks for the City

As population spread up Manhattan, open space began to disappear in the dense street grid. By the 1850s reformers warned that development would deprive New Yorkers of fresh air and greenery, while wealthy residents desired a public space for showing off their carriages and their grand civic ambitions. In 1857, partly inspired by Brooklyn's landscaped Green-Wood Cemetery (1838)—a vast rural oasis for strolling and picnicking as well as a burial ground—state lawmakers rejected the call for small parks throughout the city and acquired 778 uptown acres to create Central Park.

New Yorkers celebrated the park, designed by Frederick Law Olmsted and Calvert Vaux, as a planning and artistic feat worthy of the great European cities. The park, real estate developer Samuel Ruggles wrote in 1875, "will stand for ages before the civilized world as a noble organ of education, advancing the general culture and refinement…[of] the common metropolitan capital of the Western Continent."

Other projects followed for Olmsted and Vaux, including the beginnings of Riverside Park in Manhattan and Brooklyn's Fort Greene Park, Eastern and Ocean Parkways, and Prospect Park, created by 1,800 laborers out of 526 acres of farmland.

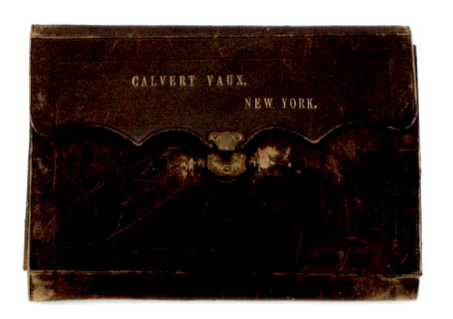

CLOCKWISE FROM TOP LEFT
**Calvert Vaux's field drafting set** c. 1865

**Buckle from Seneca Village** 19th century
The construction of the park displaced residents of Seneca Village, an African-American enclave that had come to include Irish and Germans as well.

**Map of the lands included in Central Park, showing location of Seneca Village (detail)** 1856
Map by Egbert Viele

**Andrew Haswell Green (left), Calvert Vaux (third from left), Frederick Law Olmsted (right) and others on top of Bridge No. 3 (the Willowdell Arch)** 1862

OPPOSITE
**Central Park** c. 1856
Watercolor; artist unknown

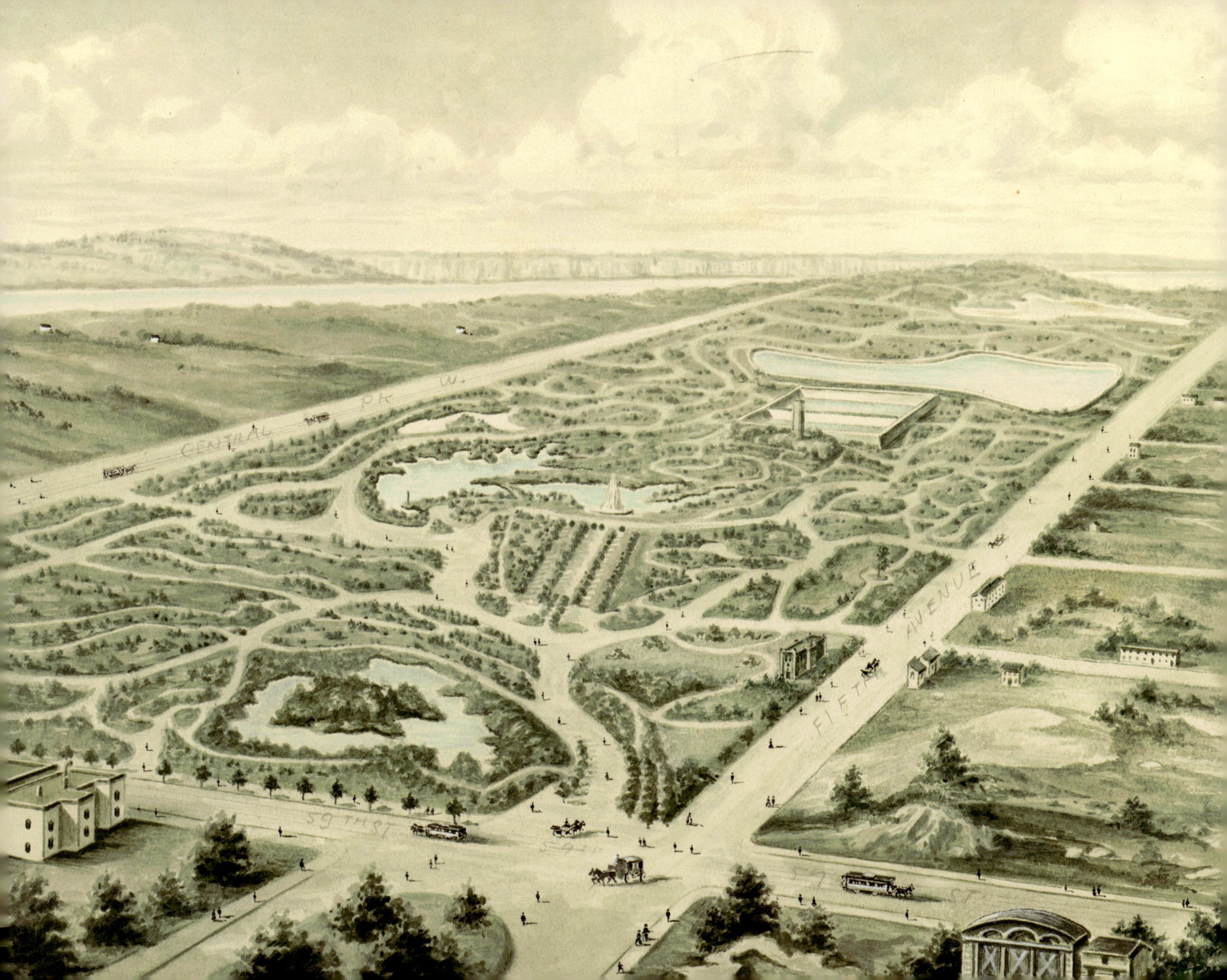

CENTRAL PK W.
FIFTH AVENUE
59TH ST

# New Yorkers 1810–1865

ABOVE
**Corner of Pearl and Chatham Streets, where Jennings boarded the streetcar (detail)** 1861

**Elizabeth Jennings Graham**
1895

## Elizabeth Jennings Graham
(c. 1830–c. 1901)
A 19th-Century Rosa Parks

In 1854 Elizabeth Jennings, one of the first black schoolteachers in the city, fought segregation in antebellum New York by resisting attempts to bar her from a streetcar on the basis of her race. After the conductor and a police officer forcibly removed her, she sued.

The jury ruled in favor of Jennings, declaring that "colored persons, if sober, well-behaved, and free from disease, had the same rights as others." After this victory desegregated the Third Avenue line, other activists launched legal challenges against other segregated rail lines through the 1850s, but the goal of full inclusion for African Americans in New York remained elusive.

## Charles T. Harvey
(1829–1912)
### Elevating Transit

New York's streets were shared by horse-drawn omnibuses, trolleys, carts and carriages, as well as pedestrians, and the occasional freight train. Charles Harvey, a self-taught engineer and inventor, came to New York in 1865 and tried to solve the city's traffic problems by inventing the first elevated railroad.

Harvey's experimental track opened to the public in 1870, the world's first elevated street railroad. But his design, in which train cars were pulled by cables, was accident-prone and Harvey was pushed out of his own company. Still, by the 1890s, steam-operated elevated railroads were a defining element of the New York City streetscape.

For Harvey, "The greatest public want of the city is a new method of transit between parts on Manhattan Island and the Northern suburban villages."

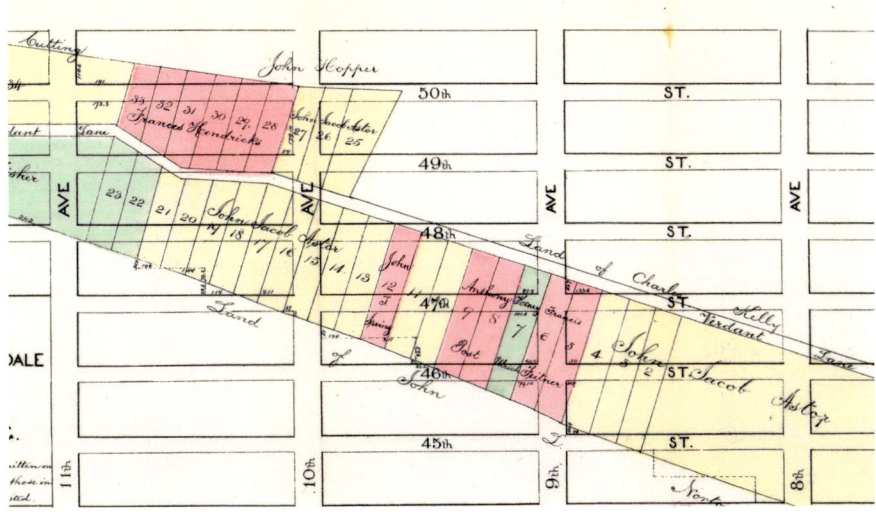

**Charles T. Harvey from *Fifty Years of Rapid Transit 1864–1917* by James Blaine Walker** c. 1918

ABOVE
**Charles T. Harvey's first experimental elevated railroad**
1867

## John Jacob Astor
(1763–1848)
### How to Get Rich in New York Real Estate

John Jacob Astor became America's first multi-millionaire by betting on the growth of New York City, buying up cheap land outside of the city and waiting for development to catch up. He increased his wealth by holding onto land while its value increased, allowing future generations of Astors to become one of New York's most elite families.

In 1803 Astor purchased a farm (in yellow above) from a destitute landowner for $25,000 and passed it onto his heirs. By 1905 it was worth $20 million and by 1929, $50 million.

He once said, "Could I begin life again, knowing what I now know…I would buy every foot of land on the Island of Manhattan."

**John Jacob Astor (detail)** 1842
Engraving by C.W. Chadwick from a drawing by Pierre Morand

ABOVE
**Map of the Farm at Bloomingdale, belonging to J.J. Astor and Wm. Cutting (detail)** 1881

49

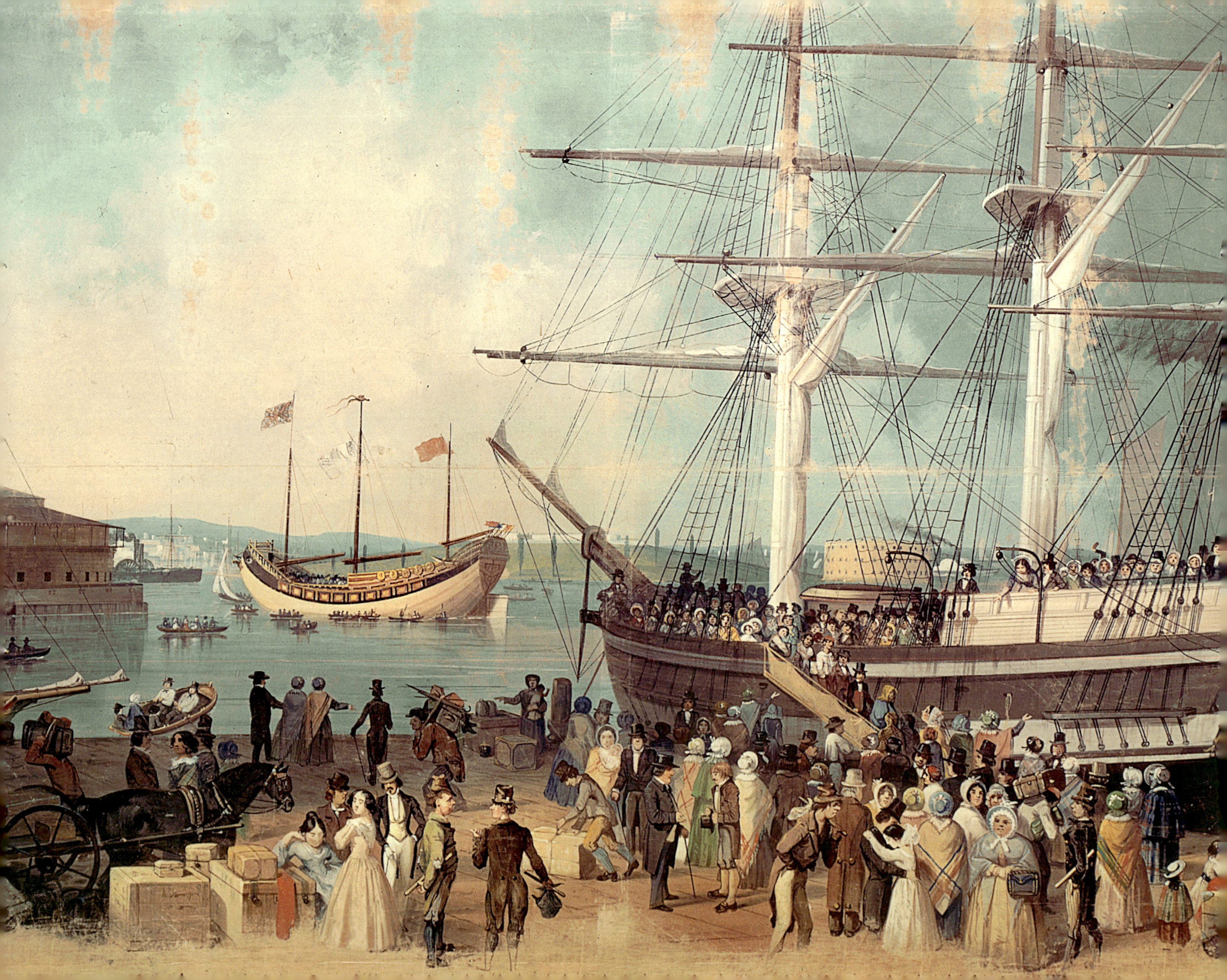

# 1830–1865

## The New Diversity

Immigrants from Europe transformed New York City in the 1840s and '50s. A deadly famine in Ireland and economic and political unrest in Germany combined with urbanization and improved transportation to drive millions of people to the United States, two-thirds of them through New York Harbor. By 1855 over half of New York City's 630,000 people were immigrants, the highest percentage in the city's history. More than one in every four New Yorkers was Irish-born, and Catholics, who had earlier been banned, were now one-third of the population. German Jewish arrivals made New York's Jewish community—numbering 30,000 by 1856—the nation's largest.

Despite the obstacles they faced, including lack of housing, poor sanitation, and subsistence living, the newcomers often made their way up in the world. In the process, they reshaped New York. Immigrants provided muscle to unload ships, build streets, and produce vast quantities of goods, and they became entrepreneurs who created jobs for others. Collaborating with white and black native-born New Yorkers—even as they competed with them for jobs and housing—the new arrivals also created a new, ethnically inflected urban culture, expressed in music hall songs, street slang, and mass politics with a distinctive New York flavor.

OPPOSITE
***The Bay and Harbor of New York*** **(detail)** c. 1855
Oil on canvas by Samuel Bell Waugh

In the final panel of a 50-scene panorama called *Italia* Waugh depicts the immigration depot at Castle Garden at left, a visiting Chinese junk called Keying, and new immigrants disembarking at right.

## 1830–1865

# Immigration

During the Irish potato famine (1845–52) New York–based shippers saw an opportunity to fill the holds of packet ships on their return trips across the Atlantic with famine refugees, who crowded into airless, disease-filled quarters below decks. By 1855, 176,000 Irish-born men, women, and children had become New Yorkers. The newcomers were often associated with stereotypes such as drinking alcohol, Sabbath-breaking, disorder, and unruly children.

In the same era, thousands of Germans, fleeing economic dislocation, famine, or political upheaval, also arrived in New York. By the Civil War, an entire section of the East Side was known as Kleindeutschland—"Little Germany"—for its dense concentration of German-American residences, businesses, churches, and cultural institutions.

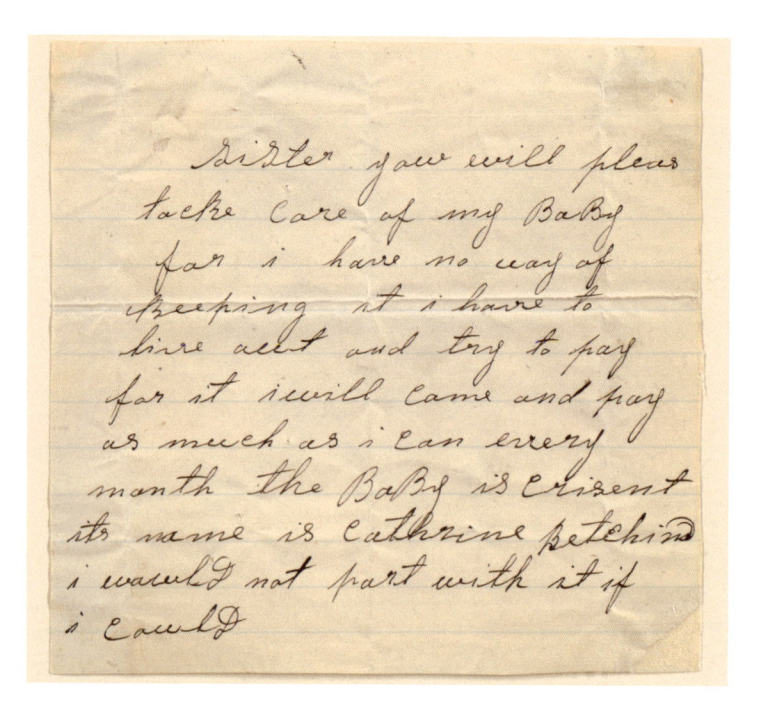

CLOCKWISE FROM TOP LEFT
**Model of a sailing ship ("*Erin's Isle*")**
early 20th century

**Note left at New York Foundling Asylum** c. 1869

Poor parents sometimes felt they had no choice but to give up their children. This mother's note entreated the nuns to raise the child as a Catholic.

**"Sunday Morning in the Fourth Ward" from *Harper's Weekly*** August 8, 1868

## 1830–1865
# New Urban World

Immigrants sailed into a harbor that was already changing, as the port city became an industrial one. New Yorkers discarded old regulations governing prices, employment, and markets; the new, freer economy opened possibilities for enterprise and exploitation alike. By the 1830s entrepreneurial artisans were expanding their production, hiring unskilled and semi-skilled men, women, and children to produce shoes, shirts, furniture, and tools in workshops and homes.

A new working-class world was emerging in New York, with its own neighborhoods and boisterous street life on the Lower East Side. While white working-class theater audiences—both native and foreign born—sometimes became stage caricatures themselves, this culture was often formed at the expense of the city's recently freed African Americans, who competed with them for jobs and status. Racist entertainments such as minstrel shows reinforced white status through stereotypes that put black New Yorkers on the lowest rungs of the city's social order.

CLOCKWISE FROM ABOVE

**Thomas D. Rice performing "Jump, Jim Crow" at the American Theatre, Bowery** 1833
Oil on canvas; artist unknown

Thomas D. Rice—a white actor performing in blackface as a caricatured African-American character named "Jim Crow"—made the minstrel show a popular attraction at the American Theatre.

***The Hot Corn Seller*, from the series "Cries of New York"** 1840–44
Watercolor by Nicolino Calyo

Discrimination often shut African Americans out of jobs, and many took to the streets as vendors. At the same time, New York's free black community included merchants, teachers, publishers, and ministers who organized to provide mutual support, fight against the southern slave system, and aid fugitive slaves arriving in the city from the South.

**F.S. Chanfrau in the Character of "Mose"** 1848
Illustration by E.J. Brown

In 1848 actor Frank Chanfrau created the role of Mose for the hit play *A Glance at New York*. Chanfrau fashioned an image of the "Bowery Boy" as a rough-and-tumble urban workingman with a heart of gold.

53

## 1830–1865

# The Five Points

Many poor New Yorkers settled in the crowded tenements of lower Manhattan's Five Points slum. Middle-class Protestants denounced the neighborhood as the epicenter of urban chaos: a place of alcoholism, brothels, crime, Catholic foreigners, and racial mixing. By the 1850s visitors warned that the district rivaled London's slums as the most densely populated place on earth.

Seeking a better life, the new arrivals created a system of institutions rooted in their own parish churches, schools, hospitals, and asylums. In the Five Points and other neighborhoods, immigrants turned saloons and firehouses into informal community centers and political clubhouses, headquarters for local street gangs, and sources of jobs in the expanding city.

CLOCKWISE FROM ABOVE
**Miniature porcelain teacup**  c. 1860

**Clay smoking pipe**  c. 1850
Made by P. Goedewaagen & Son

**Clay smoking pipe**  c. 1860
Made by Mullenbach & Thewald

**Earthenware teacup depicting Father Theobald Matthew, a leader of an Irish temperance movement**  c. 1850

**Marbles**  c. 1860

Five Points residents' varied lives came to light in 1990–91 when archeologists unearthed thousands of artifacts. These smoking pipes, teacups, and marbles are among a handful that survive; the rest were stored in the World Trade Center and were destoryed on September 11, 2001.

**Stoneware beer mug incised "Atlantic Garden/50 Bowery"**  c. 1858

A few blocks from the Five Points, the Atlantic Garden catered to German immigrants during the 1850s.

OPPOSITE
**Five Points depicted in 1827 (detail)**  c. 1850
Lithograph by McSpedon & Baker for D.T. Valentine's Manual

GROCERY
ANTHONY ST
LIQUORS
GROCERY
SOFT
SHELL
CLAMS
GOOD
FAT
HAMS
ORANGE ST
GOOD LIQUORS
GROCERY
CLAMS
ANTHONY ST
GROCERY
GROCERY
LIQUORS

SACKING A DRUG STORE IN SECOND AVENUE.

HANGING A NEGRO IN CLARKSON STREET.

RUINS OF THE PROVOST-MARSHAL'S OFFICE.

# 1830–1865

# Tammany Hall

The frustrations of poor workers exploded in 1863 in the Draft Riots, the worst civil unrest in American history. Enraged by a Civil War draft lottery that allowed rich men to pay for substitutes to serve in their place, immigrants rioted for four days, attacking African Americans and wealthy Republicans, both of whom they blamed for the war. One hundred buildings were burned, including the Colored Orphan Asylum. Over 100 New Yorkers died, and hundreds more were injured.

Sensing political opportunity, Tammany Hall, the city's Democratic Party organization, backed a plan to pay for draft substitutes for poor men. Even before the war, Tammany welcomed Irishmen, rewarding their votes with jobs and favors. Under "Boss" William M. Tweed, Tammany now became a base for Irish-American political power. The Boss was toppled from power in 1871, but Tammany remained a stronghold for the city's voting immigrants.

CLOCKWISE FROM ABOVE
**Glass globe ballot box** c. 1856
Made by Samuel C. Jolie

Glass ballot boxes like this one replaced wooden boxes sometimes equipped with hidden sliding panels that allowed ballot-stuffing. But the glass box's transparency underlined another dynamic of the political system: the visible ballots enabled Tammany Hall to track who voted for whom.

**William M. Tweed** c. 1871
Carte de visite by Sarony & Co.

**William M. Tweed's wood cane with gold, ruby, and enamel decoration** 1869

**William M. Tweed's diamond, onyx, and gold cuff buttons** c. 1868

Tweed's "Tammany tiger" cane and his personalized cuff buttons illustrate how he enriched himself on the city's money. The projects he funded also provided thousands of jobs and transformed the city.

OPPOSITE
**Illustrations from "The Riots at New York"** from *Harper's Weekly* August 1, 1863

# New Yorkers

## 1830–1865

ABOVE
***R. P. Robinson, the "Innocent Boy"* a depiction of Helen Jewett's murder (detail)** 1836
Print by Alfred M. Hoffy and John T. Bowen

***The Real Ellen Jewett* (detail)**
1836
Lithograph by Henry R. Robinson

### Helen Jewett
### (1813–1836)
### Sex, Murder, and a Media Revolution

On April 10, 1836 Helen Jewett was found dead in a bedroom of the brothel where she worked. Born a working-class girl in rural Maine, she had achieved a glamorous reputation as a sought-after courtesan, "the acknowledged queen of the promenade."

The crime made numerous headlines, and ordinary people devoured newspapers and printed images like never before. At the time of the murder, the city's most popular newspaper sold 4,000 copies per day. Four years later, multiple papers were selling at least 20,000 copies. Sensationalization of Jewett's death helped spark a revolution in the newspaper industry, changes that would help transform New York into the media capital of the country.

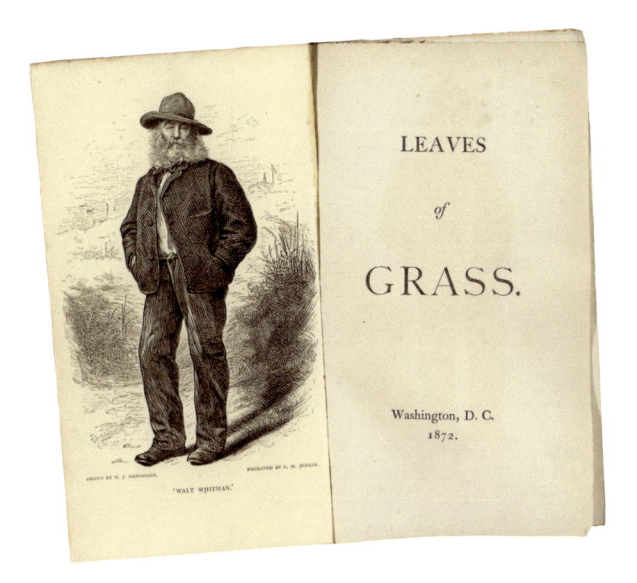

## David Ruggles
(1810–1849)
Practical Abolitionist

David Ruggles settled in New York in 1828, right after statewide emancipation. Ruggles was committed to fighting southern slavery, and he carved out a variety of spaces in the city to advance his cause.

He opened a grocery store that sold only food made without slave labor; his bookshop sold and loaned antislavery books; and he founded the New York Committee of Vigilance, which focused on helping free African Americans who had been kidnapped and accused of being fugitive slaves. And he became a key contact for the Underground Railroad in New York City, reportedly aiding as many as 600 people to reach freedom, including Frederick Douglass, who became one of the nation's leading voices for abolition of slavery.

**David Ruggles** c. 1840

ABOVE
**"The Disappointed Abolitionists," cartoon based on a legal fight between Ruggles and his associates and a slave owner** 1838
Print by H.R. Robinson

## Walt Whitman
(1819–1892)
Poet of the People

In 1835, 16-year-old Walt Whitman moved to Manhattan, seeking a job in the growing newspaper business. For the next 15 years he worked variously as a printer, editor, and writer. His work included poems, fiction, and articles about labor, women's property rights, and immigration.

The city was Whitman's muse. The places he worked, walked, and frequented—and the people he met—all inspired his poetry. This largely self-taught working man seized the opportunities and energy offered by New York and Brooklyn—in their printing offices and on their streets—spinning their diverse, churning mass of humanity into verse that captured the spirit of the city, and making his legacy as "America's poet."

**Walt Whitman** 1862
Photograph by Matthew Brady

ABOVE
**Frontispiece to *Leaves of Grass* by Walt Whitman with engraving by W.J. Hennessey, fifth edition** 1872

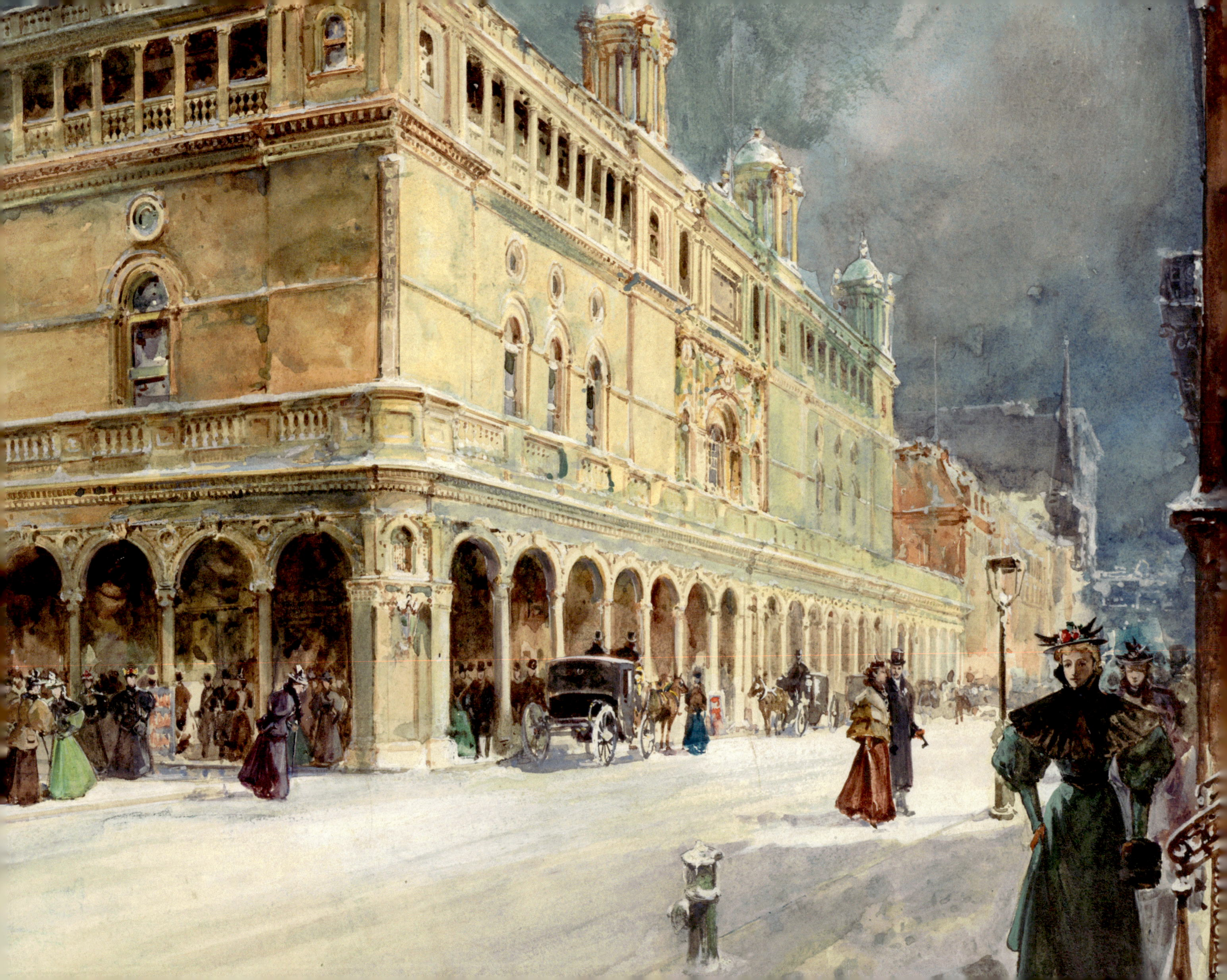

# 1865–1898

## The Gilded Age

The Civil War (1861–65) helped to catapult New York's factories, sweatshops, brokerages, and banks to the leading edge of America's economy. By 1880 New York City was the nation's largest producer of manufactured goods and the city of Brooklyn, at number four, was not far behind. On Wall Street New York financiers controlled one-quarter of all American bank deposits, money they loaned to speculators who made fortunes on the New York Stock Exchange. The city's bounty glittered in department stores and specialty shops that made New York the nation's leading retail center.

Meanwhile, conflict between "haves" and "have-nots" frequently pitted New Yorkers against each other. Forty-two percent of all American millionaires lived in or near New York City by the 1890s, and growing numbers of upwardly mobile middle-class families filled new row house and apartment neighborhoods. But the nation's wealthiest city also had an outsized share of its poorest people, many of them toiling at manufacturing jobs in crowded tenements. A growing labor movement was starting to organize poorly paid workers. By 1880 New York was home to over one hundred labor unions seeking higher pay and shorter hours for the city's 350,000 wage earners, making it an important center of the emerging American labor movement.

## 1865–1898

# Wall Street

As Wall Street bankers loaned Washington tens of millions of dollars to fight the Confederacy, they consolidated their own dominance in the nation's economy. New York emerged from the Civil War as the center of a new national banking system. The city's markets boomed as brokers, investors, and speculators made fortunes trading railroad and industrial stocks and bonds.

The nation's economy was tied to New York through the stock ticker, unveiled by Brooklyn inventor E.A. Calahan in 1867. Each ticker received prices from the New York Stock Exchange by telegraph and then printed out the information on paper "ticker tape." Distant investors could then telegraph their buy and sell orders back to New York. By the 1880s, 1,000 tickers dotted the city's offices, with thousands more at work across the country.

Newly wealthy business tycoons and their families built mansions on Fifth Avenue, vied to marry their daughters to English noblemen, and funded museums and opera houses in a quest to establish New York's place among world cities. By 1897, English journalist G. W. Steevens sneered that New York was "uncouth, formless, piebald, chaotic," but conceded that it "stamps itself upon you as the most magnificent embodiment of titanic energy and force."

OPPOSITE
**Stock ticker** 1867
Made by New York Quotation Company

LEFT
**Clerks at E.L. Oppenheimer & Co. with stock tickers and price boards** c. 1899
Photograph by Mercantile Photograph Company

BELOW
**Pieces of the Atlantic Telegraph cable** 1858–66
New York's international importance as a financial center grew when the transatlantic telegraph enabled virtually real-time communication between the stock market and European investors seeking to buy and sell American stocks and bonds.

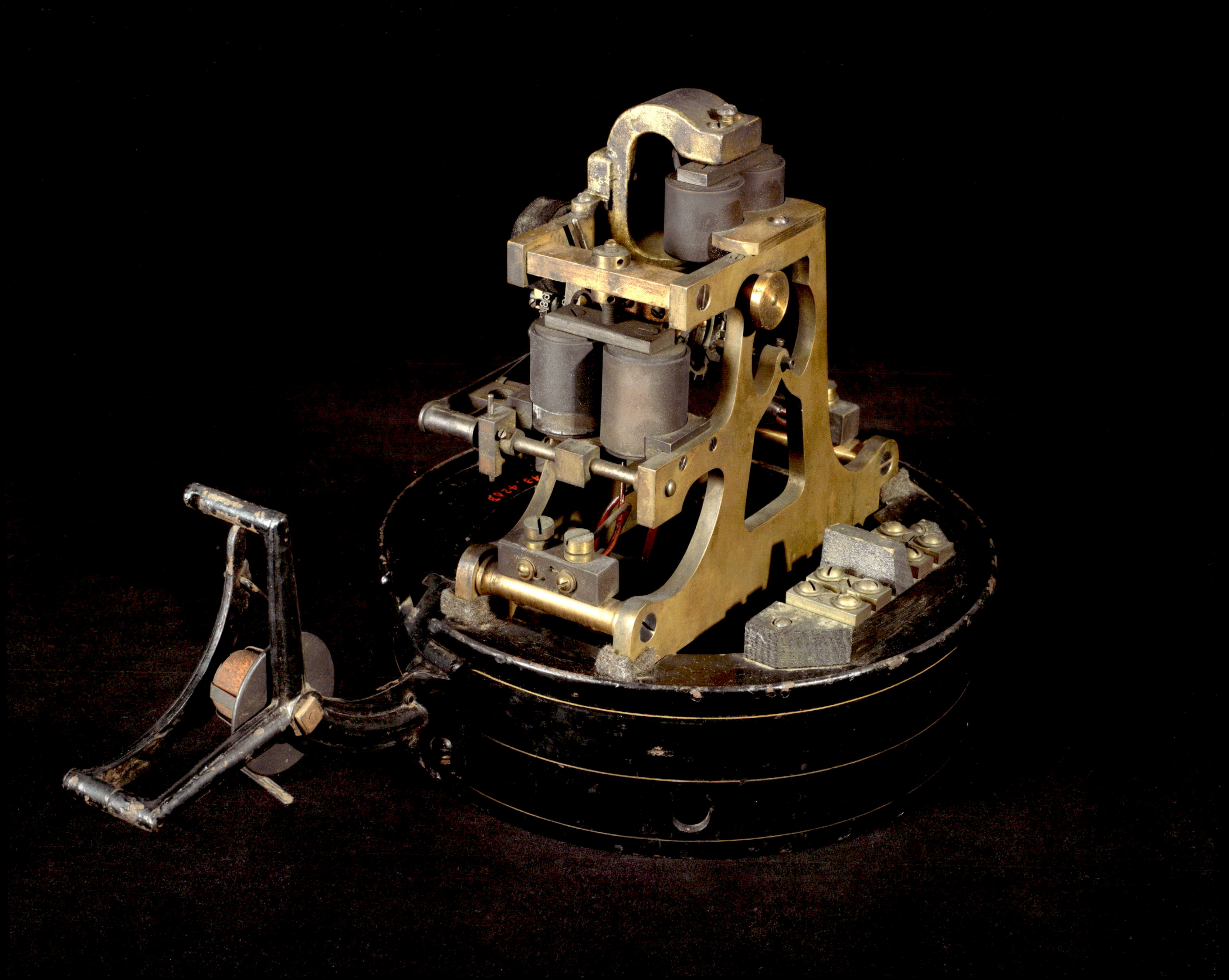

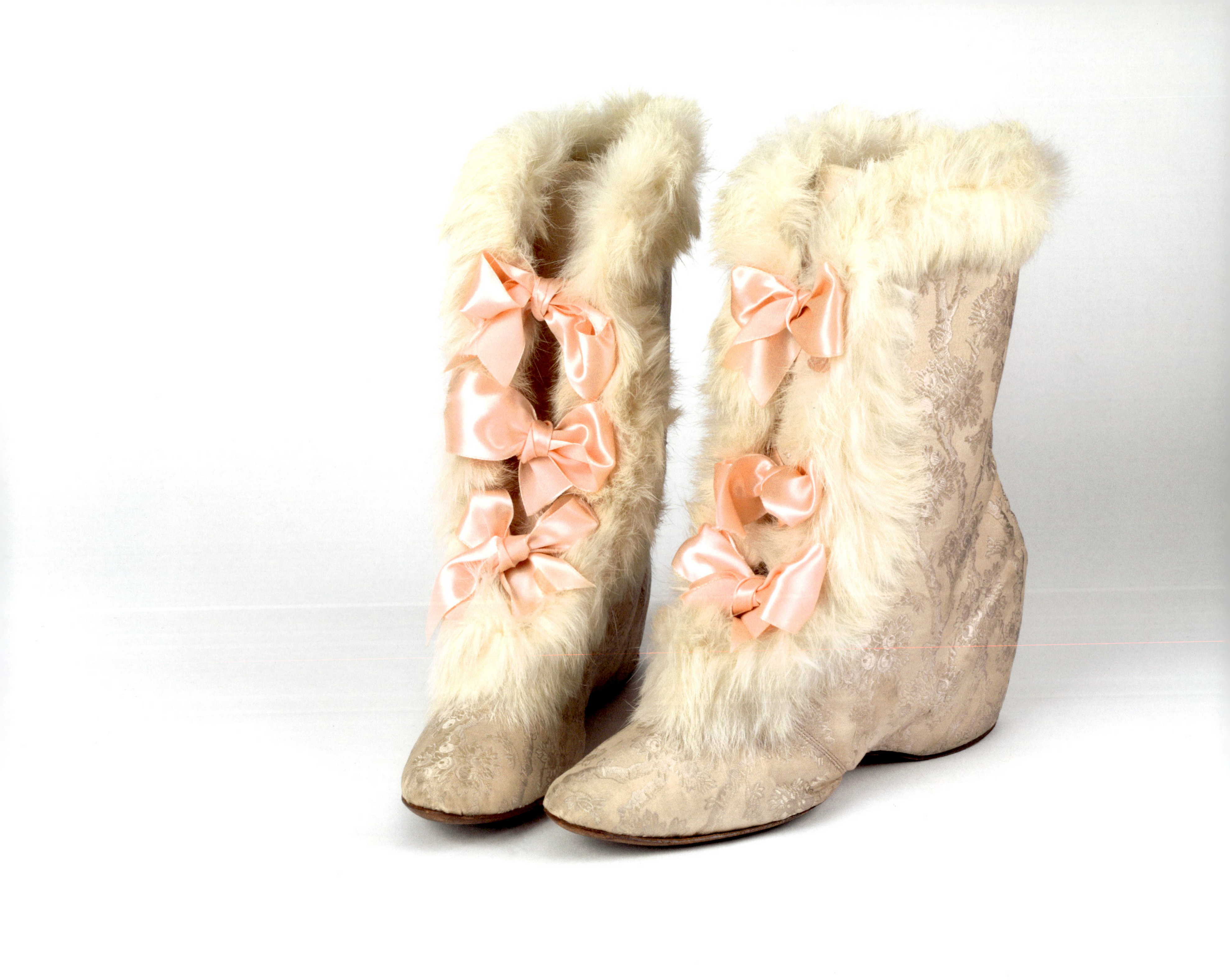

## 1865–1898

# Palaces for Shoppers

By the 1870s women with spending money gravitated to Union Square and "Ladies' Mile" between Broadway and Sixth Avenue and 15th and 24th Streets, the continent's most densely packed zone of upscale retail stores. Department stores like A.T. Stewart, B. Altman, and Lord & Taylor helped pioneer a new style of retailing that used advertising, fixed prices, shop displays, catalogs, and large inventories to reach a far-flung public in and beyond the city. A New York label became a mark of fashion and elegance to customers across the country, and New York shopping became a leisure experience in its own right.

These New York shops were also at the nexus of a changing landscape for women's employment. Working-class women made the garments that were offered for sale, while department stores provided work to "shop girls," offering some young women the opportunity to find independence in the city.

ABOVE
**Sixth Avenue entrance to Siegel-Cooper Company department store** 1900
Photograph by Byron Co.

OPPOSITE
**Women's brocaded silk and fur trim carriage boots** c. 1900
Made by and sold at Lord & Taylor

## 1865–1898

# A Growing Middle Class

Postwar New York supported an expanding middle class. A growing "white-collar" economy provided office jobs in banking, insurance, publishing, law, medicine, education, commercial and industrial management, and other fields, employing middle-class professionals as well as clerical workers. Professionals, small businessmen, office workers, and their families filled new row house neighborhoods stretching across upper Manhattan and parts of the Bronx, Brooklyn, Queens, and Staten Island.

By the 1880s typewriters were the daily tools of many middle-class men—and, increasingly, women—who worked in the city's offices, stores, schools, and public agencies. The machines revolutionized the workplace, replacing the age-old institution of clerks who hand-wrote all records.

ABOVE
**Police parade in a row house neighborhood in Brooklyn** 1896
Photograph by Byron Co.

LEFT
**Crown Typewriter** c. 1888
Made by National Meter Co., New York

This early typewriter used a dial to type one letter at a time, with keys to choose between lower and upper case.

## 1865–1898

# Cigars and Workers' Rights

Cigar makers were at the forefront of the growing labor movement in New York, where Samuel Gompers of the Cigar Makers' International Union founded the American Federation of Labor (AFL) in 1886. Joining together, skilled male workers in the AFL sought to win concessions from employers through negotiations or strikes.

But, while Gompers's skilled rollers worked in unionized workshops making "quality" cigars for higher wages, German, Bohemian, and Jewish immigrants worked for lower wages in their tenement homes, using cigar molds to mass-produce cheap cigars. In many industries, in fact, unskilled and semi-skilled workers—immigrants, women, and children—who could be easily replaced were less successful in gaining better conditions or pay. Many unions saw them as mere "tools" of employers.

As labor activism grew, some New Yorkers feared unionism could lead to revolution. Their fear was seemingly fulfilled by violent conflicts like the 1895 Brooklyn streetcar strike, which brought clashes between the National Guard and workers. Anxiety about unrest helped fuel middle-class and official support for proposals to improve living conditions for New York's poor; it also spurred the creation of fortress-like armories across today's five boroughs to guard against uprisings.

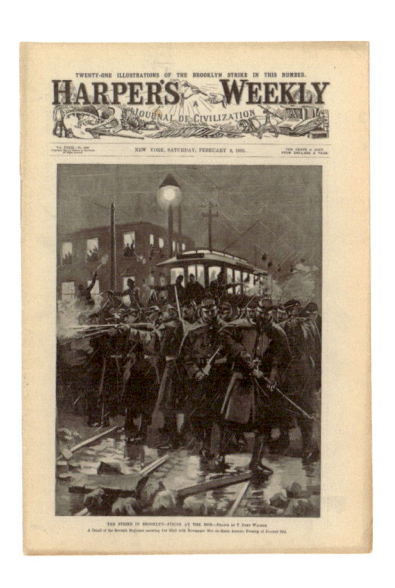

CLOCKWISE FROM ABOVE

**"The Strike in Brooklyn—Firing at the Mob," illustration by T. Dart Walker from *Harper's Weekly*** February 2, 1895

**"Union Workers," cigar box label** c. 1902
Lithograph by Consolidated Lithographing Corporation

This cigar box label celebrates unionized workers and also two New Yorkers—President Theodore Roosevelt and Mayor Seth Low, both of whom fought to eliminate low-wage tenement "home work."

**Wood cigar mold** late 19th century

The cigar mold was invented in the 1860s; it allowed less skilled workers to make cigars by pressing tobacco into the grooves of the mold.

***Bohemian Cigar Makers at Work*** 1889–90
Photograph by Jacob A. Riis

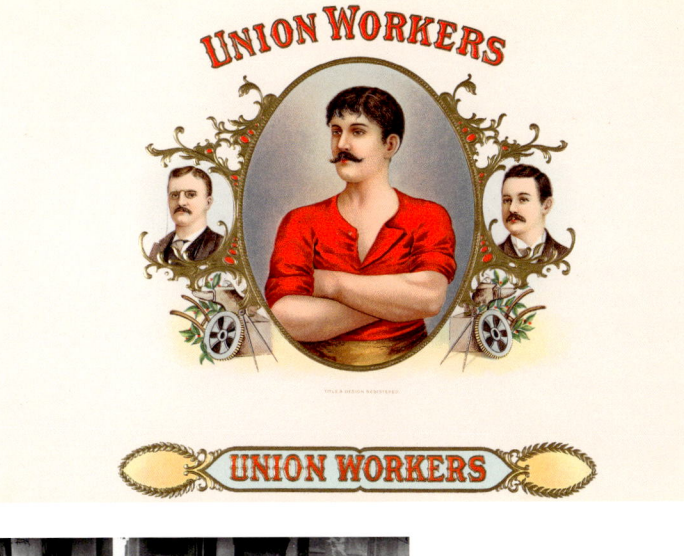

## 1865–1898

# Documenting the Tenements

Newspaperman Jacob A. Riis, a Danish immigrant, used words and photographs to expose "how the other half lived" in the tenements and shanties of lower Manhattan and beyond. Riis revealed the bleak conditions of slum poverty to a broad middle-class public, even as he also embraced negative stereotypes of Chinese, African Americans, Jews, and Italians in describing New York's poor. He helped to rally support for a 1901 state law that required more light, air, space, and sanitation in the city's new housing.

Riis's advocacy extended beyond housing reform. He lobbied for parks and playgrounds to offset the density of the tenement districts and fought for government action to address these problems at a time when New York's government, under the control of Tammany Hall, was seen by many middle-class New Yorkers as an enemy of reform.

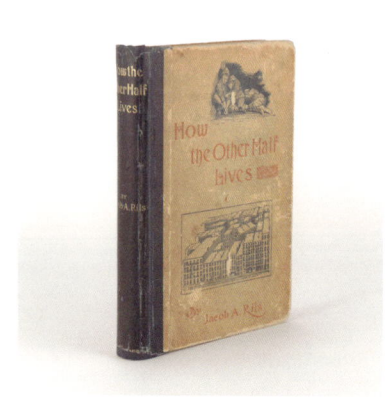

CLOCKWISE FROM ABOVE
**Jacob A. Riis** 1903
Photograph by Pach Brothers

***How the Other Half Lives: Studies Among the Tenements of New York* by Jacob A. Riis, published by Charles Scribner's Sons, New York** 1894

Riis's 1890 bestseller was based on an illustrated lecture he gave in 1888 and an article he wrote for *Scribner's* magazine in 1889.

***Sweatshop in Hester Street*** 1889–90
Photograph by Jacob A. Riis

***Five Cents a Spot*** 1888–89
Photograph by Jacob A. Riis

OPPOSITE
***Street Arabs in Night Quarters*** 1888–89
Photograph by Jacob A. Riis

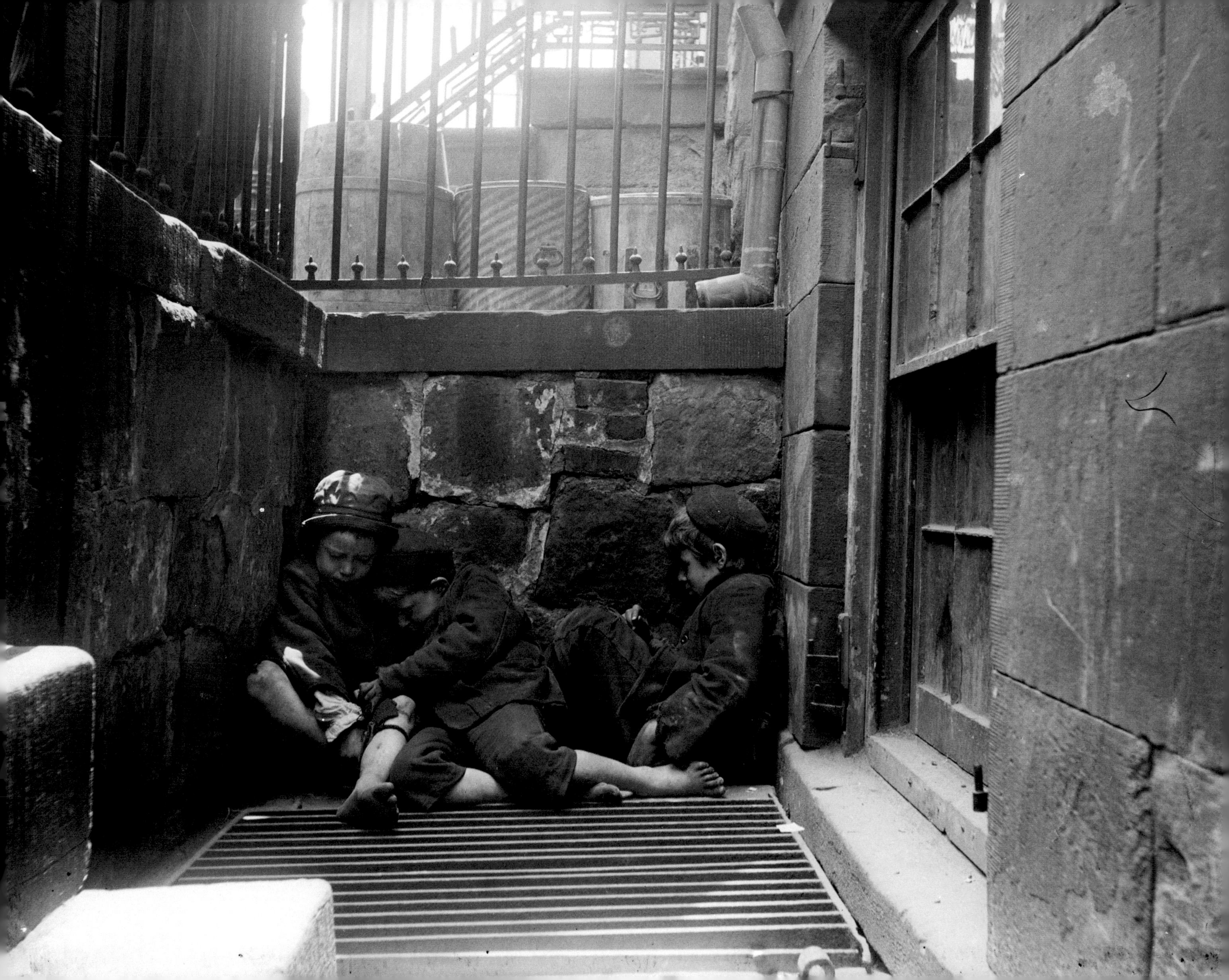

# New Yorkers 1865–1898

**Fredericka "Marm" Mandelbaum, from *Sins of New York* by Edward Van Every, published by R.A. Stokes Co., New York** 1930

## Fredericka "Marm" Mandelbaum
### (1811–1894)
Mother of Crooks

Fredericka "Marm" Mandelbaum was one of the most powerful criminals in late 19th-century New York. For nearly 20 years, the German-Jewish immigrant reigned over a far-reaching ring of burglars, pickpockets, con artists, and thieves.

Mandelbaum saw an opportunity in the immigrant communities of the Lower East Side, and she seized it. Her strategy was to recruit a diverse network of thieves—men and women, young and old, of various ethnicities—who could operate freely across cultures and blend into the background of the city when necessary. Over the course of her career, Mandelbaum handled an estimated $5–10 million in stolen property, buying "hot" merchandise, storing it in secret warehouses, then reselling it once the heat had died down.

ABOVE
**A dinner party thrown by Marm Mandelbaum (depicted with fan at right) from *Recollections of a New York Chief of Police* by George Washington Walling, published by Caxton Book Concern, New York** 1887

## Cornelius Vanderbilt
### (1794–1877)
### Empire Builder

In 1800 it took about six weeks to go from New York to Chicago. By 1857, the same trip took a day and half. No American contributed more to this transportation revolution than a Staten Island farm boy named Cornelius Vanderbilt—and no one got richer in the process.

Vanderbilt began his career as a teenage ferryboat captain, reinvested all his profits into the steamboat business to create a regional transportation network, and then traded it all in for another up-and-coming technology: the steam-powered railroad. Over the next decades, Vanderbilt would consolidate control over a sprawling web of tracks centered on New York and stretching deep into the American continent. "Commodore" Cornelius Vanderbilt epitomized both the tremendous growth and the stunning accumulation of wealth that culminated in the Gilded Age.

**Cornelius Vanderbilt** c. 1875
Photograph by William R. Howell

ABOVE
**Map of the New York Central and Hudson River Railroad and its principal connections (detail)** 1876

## Emma Goldman
### (1869–1940)
### Anarchy on the Lower East Side

Emma Goldman arrived in New York in 1889, and within a few short years this Russian-Jewish immigrant had become a lightning rod for passionate debates about the future of New York's—and America's—capitalist system.

In the densely packed tenements of New York's Lower East Side, Goldman had found a world of Jewish and German socialism and anarchism, where immigrants worked in often terrible conditions by day and read and talked about radical responses by night. Goldman became an outspoken opponent of their oppression, advocating solutions ranging from birth control to workers' rights. Though she was arrested, imprisoned, and eventually deported, for a time Goldman and other radicals found a ready audience in working-class New York.

**Emma Goldman** 1911
Photograph by Bain News Service

ABOVE
**"Miss Goldman, the high priestess of Anarchy!" from** *Harper's Weekly* August 20, 1892

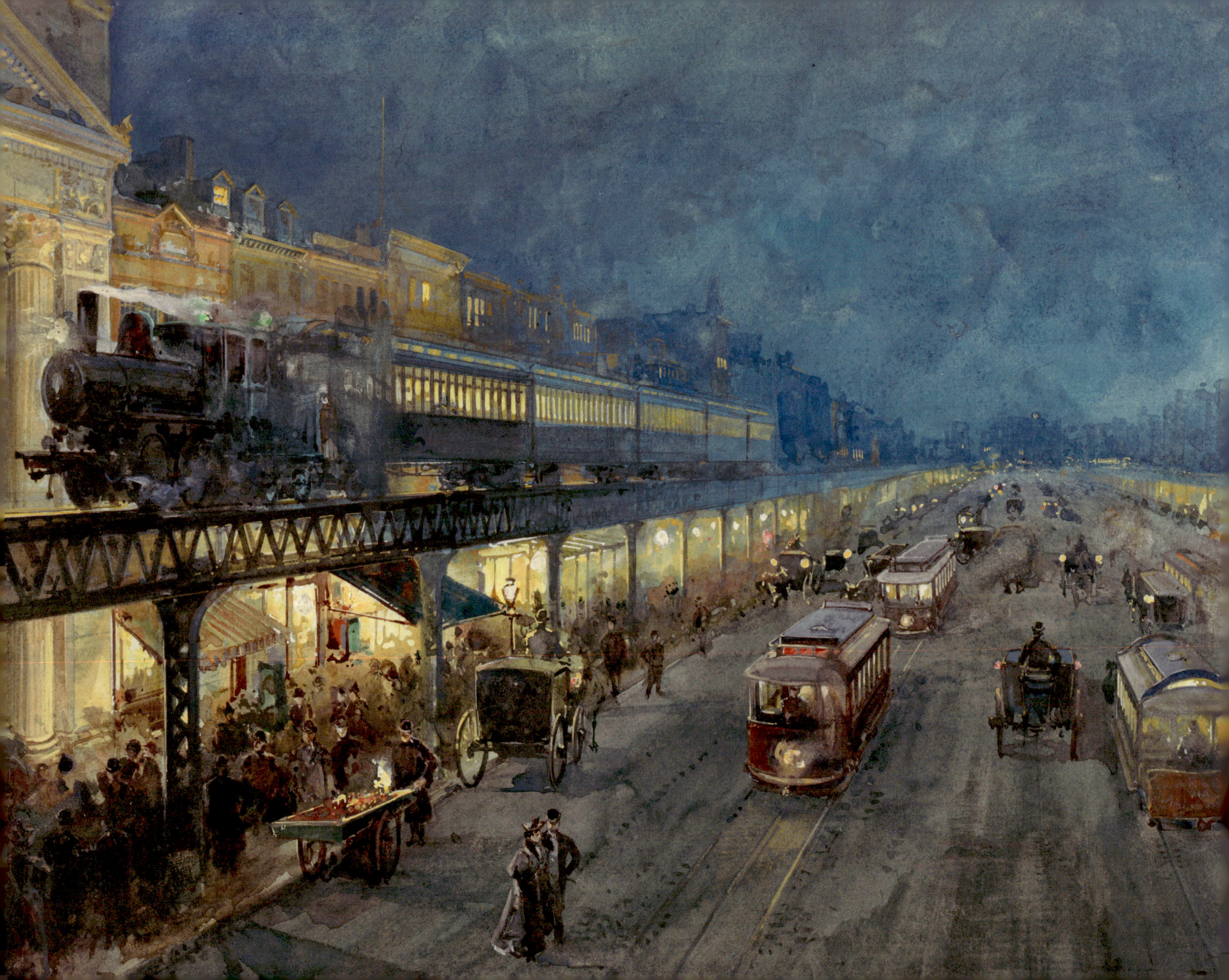

# 1880–1898

## Ethnic New York

In the late 19th century New York City became even more diverse as its population swelled with new arrivals from eastern and southern Europe. By the time Ellis Island replaced the Battery's Castle Garden as the official immigrant depot in 1892, new waves of arrivals—Italians, Yiddish-speaking Jews from Eastern Europe, Poles, Greeks, Syrians, and others—were crossing the Atlantic and making New York their home. Most settled into the old Irish and German tenement neighborhoods of the Lower East Side, where African-American and Chinese newcomers joined them. By century's end, newspapers in at least 13 languages served over one million foreign-born residents in Manhattan and Brooklyn.

Together, these men and women reshaped New York—transforming neighborhoods, workplaces, union halls, and political loyalties. For many outsiders, the most visible impact was cultural, as Yiddish, Italian, "Yankee," Irish, German, Chinese, and African-American influences all mixed on the stages of the city's music halls and cheap theaters. From the working-class crossroads of the Bowery and the new recreation zone of Coney Island came "ethnic" plays, songs, slang, jokes, games, and images that would help define New York's character for decades to come. Seizing the opportunity to make money, publishers and manufacturers marketed the city's diversity to tourists and the rest

## 1880–1898

# New Immigrants

Social and economic hardships in Europe transformed late 19th-century New York. Poverty unsettled peasants and villagers across southern and eastern Europe, while deprivation and violence in the Russian Empire and Rumania led many Jews to seek refuge in America. The result was the "new immigration," which added to New York's existing population mix dominated by Protestant northern Europeans, Catholic Irish and Germans, and German Jews.

The new arrivals remade the city's life as dramatically as Irish and Germans had a half-century earlier, transforming the urban economy and cultural landscape. They provided new labor to run the expanding city, working in the construction industry and mass transit, flocking to the booming garment-making industry, and opening thousands of small shops that provided food, clothing, and other necessities to their fellow newcomers.

CLOCKWISE FROM TOP LEFT
**Commercial postcards highlighting the "exotic" street life of new Americans** 1905–25

***The New Messiah or David Alroy* (*Der nayer moshiakh oder David Alro'i*), theater program**
c. 1910

**Rokeach Kosher Scouring Powder container**
c. 1912

Russian-born Israel Rokeach arrived in New York in 1890 and that same year started a soap-making company, which expanded to sell kosher scouring powder and other household products by the early 20th century.

OPPOSITE
**Mulberry Street** 1900
Hand-colored photograph by Detroit Photography Co.

MULBERRY STREET, NEW YORK CITY
COPYRIGHT 1900,
BY DETROIT PHOTOGRAPHIC
BANCA

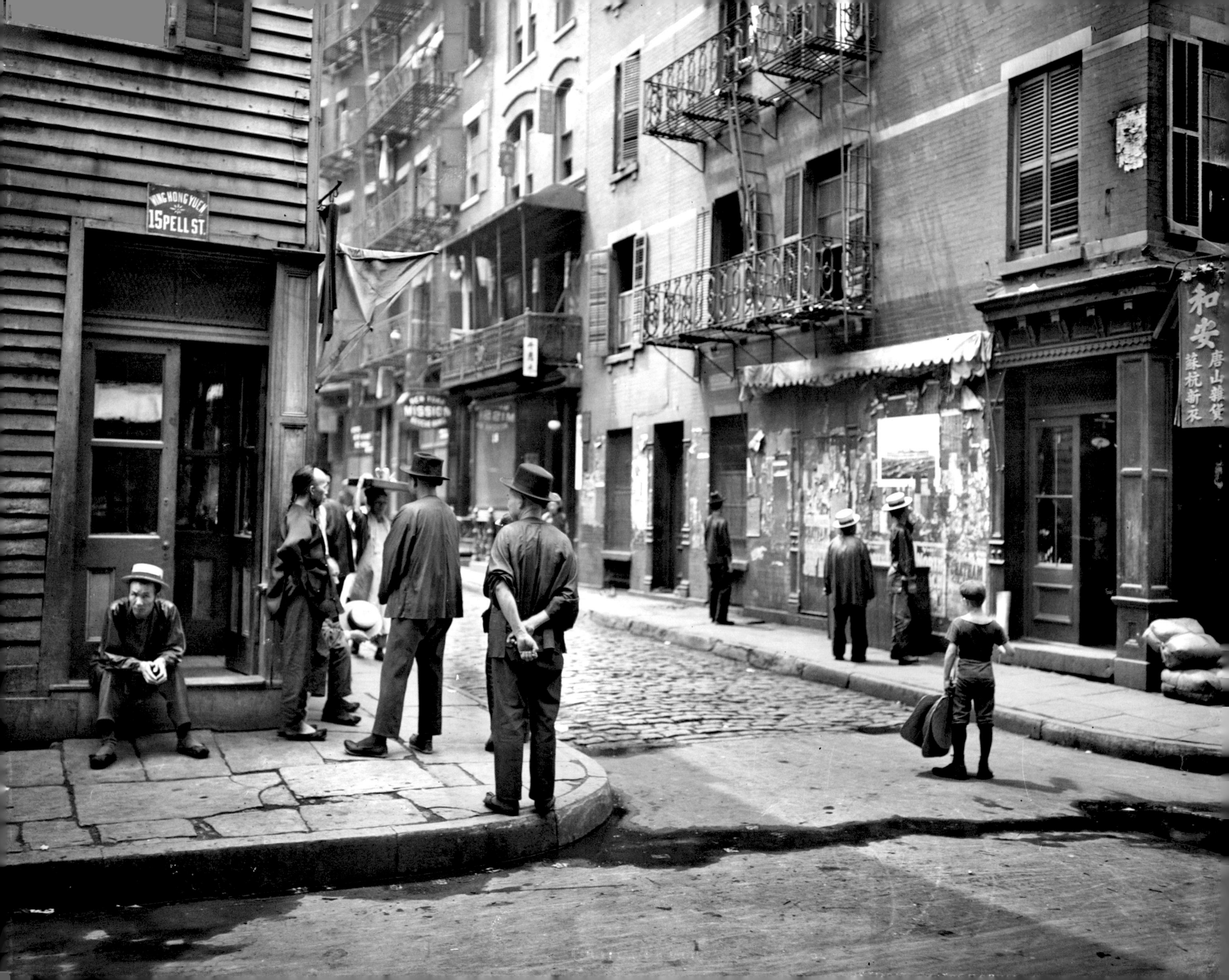
WING HONG YUEN
15 PELL ST.
MISSION
和安
唐山雜貨
蘇杭新衣

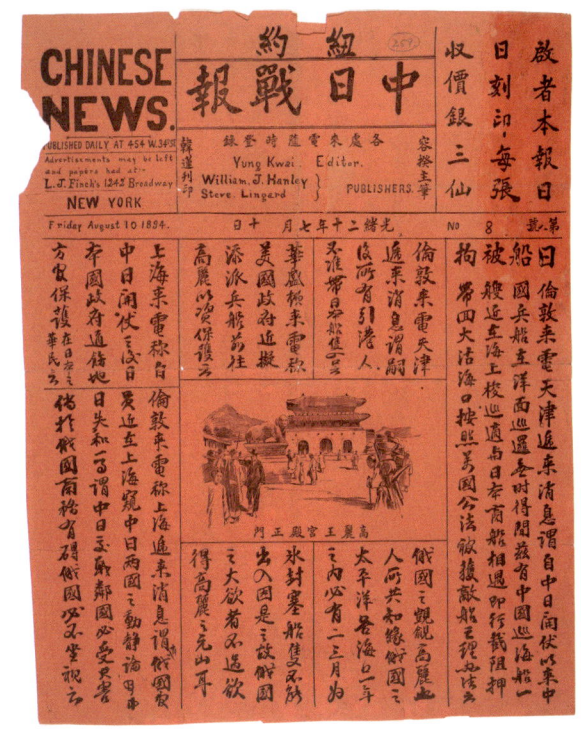

## 1880-1898

# Chinatown

A small number of Chinese men, mostly seamen, lived in 1850s New York. By the 1870s Chinatown, near the Bowery, was home to over 2,000 people, making it the second most populous Chinese community in North America, after San Francisco's Chinatown. Immigrants, still mostly male, worked as laborers, shopkeepers, and laundrymen, scattered across Manhattan.

Caricatured in the English-language press and condemned by white reformers for their gambling and opium dens, Chinese New Yorkers created their own institutions. These included merchants' societies, newspapers, and traditional Chinese opera companies. Chinatown residents such as journalist Wong Chin Foo also spearheaded efforts to repeal the 1882 federal law that excluded most Chinese, including women, from entering the United States—but the law was not repealed until 1943.

CLOCKWISE FROM ABOVE
**Chinese Theater** c. 1905
Oil on canvas by Howard McLean

The Chinese Theater at 5-7 Doyers Street, founded by Chinese performers and promoters in 1893, was the first permanent Chinese-language theater east of San Francisco.

**Satin Chinese men's slippers worn by Chinatown merchant Lee B. Lok** c. 1897

**Chinese News** August 10, 1894

OPPOSITE
**Pell Street, Chinatown** c. 1900

## 1880–1898

# The New Bowery

By the 1890s new immigrants were bringing fresh life to the Bowery. Yiddish, Italian, and Chinese theaters joined older German beer halls and Irish-American music halls. Saloons, dance halls, dime museums, and tattoo parlors added to the street's working-class allure, which drew out-of-town tourists and uptown New Yorkers eager for "slumming parties." The Bowery's polyglot medley shaped New York's evolving stage and music industries, ultimately influencing the Broadway stage and 20th-century Hollywood.

The energy of the new multiethnic New York had a dark side as well. Despite the cultural mixing of the Bowery, New York's varied peoples did not always mingle harmoniously. "Scientific" theories of racial hierarchy were matched by ready-at-hand racism expressed in popular culture, including a series of locally published joke books that openly lampooned "drunken" Irishmen, "cheap" Jews, "hot-tempered" Italians, and "silly" African Americans and Chinese.

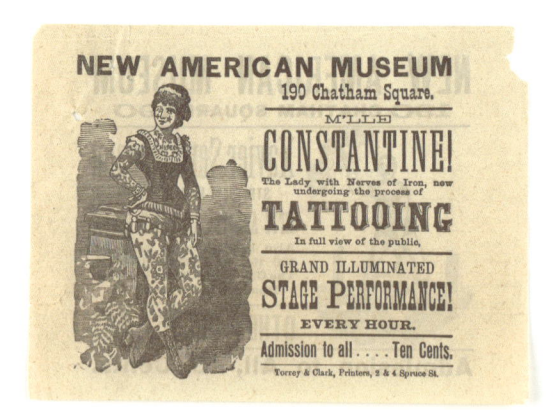

CLOCKWISE FROM TOP LEFT
**New American Museum handbill** 1883

The Bowery's southern end at Chatham Square became the site of tattoo parlors and the New American Museum (a business displaying "freaks" and sideshows).

**Electric stencil pen** c. 1877
Made by Edison's Electrical Pen & Duplicating Press Co.

In 1891 Bowery tattoo artist Samuel O'Reilly repurposed Thomas Edison's "electric pen"—invented in 1876 for cutting stencils to use in copying documents—as the first electric tattoo machine.

**"The Bowery Burlesquers," theater poster**
c. 1898
Lithograph by H.C. Litho. Co., New York

## 1880–1898

# Coney Island

In the late 19th century developers turned the beach resort of Coney Island on Brooklyn's Atlantic shore into a hotel and saloon district reachable by streetcar, railroad, and steamboat. Seeing an opportunity, businessmen soon further transformed the island with dazzling amusement parks—Sea Lion Park (1895), Steeplechase Park (1897), Luna Park (1903), and Dreamland (1904)—with electric lights, mechanical rides, and performances by such stars as the escape artist Harry Houdini and the exotic dancer called Little Egypt.

The parks attracted millions of visitors, as sideshows, dime museums, and tattoo parlors brought Bowery pastimes to the island. Generations of workers spent their free afternoons and nickels on Coney's pleasures, escaping tenement life and factory labor for a few hours. A new form of urban recreation—commercial, boisterous, and democratic—had been born.

CLOCKWISE FROM ABOVE
**The Algerian Theatre, Coney Island** 1896
Photograph by Byron Co.

**Excursion to Coney Island game** 1875–1900
Made by Milton Bradley & Co.

**Steeplechase Park tickets** c. 1890

# New Yorkers
## 1880–1898

ABOVE
**Barnum's American Museum (detail)** 1853
Engraving by John Ruben Chapin and Samuel Putman Avery

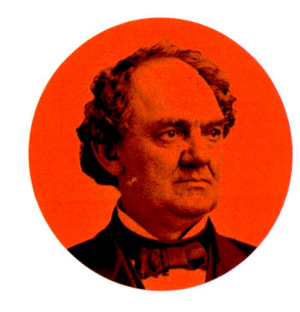

**P.T. Barnum** c. 1860

### P.T. Barnum
### (1810–1891)
### Entertainment as Big Business

Before Phineas Taylor Barnum ever stepped into a circus ring, he learned how to sell fun like no one else had before. Barnum invented a new kind of mass culture by catering to public tastes, creating spectacle, and promoting relentlessly. In the process, he made himself rich and New York the entertainment capital of the country.

The epicenter of this revolution was Barnum's American Museum on the corner of Broadway and Ann St. in Manhattan. Part zoo, part funhouse, part theater, and part scientific emporium, Barnum's Museum became the most visited place in America. Through this and his other endeavors, including concerts and circuses, Barnum helped spark (and capitalized on) a transformation in American culture: entertainment as big business.

### Wong Chin Foo
### (Wang Qingfu 王清福)
### (1847–1898)
### Speaking Up for Chinese New York

Wong Chin Foo came to New York in the 1870s looking for opportunity. Instead, he found a city where many people held racist stereotypes about immigrants like him. Wong became one of the most famous Chinese Americans of his day, devoting himself to fighting for Chinese rights as a writer, lecturer, and organizer.

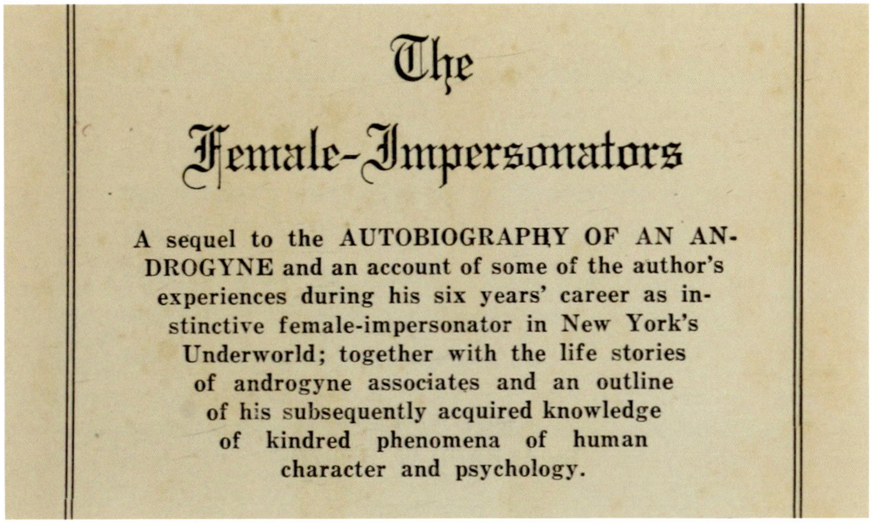

Wong's efforts did not end anti-Chinese bias. But the enclave that Wong helped build in New York kept growing—up to a population of 6,300 by 1900. Chinatown became a haven, one of the few places with a dense enough Chinese population to offer a familiar language, culture, and the hope of economic support, and to plant the seeds for growth in the 20th century.

**Wong Chin Foo from *Harper's Weekly*** May 26, 1877

ABOVE
**The *Chinese-American* newspaper published by Wong Chin Foo** February 3, 1883

### Jennie June/Ralph Werther
### (1874–?)
### Transgender in Gilded New York

The author known as Jennie June was, in her own words, an "androgyne," maintaining a professional life as a man while living much of the time as a woman. Her move to New York City was the decisive turning point in her life, offering her spaces to explore her gender and sexuality in ways she could not in the small Connecticut town of her birth.

June also took the nearly unprecedented step of writing about her life; her two books are some of the earliest surviving accounts in the words of someone whom we might now call transgender. They allow us to reconstruct the city that she moved in, from the university to the Bowery, where she both found community and faced the daily possibility of harassment or violence.

**Jennie June from *The Female-Impersonators* by Ralph Werther/Jennie June, published by Medico-Legal Journal, New York** 1922

Jennie June never sat for a traditional portrait.

ABOVE
**Title page of *The Female-Impersonators* by Ralph Werther/Jennie June** 1922

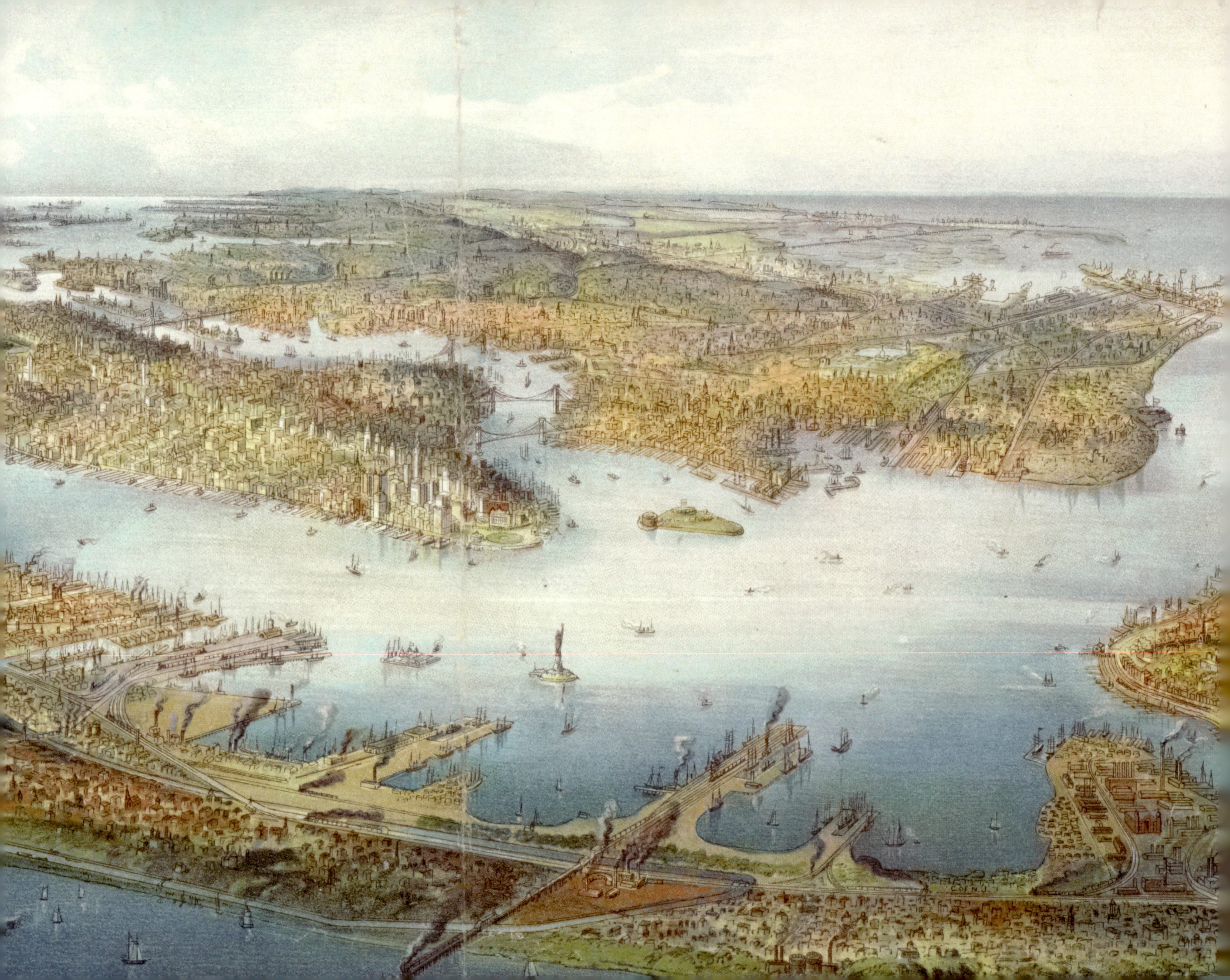

# 1880–1898

## Making Greater New York

By 1880, with over 1.2 million people, New York was the world's third most populous city, after London and Paris. The cities of New York and Brooklyn shared the Western Hemisphere's busiest harbor. Manhattan, the nation's economic and cultural capital, was also its most ethnically diverse place. The city's preeminence was soon symbolized by two monumental structures in the harbor: the Brooklyn Bridge and a statue called "Liberty Enlightening the World." City leaders had high ambitions for future growth, proclaiming New York "the commanding, commercial, and financial center of the civilized world."

Nothing expressed this expansive vision more than the movement to unite the Bronx, Brooklyn, Manhattan, Queens, and Staten Island under a single city government. Advocates argued that "consolidation" not only would allow efficient planning, and the sharing of resources like fresh water, but would fulfill New York's destiny of scale and grandeur. Despite resistance, particularly from devoted Brooklynites, their arguments prevailed at the ballot box and in the statehouse. On January 1, 1898, the five-borough city of Greater New York came into being. The city's population jumped overnight from 1.8 million to 3.4 million, passing the size of its rival, Paris.

OPPOSITE
*Greatest New York* (detail) c. 1911
Illustration by H. Wellge, lithograph by Julius Bien

## 1880–1898

# The Great Bridge

In 1883 the world's longest suspension bridge linked the cities of Brooklyn and New York. The sheer size of the "New York and Brooklyn Bridge"—with its main span of 1,595 feet—proclaimed the ambitions of the two cities it joined. Its two 276-foot high towers were the tallest structures in Brooklyn and Manhattan.

The construction of the bridge required a massive human effort. Between 1869 and 1883, several thousand laborers and engineers worked above, below, and along the East River to complete the structure. Many were Irish, German, Italian, African American, or Chinese. Most worked for a daily wage of $2.00 or $2.25; a strike for $3.00 was put down in 1872. At least 20 men died, several from "the bends," a sickness caused by toiling in underwater caissons deep below the East River, while building the "Great Bridge."

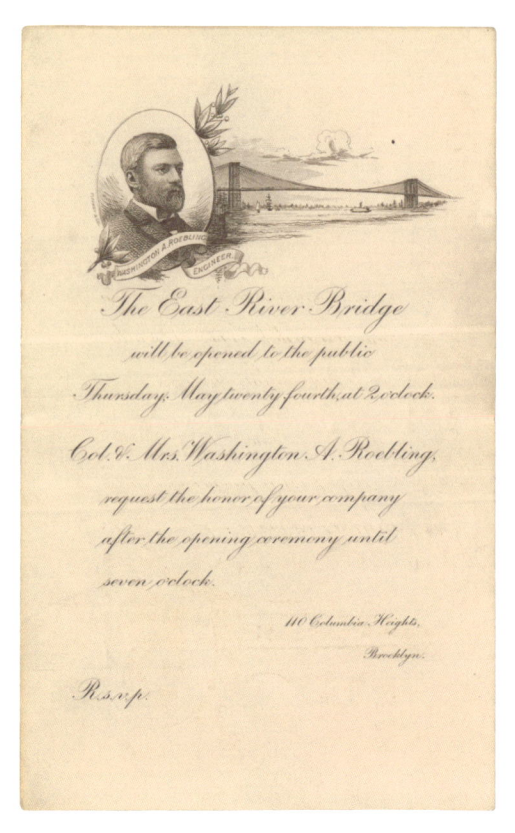

CLOCKWISE FROM LEFT
**Top of Brooklyn Pier at Fifth Course Above Roadway** 1872
Photograph by Silas A. Holmes

**Pulley, wire brush, and nut used in the construction of the Brooklyn Bridge, the pulley is marked "NY&BB" for the New York & Brooklyn Bridge** 1869–83

**Invitation to a reception given by Col. and Mrs. Washington A. Roebling following the opening of the Brooklyn Bridge** May 24, 1883

OPPOSITE
**Brooklyn Bridge under construction** 1881

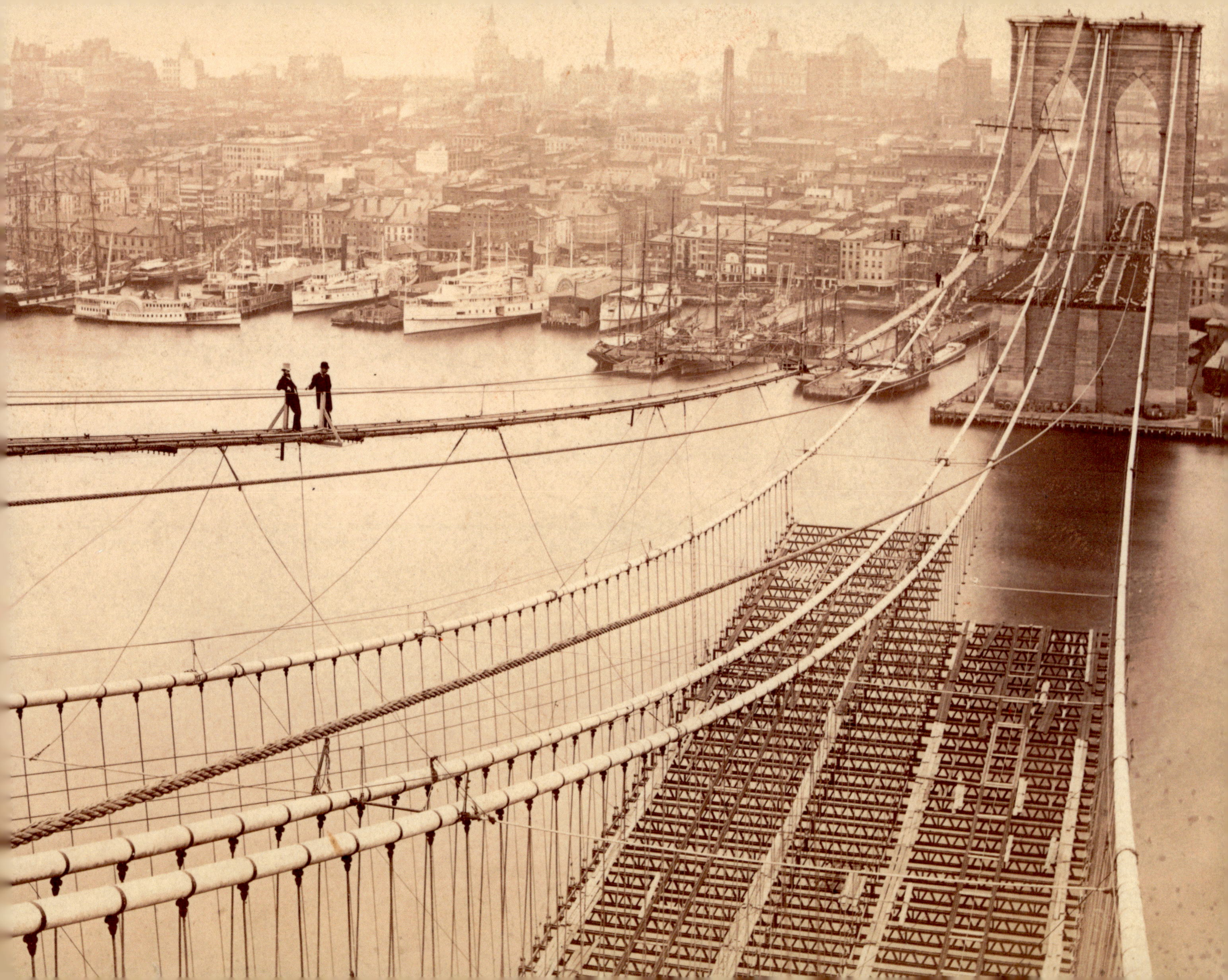

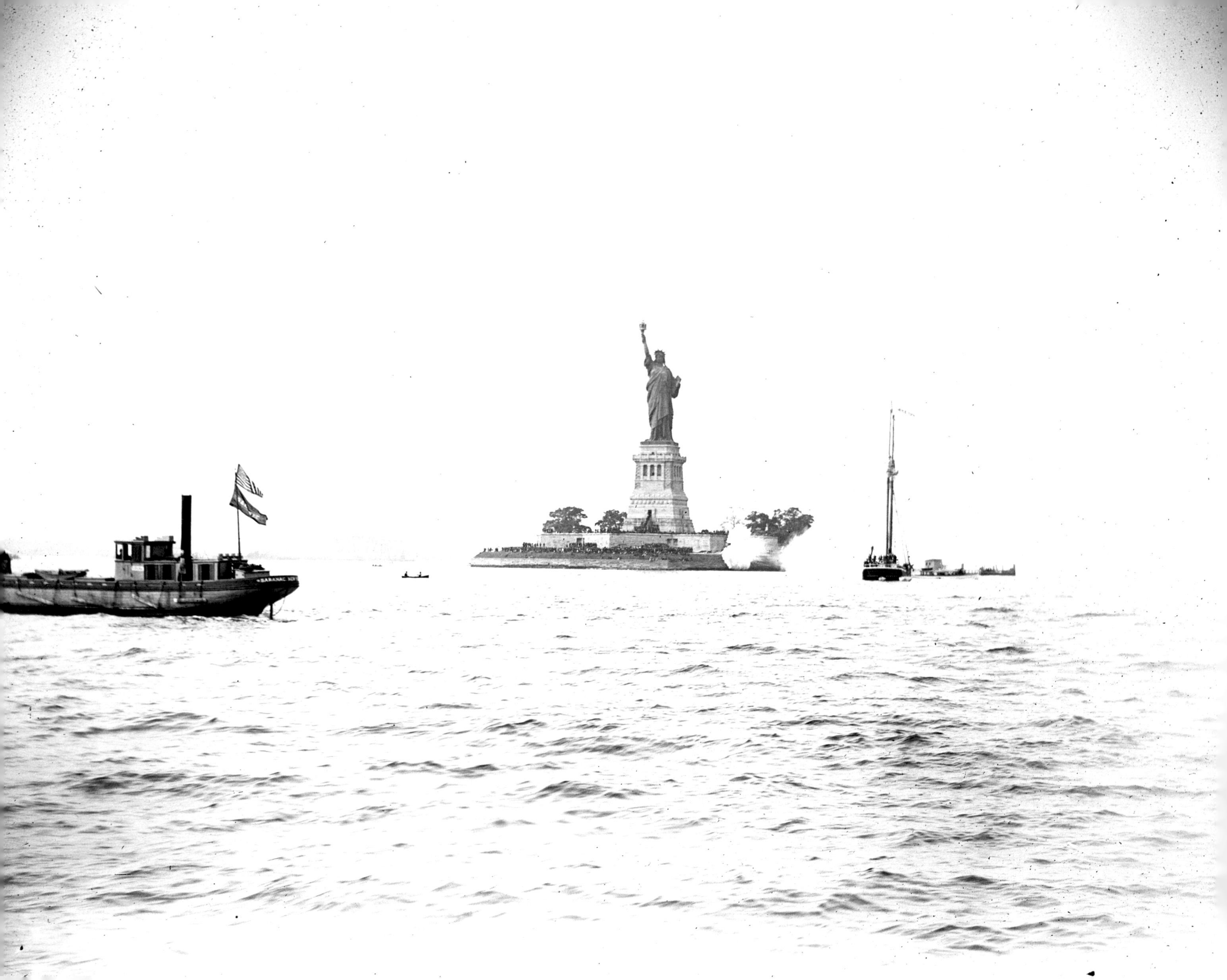

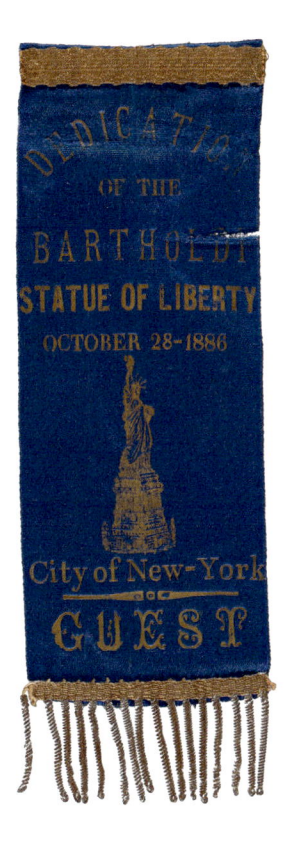

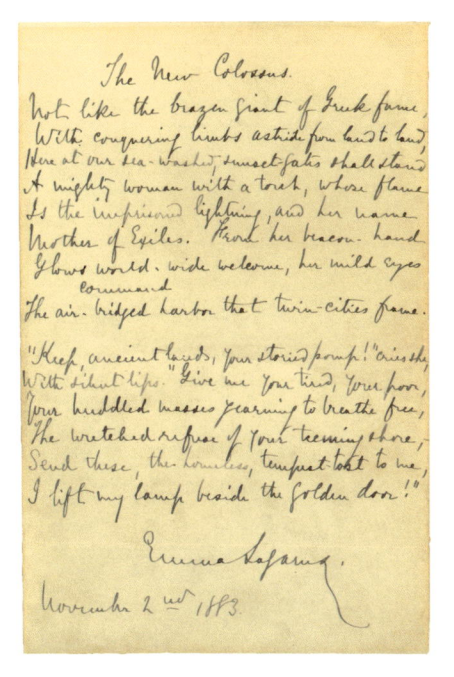

## 1880–1898

# Liberty Enlightening the World

Parisian sculptor Frédéric Auguste Bartholdi chose Bedloe's Island in New York Bay as the site for his statue of "Liberty Enlightening the World," proposed as a gift from France to the United States in 1875. Americans donated over $100,000 to pay for its pedestal, designed by architect Richard Morris Hunt.

Towering 305 feet over the harbor after its completion in 1886, the statue of Franco-American friendship became an icon of national freedom and of New York's role as the country's dominant metropolis. In an era when about three-quarters of all European immigrants landed in New York, the statue also became a symbol of the city as a gateway to America.

CLOCKWISE FROM TOP LEFT
**Guest ribbon badge for the dedication of the Statue of Liberty** October 28, 1886

**Terracotta maquette for the Statue of Liberty**
c. 1870
By Frédéric Auguste Bartholdi

**Bronze maquette for the Statue of Liberty**
c. 1870
By Frédéric Auguste Bartholdi

**Manuscript for "The New Colossus" by Emma Lazarus** 1883

New Yorker Emma Lazarus, a descendant of some of the city's earliest Jewish settlers, wrote this sonnet in 1883 to help raise funds to build the Statue's pedestal. The poem recast the statue as the "Mother of Exiles," welcoming "huddled masses yearning to breathe free."

OPPOSITE
**Statue of Liberty on Bedloe's Island** c. 1886
Photograph by Robert L. Bracklow

## 1880–1898

# Connecting the Region

Before the five boroughs officially became a single city, they were already knit together by new infrastructure, including gas, electric, and especially transit lines. Cable cars and electric-powered trolleys joined horse-drawn streetcars and omnibuses on the streets. Overhead, elevated trains—pioneered in Manhattan in the late 1860s—soon crisscrossed the region, creating outcries about noise, dirt, shadows, and the unsightly transformation of urban streets.

Expanding transit drove development in Brooklyn, the South Bronx, and upper Manhattan, as neighborhoods like Crown Heights, Melrose, and the Upper West Side filled with row houses and early apartment "flats" for middle-class families. By 1898, 100,000 commuters a day poured into Manhattan via bridge and ferry from Brooklyn. Hundreds of thousands more came by ferry from Staten Island and New Jersey or by commuter rail from Westchester, Long Island, and Connecticut.

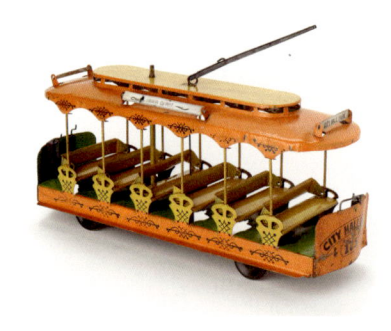

CLOCKWISE FROM TOP LEFT

**Broadway with cable car, looking north from 23rd Street** 1895
Photograph by Byron Co.

**Mechanical toy trolley car** c. 1885

**Third Avenue Elevated railway destination sign** c. 1900

When the Third Avenue Elevated railway extended its route from Manhattan into the Bronx in 1886, it immediately spurred construction along its tracks and around its stations.

**Daily schedule for the Narrows Ferry**
August 22nd to November 1st, 1897

Steam-powered ferries remained an important means of transportation in an urban region divided by waterways.

CLOCKWISE FROM RIGHT
**Surveyors, Bronx** 1895

Large areas of the Bronx became part of New York City in 1874 and 1895. Across the borough, surveyors laid out lines for streets and avenues through rural farmland.

**Souvenir badge for the "Inauguration of Greater New York"** Jan. 1, 1898

**"Up with the Flag of Brooklyn," sheet music published by F.H. Chandler** 1895

This anti-consolidation song sheet features Brooklyn's City Hall, which became Borough Hall in 1898.

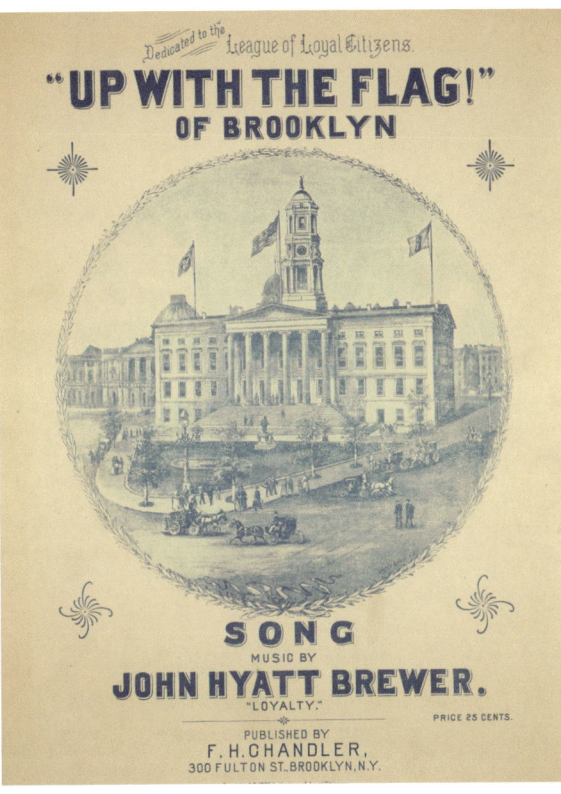

## 1880–1898

# Establishing the Greater City

Lawyer-planner Andrew Haswell Green spearheaded the movement to add surrounding areas to New York City in order to create a greater municipality. Green and others argued that shared taxes, harbor facilities, police, fresh water, and other resources would secure a more livable and prosperous metropolis. In 1894 residents of the Bronx, Brooklyn, Manhattan, Queens, and Staten Island voted by 176,000 to 132,000 to consolidate as Greater New York City.

But the referendum was non-binding and anti-consolidation forces from Brooklyn blocked it in the state legislature until machine politicians took the reins. Thomas Platt, "boss" of the state Republican Party, decided that an enlarged city offered better opportunities for Republican control and patronage, and he secured the Republican governor's signature in 1896.

With 3.4 million people and 305 square miles, Greater New York City was the world's second largest metropolis, ready to play an even more momentous role in the 20th century.

# New Yorkers
## 1880–1898

ABOVE
**East 5th St., before and after George E. Waring took over New York's street cleaning services**
1893 and 1897
Photographs by Jacob A. Riis

### The Horse
#### The Poop Problem

For most of the city's history, New Yorkers used horses to haul just about everything and to provide essential city services, from fighting fires to cleaning the streets. But their sheer numbers—some 160,000 in late 19th-century Brooklyn and Manhattan—created problems. The average horse produced about 22 pounds of manure and a quart of urine each day; much of it ended up on the streets.

In 1894 reform-minded mayor William Strong appointed George E. Waring to reinvent the city's woefully inadequate sanitation system. Waring hired 2,700 men, drilled them in military precision, and set them to work removing waste from the streets—just one of the creative responses to the challenges of growing urban density.

## Emily Warren Roebling
(1843–1903)
### Unsung Hero of the Brooklyn Bridge

Emily Roebling helped oversee one of the most important technological feats of her time—the creation of the Brooklyn Bridge. When tragedy disabled her husband, chief engineer Washington Roebling, Emily took over to manage the bridge's construction. Defying the limitations placed on women of her time, Roebling secured her family's legacy as the builders of New York's first great bridge.

Acting as her husband's eyes, ears, and voice and winning the confidence of the men she worked with, Emily Roebling quickly became the public face of the chief engineer. The result was an engineering marvel that linked the cities of New York and Brooklyn— the first and third largest cities in the United States— creating a vital strategic connection and paving the way for their eventual merger.

**Emily Warren Roebling** c. 1870

ABOVE
**President, Treasurers, Engineers, and Foremen at the Brooklyn Bridge construction site** 1878

## Andrew Haswell Green
(1820–1903)
### Father of Greater New York

In the second half of the 19th century, New York remade itself to compete with European capitals—creating grand parks, major cultural institutions, and stately boulevards. One man had an outsized role in this transformation: Andrew Haswell Green, lawyer, public servant, and city visionary.

Among the many projects Green was instrumental in creating were Central Park, Riverside Park, Morningside Park, Fort Washington Park, the New York Public Library, the Bronx Zoo, the American Museum of Natural History, and the Metropolitan Museum of Art. But his most lasting legacy is probably the five-borough city. His vision of uniting the City of New York, the City of Brooklyn, and the surrounding counties was fulfilled when the city of Greater New York came into existence on January 1, 1898.

**Andrew Haswell Green** c. 1868

ABOVE
**"The Raid on the City Treasury the Mangy Curs Running Away from Watch-dog Green" a political cartoon depicting Andrew Haswell Green as New York City's comptroller** c. 1870

M
CUNEO IMPORTING CO
BANANAS
NEW YORK
DISA ★ GEFLE
SAIL MAKERS

# 1898–1914

## The World's Port

As the 20th century began, people and goods streamed into what was now the world's second most populous city after London. By 1914 more than half of the entire nation's imports and 40 percent of its exports were passing through New York's seaport. Tens of thousands of mostly small factories created more than two billion dollars in goods each year, almost double that of New York's nearest U.S. competitor, Chicago. Office towers soared into the sky. Along with record-level immigration, these transformations helped make New York the signature metropolis of the modern age—a global city of formidable energy and intense ambitions.

The city's rapid growth brought new scrutiny to old but increasing urban problems—crowding in tenement districts, low wages and dangerous working conditions, financial volatility, racial discrimination, and unequal concentrations of economic and political power. A generation of New Yorkers embraced the idea that these urban ills could be solved by collective action. An alliance of union members, journalists, social workers, academics, and middle-class women rallied for a new kind of "progressive" government activism to rein in private interests for the sake of the public good. This coalition and its ideas about activist government would shape urban politics—and American liberalism—for most of the 20th century.

OPPOSITE
**Dockworkers unloading bananas in**

## 1898–1914

# Capital of Enterprise and Finance

New York's economy was strikingly diverse. Shippers and dockworkers moved goods through the bustling port; men and women churned out an astonishing variety of goods, from garments and lace to solvents, furniture, and linoleum (manufactured in Linoleumville, Staten Island); and new corporate headquarters in towering skyscrapers offered employment to white-collar workers from executives to mailroom clerks.

This economic energy was underwritten by Wall Street bankers, who reinforced New York's pivotal role in the global economy by merging far-flung railroads and steel-making firms into corporations larger than any ever seen before. About 60 percent of all American commercial banks kept deposits in New York banks, which in turn loaned millions of dollars to traders on the New York Stock Exchange.

The outbreak of World War I in 1914 was a watershed, as New Yorkers supplied arms, goods, and credit to the Allied combatants. By the war's end, New York surpassed London to become the world's busiest seaport and leading lender, whose influence stretched to the farthest reaches of the globe.

CLOCKWISE FROM TOP LEFT
**Metropolitan Life Insurance Co. postcards depicting clerical workers in a skyscraper office** c. 1910

**Cigar owned by J. P. Morgan with "JPM" monogram** c. 1900

"Captains of finance" like John Pierpont (J. P.) Morgan, George F. Baker, and Jacob Schiff controlled the flow of money, providing credit not just to private industries, but also to governments at home and abroad. New York City itself turned to J. P. Morgan for a loan to prevent municipal bankruptcy during the financial crisis of 1907.

**Brooklyn sugar refineries** 1900

OPPOSITE
***Wall Street*** 1915
Photograph by Paul Strand

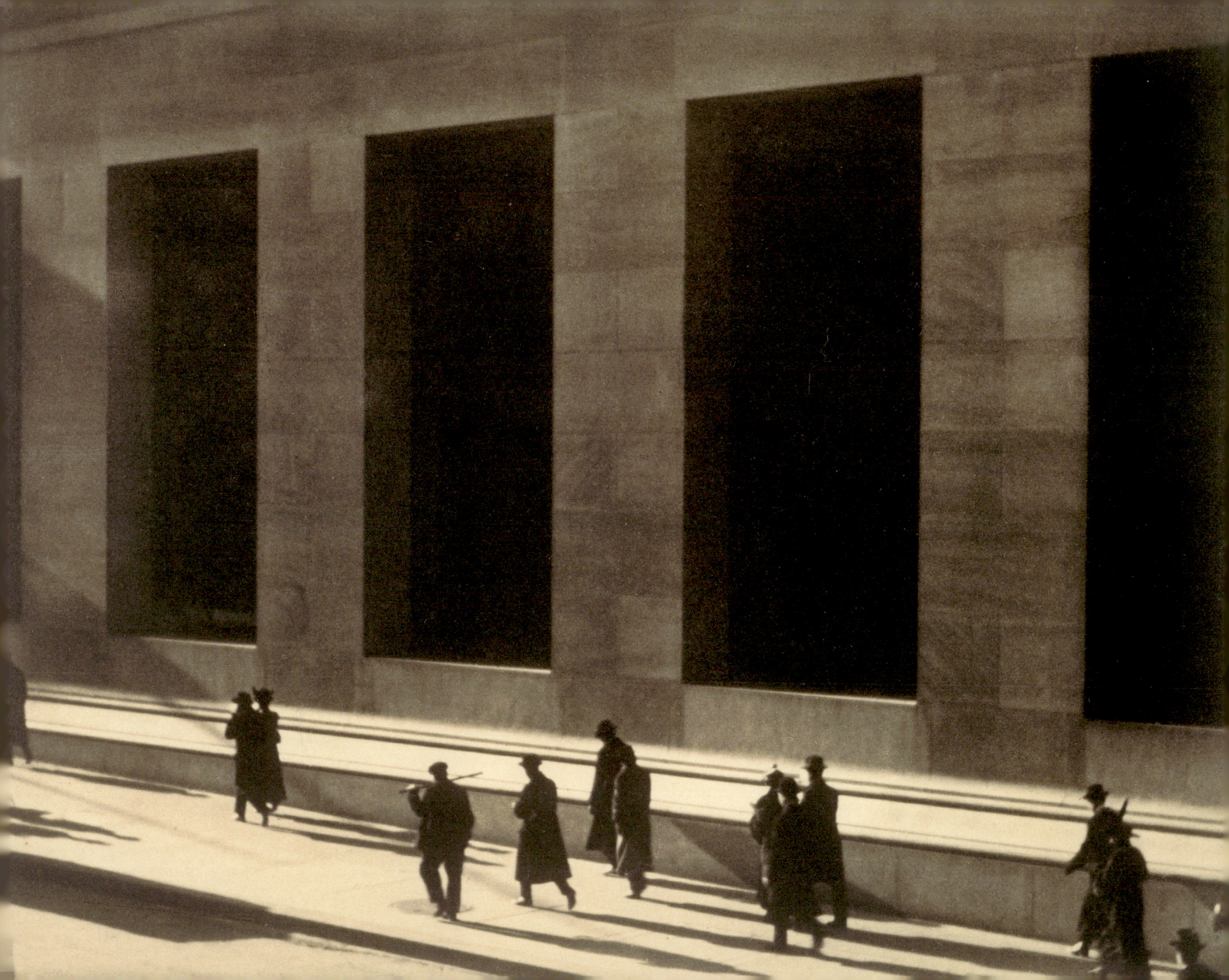

SAHADI'S
EL-AHRAM
BRAND
DELICIOUS
FOOD
NET CONTENTS 15 OUNCES
CONTAINS:
GROUND SESAME SEEDS
CORN SYRUP
CANE SUGAR
EGG ALBUMEN
FLAVOR BERGAMOOT
REG. U. S.
PAT. OFF.
No. 270
No. 510
Class 46
"IT MELTS IN YOUR MOUTH"
A1
HALWAH
A. SAHADI & CO., INC., MFRS. — 195 WASHINGTON ST., N.Y.C.

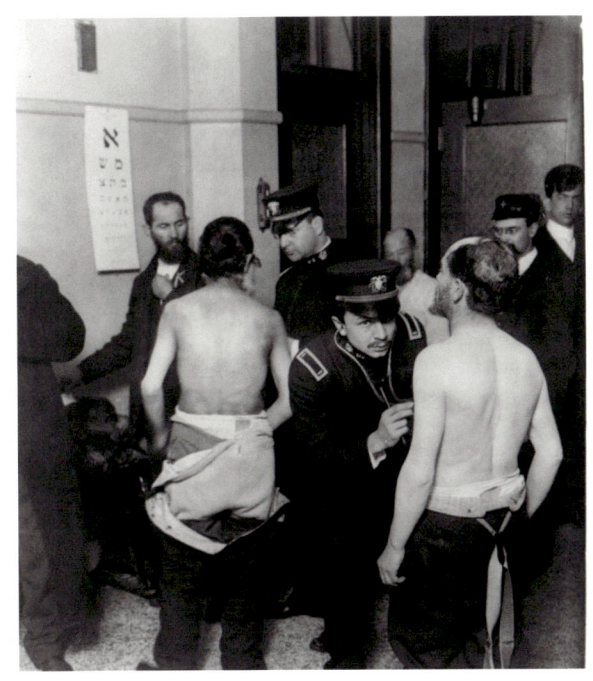

CLOCKWISE FROM ABOVE
**Physicians examining a group of Jewish immigrants at Ellis Island** c. 1907
Photograph by Underwood & Underwood

**Silver candlesticks with bullet hole brought to New York by the Grossman family, Jewish immigrants from Kiev** c. 1905

**Apple peeler and corer used by immigrant entrepreneur Joel Russ in his Lower East Side appetizing shop, Russ and Daughters**
early 20th century

OPPOSITE
**Halvah tin, sold by the Sahadi family in "Little Syria" in downtown Manhattan**
early 20th century

## 1898–1914

# Immigration

In 1907, as manufacturing boomed, immigration to the United States hit a new high of a million people in a single year, most of them arriving in New York. By 1910 immigrants accounted for 40 percent of the city's population, the highest since before the Civil War. Most newcomers were from eastern and southern Europe— Russian Jews, Italians, Poles, Greeks, and others. They brought new languages, customs, and political ideas to the nation's most diverse metropolis.

The new arrivals powered the economy, providing the labor that kept the city's workshops running, and they started an array of new businesses that served their communities. By 1919 New York was America's dominant manufacturing center, producing ten percent of the nation's entire industrial output. In some areas, like women's clothing, New York was responsible for the vast majority of all U.S. production. But, unlike Pittsburgh or Detroit, New York City had no single dominant industry and most shops were small. In this varied economic environment, it often required only a small amount of savings for New Yorkers to start their own small businesses and add to the entrepreneurial energy of the city.

## 1898–1914

# Organizing Workers

Many New York workers faced low pay and dangerous conditions. "If there is one place in America where the workers have reason to revolt," socialist Louis Duchez argued in 1910, "it is New York City." Workers reacted to conditions with organization and mobilization: in 1909, 20,000 garment workers struck for higher wages and shorter hours, and, when 146 workers died in a fire behind locked doors at the Triangle Waist Company factory in 1911, many New Yorkers responded with heightened activism.

New York was also a crucial base for radical groups, including the Socialist Party of America, which mobilized many of the city's unionized voters through rallies, the newspaper *The Jewish Daily Forward*, and political campaigns. Socialists won 145,000 votes for their mayoral candidate, Morris Hillquit, a Latvian Jewish immigrant, in 1917. Though Hillquit came in third, socialist influence remained strong in the city's labor movement.

CLOCKWISE FROM TOP LEFT
**Funeral procession for seven unidentified Triangle fire victims** 1911

**Workers in a sweatshop** c. 1911
Photograph by Lewis Hine

**Seltzer bottle, adorned with the emblem of the Socialist Labor Party** c. 1910
Labeled "Joe Netke, 374–76 E. 10 Street N.Y."

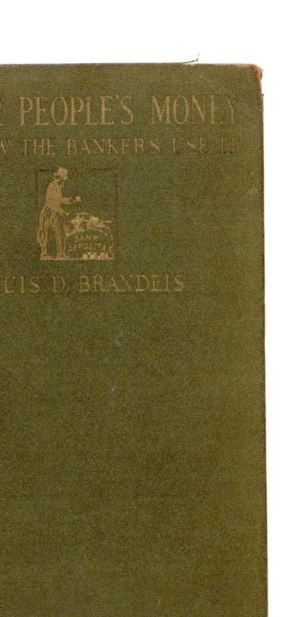

## 1898–1914
# The Power of Print

As the nation's media capital, New York became the base for "muckraking" reporters. Their critique of Wall Street spurred a movement to regulate the power of New York's banks and helped to push bankers themselves to devise one of the era's lasting reforms: the Federal Reserve System. Muckrakers Ida Tarbell, Lincoln Steffens, and David Graham Phillips became nationwide celebrities, and their investigations of powerful industrial "Trusts," Tammany Hall, and the U.S. Senate fueled sweeping movements for economic and political reforms.

Meanwhile, African-American newspapers like the *New York Age*, humor periodicals like *Puck*, and progressive magazines such as *The Survey* tackled issues ranging from racial discrimination to poverty and slum conditions.

**ABOVE**
*Other People's Money*, an exposé of Wall Street banks, by Louis D. Brandeis, published by Frederick A. Stokes, New York  1914

**RIGHT**
"Jack and the Wall Street Giants," illustration by Joseph Keppler Jr. satirizing J.P. Morgan and other financiers towering over President Theodore Roosevelt, from *Puck*  January 13, 1904

## 1898–1914

# Tammany Goes Progressive

Facing competition from the leftist politics of new New Yorkers and their unions, Tammany Hall boss Charlie Murphy pragmatically pivoted the city's Democratic political "machine" to a reform agenda. The Triangle fire of 1911 emboldened Tammany politicians, like Alfred E. (Al) Smith and Robert F. Wagner, to champion the idea that government could improve urban life. They put New York on a course to path-breaking, nationally influential laws—at both city and state level—to improve workplace safety, shorten work hours, and provide decent low-cost housing.

Smith and Wagner became New York's "twins" of reform. Their work on factory regulation as state lawmakers during the 1910s set the stage for Smith's terms as New York's governor (1919–20, 1923–28). Smith's Lower East Side accent, ever-present cigar, and brown derby symbolized his working-class urban progressivism. As U.S. senator (1927–49), Wagner would carry his dedication to working people's rights into national policy in the New Deal of the 1930s.

CLOCKWISE FROM TOP LEFT

**"E' Vietato Fumare in Questi Locali," Italian-language sign warning workers that smoking inside the workplace is prohibited, in compliance with new workplace safety regulations** c. 1915

**Derby hat owned by Al Smith** 1930s
Made by Knox Twenty/Knox New York

Al Smith's brown derby came to symbolize his Lower East Side origins and became an emblem of his 1928 presidential campaign.

**Camera-booth snapshots of Al Smith and Robert Wagner Sr.** c. 1933

OPPOSITE

**Former Governor Al Smith (at right) and Mayor James J. Walker (second from left) at the cornerstone-laying ceremony for the new Tammany Hall on East 17th Street** 1929

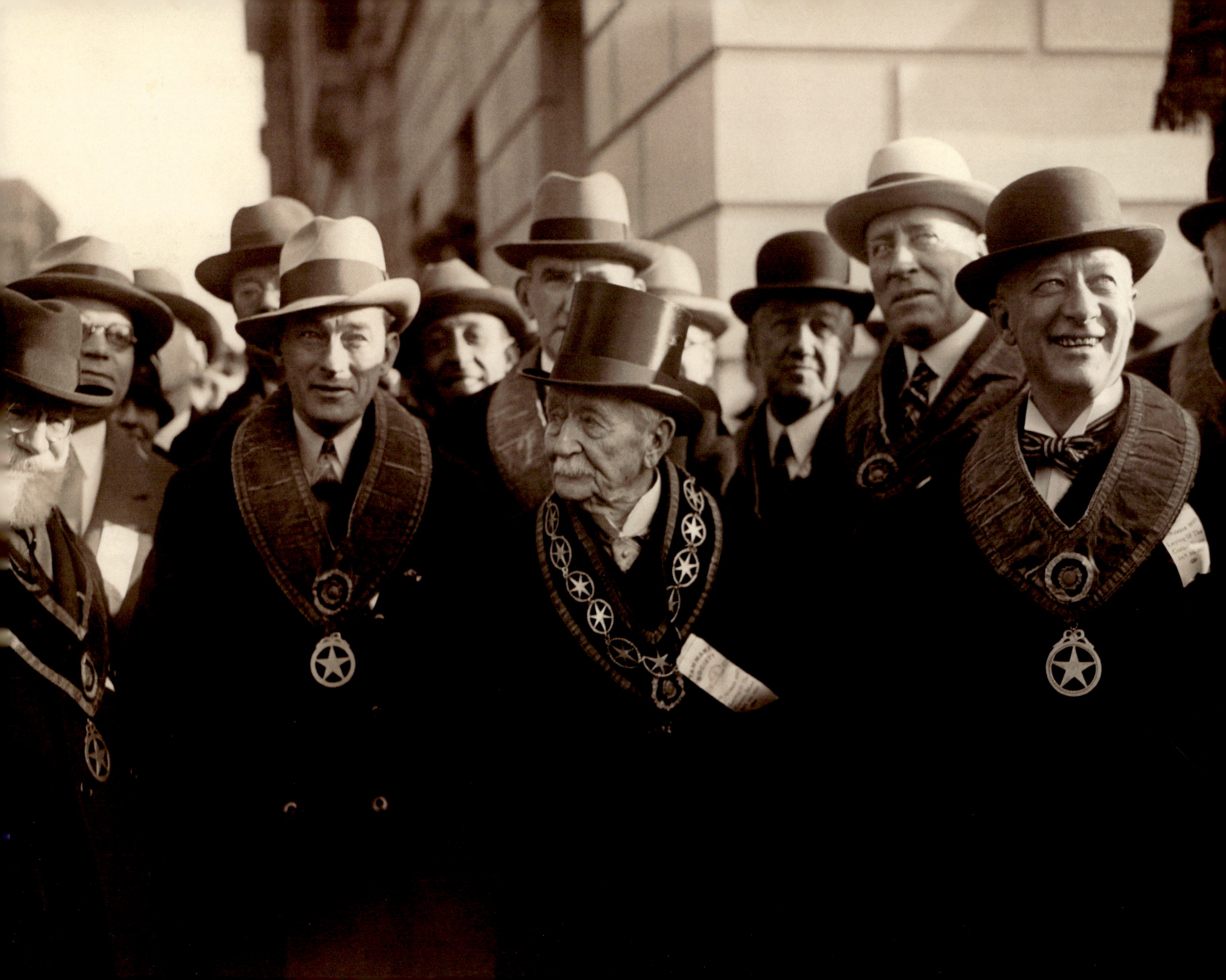

# New Yorkers 1898–1914

**Belle Moskowitz** c. 1915

### Belle Moskowitz
(1877–1933)
Progressive Reformer

A social worker, writer, and publicist, Moskowitz exemplified New York's Progressive Era. A native of East Harlem and the daughter of German Jewish immigrants, she launched one of her earliest crusades in 1908, when she led a campaign against the city's cheap dance halls, such as the Haymarket on 30th Street, which critics worried corrupted young women.

During the 1920s Moskowitz carried her reform goals into politics as the principal advisor to New York governor and presidential nominee Al Smith. She became arguably the nation's most powerful woman, shaping the liberal politics of New York City and State.

ABOVE
**The Haymarket** c. 1906
Photograph by George F. Arata

**Andrew Carnegie**
(1835–1919)
Philanthropy and the Birth of the Modern City

Steel manufacturer Andrew Carnegie spent $350 million over his lifetime on philanthropic efforts, including creating 67 libraries throughout New York City, the acoustic masterpiece Carnegie Hall, and the Carnegie Corporation of New York, founded in 1911 to "promote the advancement of knowledge among people."

Carnegie was part of a group of wealthy New Yorkers like J.D. Rockefeller, Andrew W. Mellon, and Peter Cooper who transformed the city through their philanthropy. Some critics saw the very power of their private dollars as a threat to the democratic process, but Carnegie proclaimed "My chief happiness lies in the thought that after I pass away the wealth that came to me to administer as a sacred trust for my fellow men is to continue to benefit humanity for generations untold."

**Andrew Carnegie** 1910

ABOVE
**Cartoon criticizing Carnegie's Scottish (rather than American) philanthropy, from *Puck*** 1901

**Philip A. Payton Jr.**
(1876–1917)
Building Black Harlem

Philip Payton opened the Afro-American Reality Company in 1900. For Payton, "the very prejudice which has heretofore worked against us can be turned and used to our profit." He soon seized on a housing glut in Harlem as an opportunity to meet the needs of black New Yorkers, and he drew on a network of black businessmen to purchase Harlem buildings and lease them to black tenants.

Payton's work fueled the transformation of the upper Manhattan neighborhood into the "capital of black America." By 1930 Harlem's black population had grown to 200,000 and the neighborhood became home to the "New Negro" movement and the incubator of the artistic flowering known as the "Harlem Renaissance."

**Philip A. Payton Jr.** 1907

ABOVE
**Harlem** 1932
Photograph by Arthur Vitols, Byron Co.

CHOPSUEY
Edwin's
CIGAR
STORE
EDWIN'S CIGARS
THE NEW NEGRO
HAS NO FEAR
HONOR TO THE
053-353

# 1914–1929

## New York Roars into the Twenties

In the 1910s the development of the city accelerated as subways connected four of the five boroughs and the soaring skyline became a symbol of New York's new supremacy as an international metropolis. By 1925 New York replaced London as the world's most populous city, leading port, and financial center.

By the mid-1920s New York's culture and population were dramatically different from a generation earlier. Although federal restrictions and war had sent new immigration plummeting, more than one-third of the city's population had been born abroad, and they and their children were rapidly transforming the very definition of what it meant to be American. They were joined by New York's newest wave of arrivals: African Americans leaving the South, who made Harlem the nation's largest and most famous urban black community.

New York became the capital of the "Jazz Age," as the multiethnic, multiracial city encouraged experimentation. Women stepped into the city's public life as never before, enjoying a daring new nightlife. Openly gay men and women found enclaves of acceptance that could not be found elsewhere. Black and white New Yorkers, newcomers and old-timers, mingled their cultural traditions with fresh ideas to create art forms that reshaped national tastes. Together they established the city as a beacon of the edgy, the sophisticated, and the sensational.

OPPOSITE
**Parade for Marcus Garvey's Universal Negro Improvement Association 1920**

## 1914–1929

# Mass Transit

New York's subway began in 1904 with the privately operated Interborough Rapid Transit Company. Reformers, entrepreneurs, and politicians soon joined forces to spread the subway to four of the five boroughs. Massive construction began in the 1910s, followed by the first fully public lines in the 1920s. Together with new East River crossings—the Williamsburg (1903), Manhattan (1909), and Queensboro (1909) Bridges—the new subway lines dramatically diminished crowding in lower Manhattan by enabling people to move to less congested areas across Brooklyn, Queens, and the Bronx. There, developers rapidly transformed farmland into residential districts for New Yorkers who now crisscrossed the city between work and home.

Although plans for a subway to Staten Island were foiled by the Depression, the multiple lines enabled the development of block upon block of new apartment buildings and single-family homes in neighborhoods like Riverdale in the Bronx, Sheepshead Bay in Brooklyn, and Jackson Heights in Queens where the city's religious and racial divisions surfaced as some developers sought to bar Jews, Catholics, and African Americans. By 1929 annual subway rides reached over two billion (versus 1.25 billion today).

CLOCKWISE FROM ABOVE
**First subway ticket** 1904

**Sheet music for "Bronx Express" from the comedy *Bronx Express* by Ossip Dymow** 1922

*Bronx Express* is a satire about a Jewish newcomer who falls asleep in a subway traveling from the Lower East Side to the Bronx and dreams he becomes a millionaire.

**Silver ceremonial shovel, used to break ground on the city's first subway, made of wood from a tree planted by Alexander Hamilton** 1900
Designed by Tiffany & Company, New York

# 1914-1929

# Skyscraper City

As the other boroughs built out, Manhattan built up. In the 1920s, New York became the great skyscraper city, surpassing its rival Chicago in the sheer number and height of its towers. Corporations erected the world's tallest office buildings in the borough's business districts, leveraging new techniques in steel construction and elevators that enabled skyscrapers to pass 50 stories by 1909. On Manhattan's crowded blocks, these towers became "machines for making the land pay," in the words of architect Cass Gilbert.

Reformers argued that massive buildings like lower Manhattan's Equitable Building were depriving New Yorkers of light and fresh air. In 1916 a citywide zoning law, the first in the nation, required "set back" upper floors to provide light and air at street level. The 102-floor Empire State Building, the world's tallest structure at its completion in 1931, is a classic example of the setback skyscraper, with its upper floors set back from the lot line. The setback skyscraper created the distinctive profile of New York's 20th-century skyline.

CLOCKWISE FROM TOP
**The Equitable Building under construction**
c. 1913

**Plaster model of the Empire State Building**
c. 1930
Made by Shreve, Lamb & Harmon, New York

**Empire State Building under construction** 1931
Photograph by Lewis Wickes Hine

## 1914–1929

# Harlem

The "Great Migration" that began during World War I and continued throughout the 1920s brought black newcomers fleeing oppression and economic hardship in the South to Harlem in upper Manhattan. Joining them were new American citizens from Puerto Rico, other Caribbean immigrants, and black New Yorkers leaving midtown after racist attacks in the early 1900s. By 1930 over 200,000 African Americans lived in Harlem.

The new arrivals included intellectuals, writers, artists, performers, and activists who built a new cultural movement: the Harlem Renaissance. Writers Langston Hughes, Zora Neale Hurston, and others forged a new kind of urban African-American voice in poems, novels, and magazines, while painter Aaron Douglas and photographer James Van Der Zee visually celebrated the "New Negro." Their energy opened opportunities for entrepreneurship, spawning businesses that catered to black consumers and marketed the talents of Harlem artists. Among them were restaurants, nightclubs, and record companies, including Black Swan Records, the first black-owned recording company, which launched in Harlem in 1921.

CLOCKWISE FROM TOP LEFT
**Harlem** 1933
Watercolor by William L'Engle

***The Crisis: A Record of the Darker Races***
November 1919

*The Crisis* was founded in New York in 1910 as the official magazine of the National Association for the Advancement of Colored People (NAACP). It became a leading activist periodical of the Harlem Renaissance under W.E.B. Du Bois, its first editor.

**"Oh Daddy/Down Home Blues"** 1921
Black Swan Records, Manufactured by Pace Phonograph Corp., New York

**Harlem Renaissance figures including the poet Clarissa Scott, lawyer Hubert Delany, and author and editor Jessie Fauset, at a party for the author Langston Hughes (second from left)** 1925

OPPOSITE
***Couple, Harlem*** 1932
Photograph by James Van Der Zee

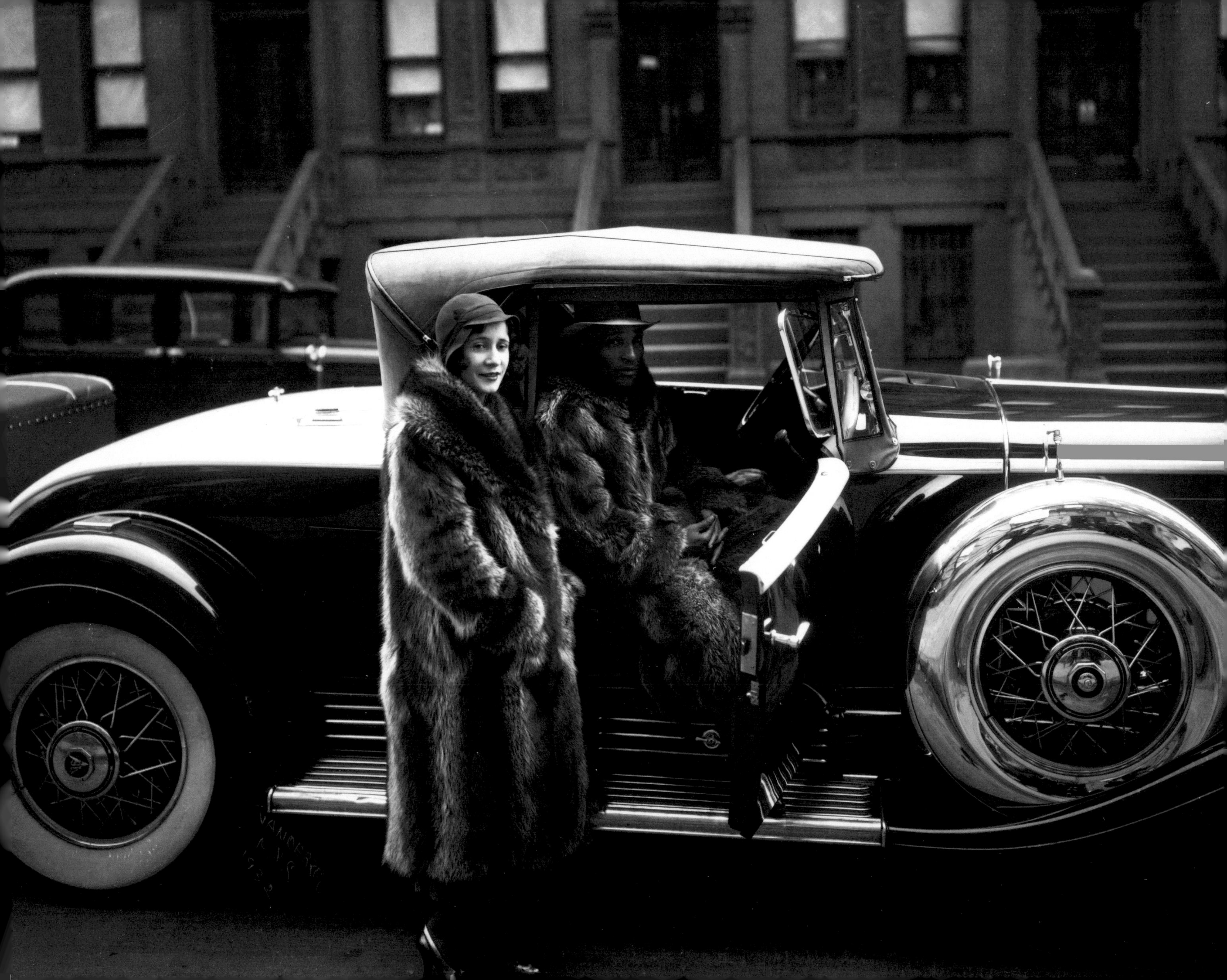
VANDERZEE

# 1914-1929
# Broadway: Cultural Crossroads

Broadway theaters and nightclubs of the 1920s promoted a jazzy, hybrid popular culture. Jewish, African-American, Irish-American, and other entertainers learned from each other's music, dance steps, and jokes on the stages of music halls, vaudeville houses, and cabarets. Sophie Tucker, the Marx Brothers, Adelaide Hall, Bill "Bojangles" Robinson, and George M. Cohan were all stars on Broadway, performing music composed in New York's music publishing district, "Tin Pan Alley," on West 28th Street.

Broadway's longest running all-black musical of its time was *Blackbirds of 1928*, produced by Russian Jewish immigrant Lew Leslie. Its stars included Brooklyn-born Adelaide Hall and Virginia native Bill "Bojangles" Robinson, the tap dancer, choreographer, and film star who went on to earn the nickname "Mayor of Harlem."

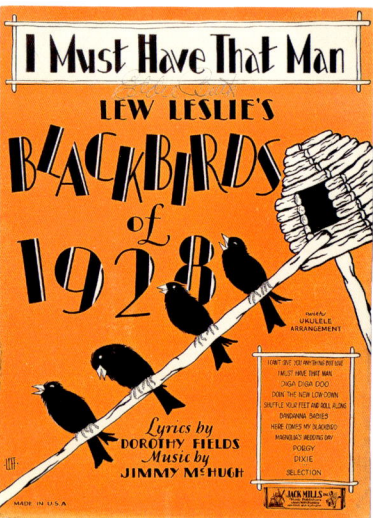

CLOCKWISE FROM TOP LEFT

**Bronzed tap shoes worn by Bill "Bojangles" Robinson** c. 1925

**"I Must Have That Man," sheet music from Lew Leslie's *Blackbirds of 1928*** 1928

**Bill Robinson** 1933
Photograph by Carl Van Vechten

CLOCKWISE FROM ABOVE
**Silk evening dress with applied beads and sequins** 1926

**Silk dance dress with gold metallic tissue, silk fringe, and applied paillets** c. 1925

**"Mixed Company," cocktail recipe book advertising liquor delivery** c. 1925

**Silver cocktail mixer and cup, inset with marble** c. 1928
Designed by Tiffany & Company, New York

## 1914-1929

# 1920s Style

Nationwide Prohibition (1920–33) made drinking illegal—and chic—and created new opportunities for making money. While Tiffany & Company met the needs of prosperous illegal drinkers with sleek cocktail sets, some New Yorkers opened secret speakeasies that marketed to those "in the know." Some underground establishments even delivered, producing menus that advertised a phone number but no street address, probably to guard against police raids—although many clubs received police or gangster protection in exchange for bribes. By 1925 the city had 35,000 illegal saloons, five times as many as Chicago. They ranged from Harlem and midtown nightclubs to Greenwich Village "nooks" and tenement kitchens.

New York nightlife helped popularize "flappers"—young women who wore short dresses, danced to jazz, smoked, drank, and enjoyed a social and sexual freedom that rejected strait-laced 19th-century values. New York's mayor, Jimmy Walker, embodied the spirit of the era by keeping an office in a flashy nightclub in the Central Park Casino, connecting politics, nightlife, and show business. His mayoralty ended under the shadow of corruption scandals, and he resigned in 1932, setting the stage for the reform Republican mayor Fiorello La Guardia.

## 1914–1929 New Yorkers

ABOVE
**Dorothy Parker (seated at right) with several *New Yorker* contributors including Wolcott Gibbs, James Thurber, St. Clair McKelway, and Russell Maloney at a cocktail party at the Algonquin Hotel for its owner and manager Frank Case (seated third from left)** 1938

**Dorothy Parker** c. 1935

### Dorothy Parker
### (1893–1967)
### The Poison Pen

Writer Dorothy Parker embodied the spirit of New York in the 1920s, especially after she joined the staff of the brand new magazine *The New Yorker* in 1925. By the 1920s publishing and printing was one of the largest industries in New York and *The New Yorker* was one of a new crop of so-called "smart magazines" that captured the Prohibition-era city's sophistication, wit, and glamor and directed it to a national audience.

Along with other members of the lunch group known as the "Algonquin Round Table," Parker violated social niceties, challenged gender norms, and broke cultural taboos with glee. In her words, "The first thing I do in the morning is brush my teeth and sharpen my tongue."

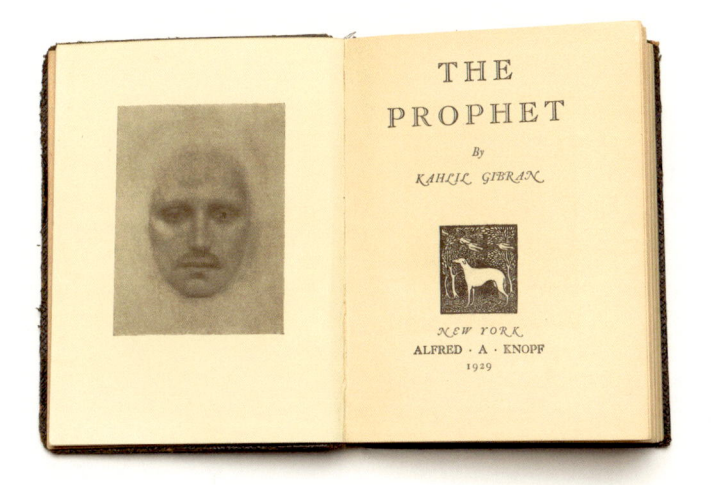

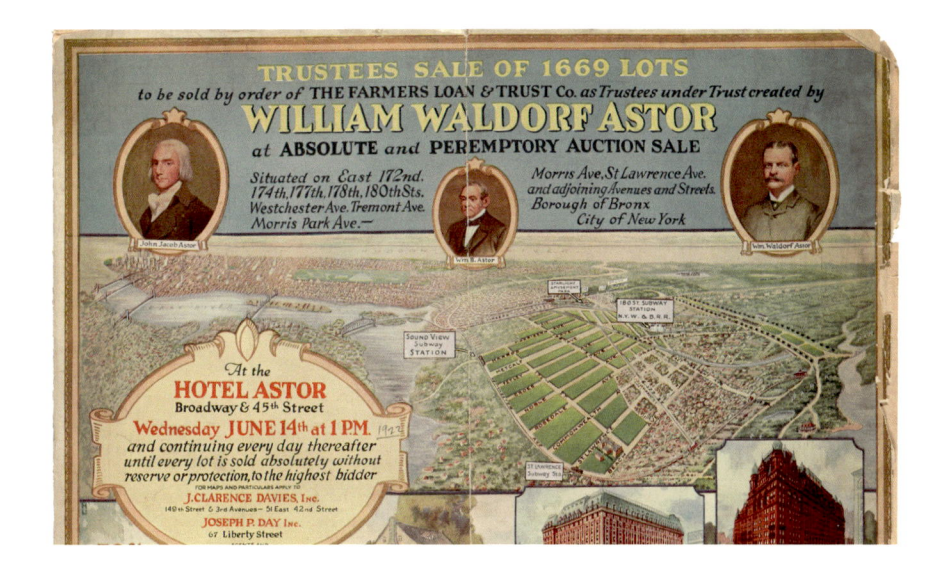

## Kahlil Gibran
### (1883–1931)
### A Prophet in New York

Lebanese immigrant Kahlil Gibran, a writer and artist who moved to New York in 1911 at age 28, became the third best-selling poet of all time. His career embodied the promise of cross-fertilization of Middle Eastern and American culture, shaped in the nation's foremost Arab-American community, located in New York.

Gibran hoped for his writing to bridge East and West, urging all Americans to live more reflective, spiritual lives. He wrote to a friend, "Westerners are weary of the phantoms of their souls and tired of themselves. They will hang onto anything exotic and extraordinary, especially if it comes from the East."

**Kahlil Gibran**

ABOVE
***The Prophet* by Kahlil Gibran, published by Alfred A. Knopf, New York** 1929

## J. Clarence Davies
### (1868–1934)
### Cashing in on the Bronx

When J. Clarence Davies opened his real estate office in the Bronx in 1889 its population was less than 100,000. But Davies saw the creation of a mass transit system as key to opening up the area to real estate development.

He joined a network of Bronx businessmen, landowners, architects, and local politicians to advocate for the expansion of the transit system, published transit maps as a tool for selling real estate, and highlighted the locations of subway stations in his advertisements for the auctions of lots from newly subdivided Bronx estates.

By 1930 the population of the Bronx had grown to 1,265,258. As Davies concluded, "History has shown that transit and population are the creators of real estate values."

*J. Clarence Davies* (detail)
1922
Oil on canvas by Paul Moschcowitz

ABOVE
**Advertisement for the sale of 1669 lots in the Bronx brokered by J. Clarence Davies, Inc. and Joseph P. Day, Inc.** 1905

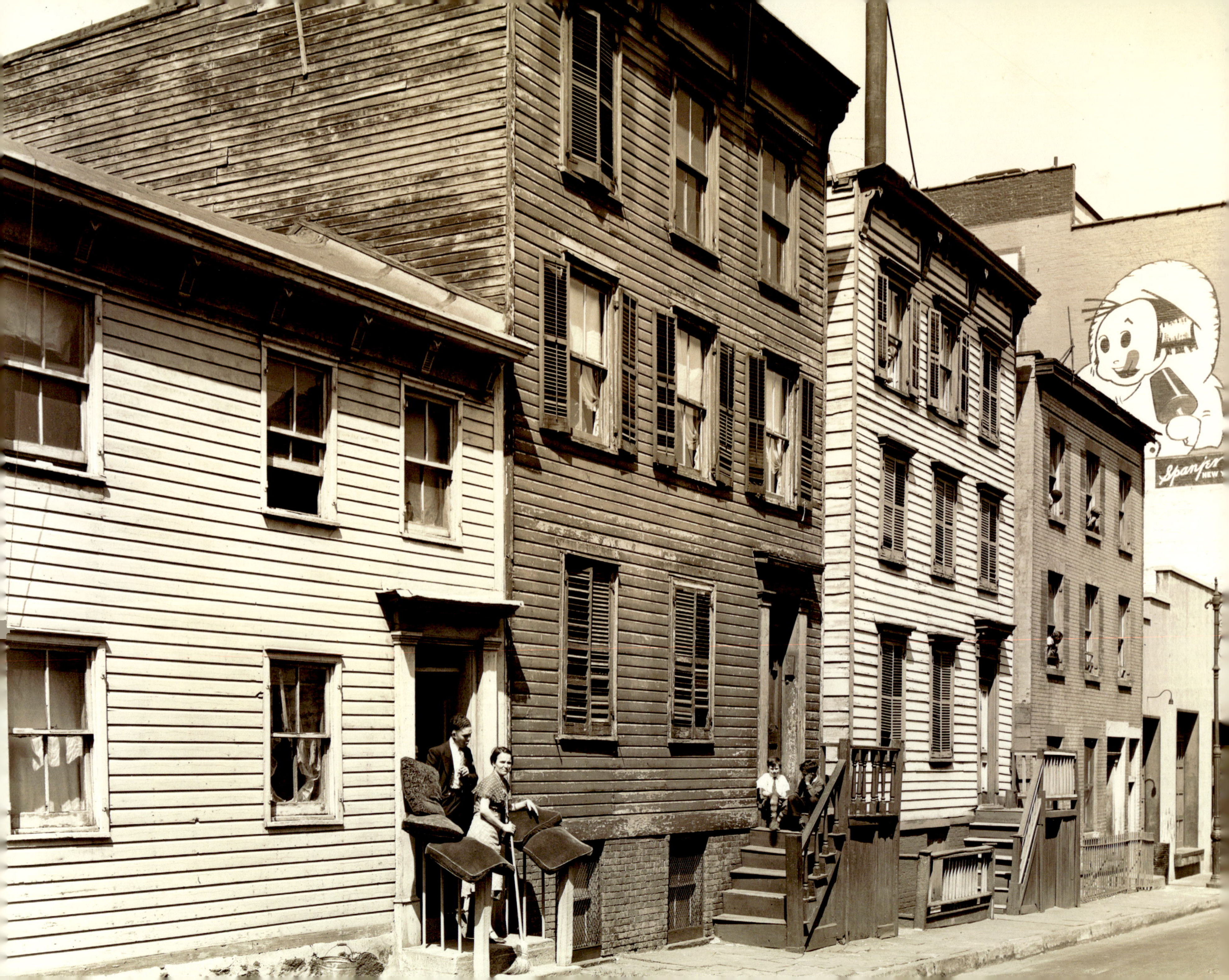
Spanjer
NEW

# 1929–1941

## New York's New Deal

Wall Street's stock market crash in 1929 abruptly ended New York's era of prosperity and exuberance. Radiating out from New York, the Great Depression brought economic growth to a halt across the country. By 1935 one-third of all employable New Yorkers—about a million people—were jobless. Journalist Martha Gellhorn summed up the city's mood as one of "fear, fear... an overpowering terror of the future." In the nation's business center, capitalism itself seemed to teeter on the brink of collapse.

In 1933 New Yorkers elected a feisty maverick as mayor, who tackled the Depression through bold experimentation. Building on the reforms of the previous generation, Fiorello La Guardia made New York the showcase for a new kind of urban liberalism, with massively expanded government spending and services. The New Deal did not cure New York's economy, but in no other American city did the crisis inspire a more far-reaching government reshaping of daily life. Its vision of a city transformed and uplifted by its government relied on the support of labor unions and a diverse coalition of voters—Jews, Catholics, African Americans, and others—that would sustain the liberal city for decades to come.

OPPOSITE
**Talman Street, nos. 57–61, Fort Greene, Brooklyn** 1936
Photograph by Berenice Abbott

## 1929–1941

# Disaster

The city's vibrant 1920s economy evaporated in 1930–31. On "Black Thursday," October 24, 1929, the American stock market lost a crushing 11 percent of its total value in the first few minutes of trading on the New York Stock Exchange, triggering the Wall Street crash. A wave of bank failures, followed by massive layoffs, spread panic throughout the city's and nation's economies. By 1932 the state had run out of relief funds, leaving 88,000 city residents without aid.

The Depression did not affect all New Yorkers equally. The city's diverse economy insulated some workers from the worst effects of the crisis. Meanwhile, jobless, homeless men set up makeshift shantytowns—called "Hoovervilles" in bitter reference to President Herbert Hoover's inability to end the Depression—throughout the five boroughs, while others swelled the population of the Bowery's Skid Row. Layoffs and poverty hit the city's African-American communities especially hard: by 1935–36, 40 percent of the city's black families were receiving public relief funds, almost twice the rate of white families. "There they are," journalist Lorena Hickok wrote of families receiving public relief, "all thrown together into a vast pit of human misery, from which a city, dazed…is trying to extricate them."

CLOCKWISE FROM TOP LEFT
**West Houston and Mercer Streets** 1935
Photograph by Berenice Abbott

**Unemployment line in Harlem** 1931

*Brooklyn Daily Eagle* October 24, 1929

## 1929-1941

# Facing the Depression

Necessity and despair drove New Yorkers to improvise. As reformers and bankers fought to remake the city's financial system, middle-class families saved pennies and doubled up in apartments, newly homeless people built shantytowns, and tenants banded together against evictions. Some were convinced that the economy had broken down completely and embraced the call for radical change by visionaries of the left and the right, including the Communist Party, the left-leaning Catholic Workers Movement, or the right-wing Christian Front.

Meanwhile, a range of private charities and public agencies sought to offset the worst effects of poverty. New Yorker Joseph Sicker, chairman of the Unemployed Relief Committee of the International Apple Association, supplied apples subsidized by donations from growers at below market price for the needy to sell as a survival strategy. Private charities like the Hadley Rescue Hall at 291-293 Bowery and the Salvation Army provided free meals and clean beds. By 1933, 1.25 million New Yorkers—more than one of every five city residents—received some form of relief to help them withstand the crisis.

CLOCKWISE FROM ABOVE
**Protest against foreclosures in Sunnyside, Queens** c. 1936

Almost 60 percent of the residents of Sunnyside Gardens, Queens lost their homes during the Depression. Here, Sunnyside families protest the role of the Equitable Life Insurance Company in foreclosing on their homes.

**"Unemployed. Buy Apples. 5c. Each" placard**
c. 1930

**Unemployed** 1930
Pencil on paper by John Sloan

**Letter from Jacob Banner to acting Mayor Corrigan** 1931

When acting Mayor Joseph Corrigan rhetorically offered to send protesters back to Russia, Russian-born Jacob Banner wrote to accept: "I will gladly leave this country with my family for a place where I can find some work."

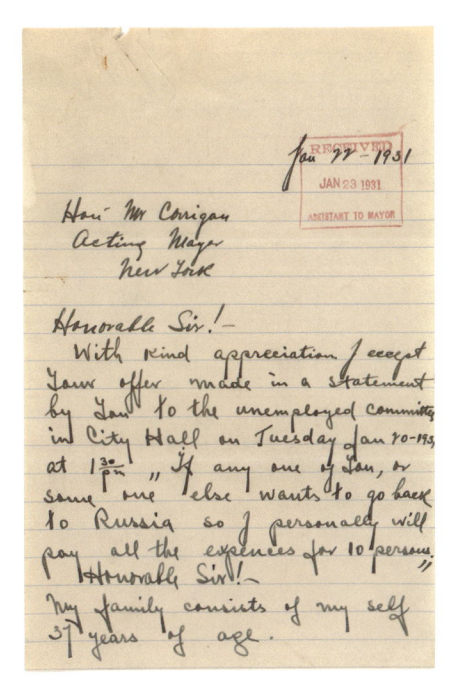

117

## 1929–1941

# La Guardia, Moses, and Roosevelt

Mayor Fiorello H. La Guardia, an Italian-Jewish Episcopalian from East Harlem, mobilized a diverse coalition of reform Republicans, liberal Democrats, and unionized workers. The Republican mayor also forged a relationship with his fellow New Yorker, Democratic President Franklin D. Roosevelt, whose New Deal programs drew heavily on the city's progressive traditions and channeled millions of federal dollars to projects in the five boroughs.

La Guardia and his administration used these funds to hire legions of workers to update and expand the city's infrastructure and public realm. The mayor and his parks commissioner Robert Moses orchestrated the construction of public housing, parks, bridges, swimming pools, health clinics, concert halls, and a public university (the City University of New York) that would provide tuition-free education and upward mobility to generations of New Yorkers. By augmenting Moses's power over public money and construction, the New Deal also clinched his role as New York's "master builder," whose massive, often controversial, construction projects would radically transform New York over the next three decades.

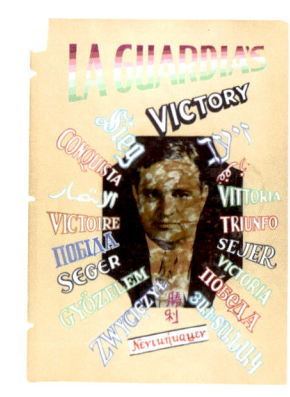

CLOCKWISE FROM TOP LEFT
**President Franklin D. Roosevelt signing the Wagner-Peyser Act** 1933

Three fellow New Yorkers—Senator Robert Wagner, Labor Secretary Frances Perkins, and Rockland/Westchester Congressman Theodore Peyser— look on as the president signs legislation creating a national system of employment offices.

**Robert Moses's Department of Parks Commissioner and Triborough Bridge Authority Chairman badges, with case** 1924–60

**Multilingual poster celebrating Fiorello La Guardia** c. 1933

La Guardia, who had served as an Ellis Island interpreter, could address voters in English, Italian, Yiddish, or Croatian.

**(Left to right) Robert Moses, Grover Whalen, and Fiorello La Guardia looking at blueprints of Flushing Meadow, site of the 1939 World's Fair** c. 1939

CLOCKWISE FROM ABOVE
**"Marine Parkway" brochure** c. 1937
Report published by the City of New York

**Scale model of Manhattan-Randall's Island section of the Triborough Bridge (now Robert F. Kennedy Bridge)** c. 1937

**Commemorative trowel from Mott Haven Health Center, a New Deal project** 1936–39

## 1929–1941
# Building Jobs

Mayor La Guardia used grants, taxes, and loans to put tens of thousands to work in construction, social services, and the arts. Though African Americans had to fight to gain access to some of these opportunities, public jobs were a lifeline for New Yorkers of all races.

The New Deal was also about more than paychecks. The mayor envisioned a metropolis where government actively enriched daily life: new public hospitals would safeguard health; new housing and community centers would end crime; and new universities and concert halls would enrich the lives of New Yorkers. His projects transformed the city: La Guardia laid the cornerstones for dozens of publicly funded New Deal projects and Robert Moses built four major city bridges during the Depression, including the Triborough (now RFK) Bridge linking Manhattan, Queens, and the Bronx, and the Marine Parkway Bridge connecting the Rockaway Peninsula to Brooklyn. By 1938 Moses had spent $182 million in federal relief money on the city's parks, and tens of millions more on bridges, parkways, and the site of the upcoming 1939 World's Fair.

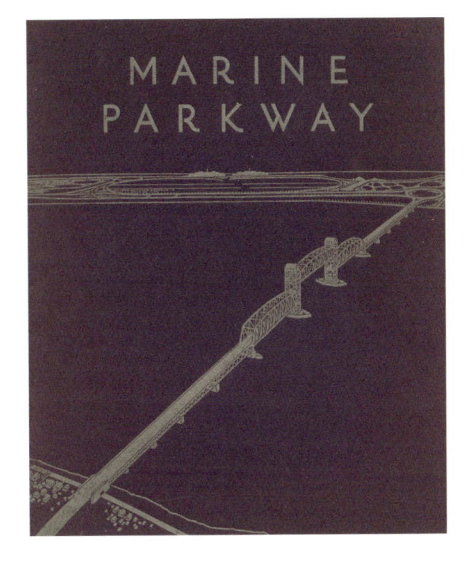

## 1929–1941

# City of Parks

Among the many changes in the city's fabric under the New Deal, none had a greater impact on the dense city than the parks programs—by far the largest in the nation. As New York's first citywide parks commissioner, Robert Moses more than doubled the amount of parkland in the city. Eleven state-of-the-art pools, accommodating 5,000 people each, opened in the summer of 1936 alone. Moses also built 255 playgrounds, 17 miles of beaches, and, in 1939, a World's Fair in a massive new park built in Queens on the site of a former ash dump. The Flushing Meadow Improvement also included the construction of a new airport (now LaGuardia), the Whitestone Bridge, and a parkway system to reach the World's Fair.

The Works Progress Administration (WPA) put artists to work making murals and posters for federally sponsored projects in the parks and beyond, including the "Learn to Swim" classes held at the city's new public pools.

CLOCKWISE FROM TOP LEFT
**West Side Improvement Project fountain** 1937
Photograph by Samuel H. Gottscho

The West Side Improvement built the Henry Hudson Parkway and expanded Riverside Park by 148 acres.

**"Learn to Swim" poster** 1940
Designed by John Wagner for the Works Progress Administration

While this WPA poster shows black and white children separately, it emphasizes the openness of New York's New Deal pools to all. In practice, use of the city's public pools and beaches reflected neighborhood conditions. At some, racial integration was the norm; at others, exclusion prevailed.

**"Flushing Meadow Improvement" brochure**
July 1938

**Turtle sculpture from Riverside Park Expansion/ West Side Improvement Project fountain** 1937

OPPOSITE
**A swimming contest at Astoria Pool, Queens**
1936

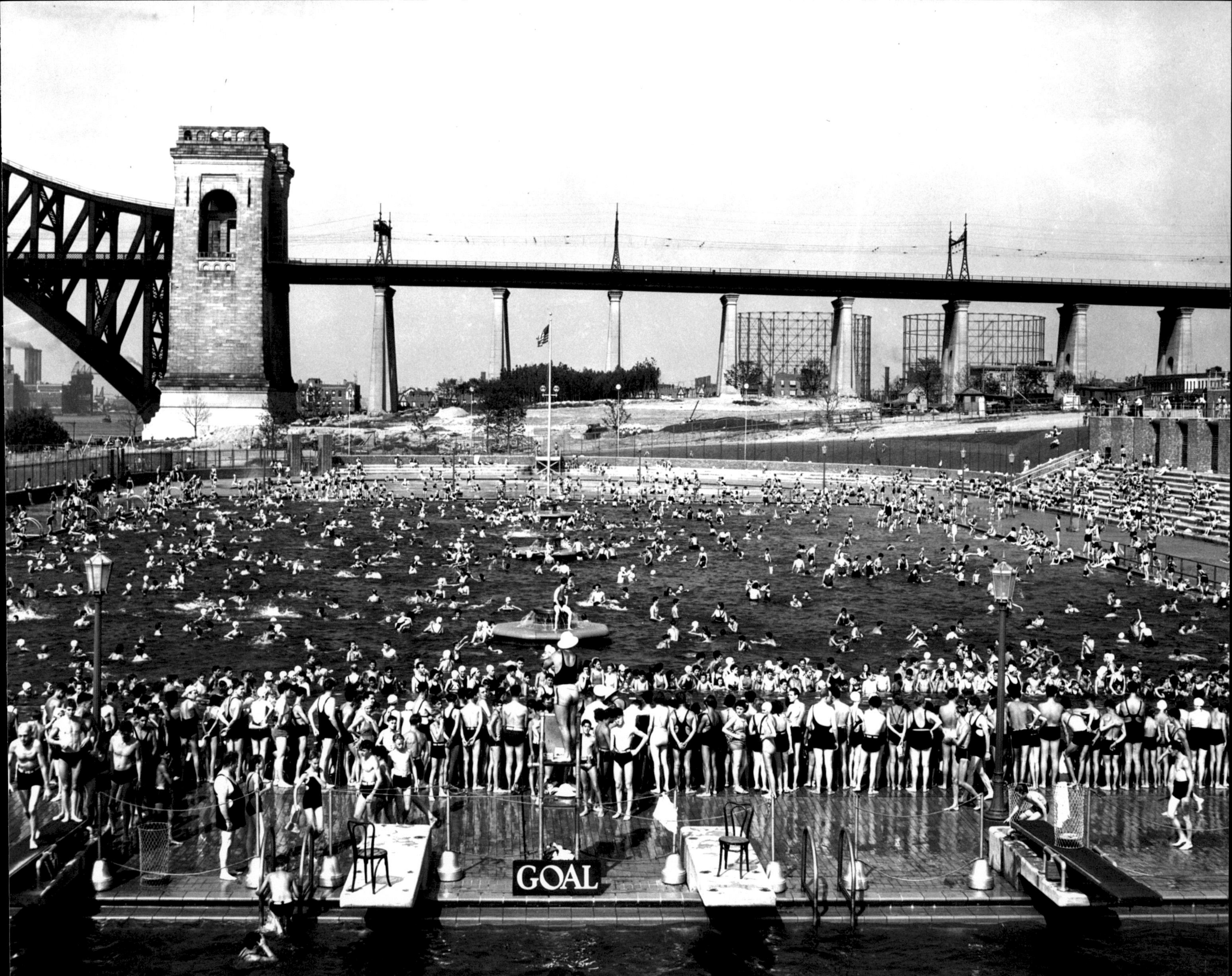
GOAL

## New Yorkers 1929–1941

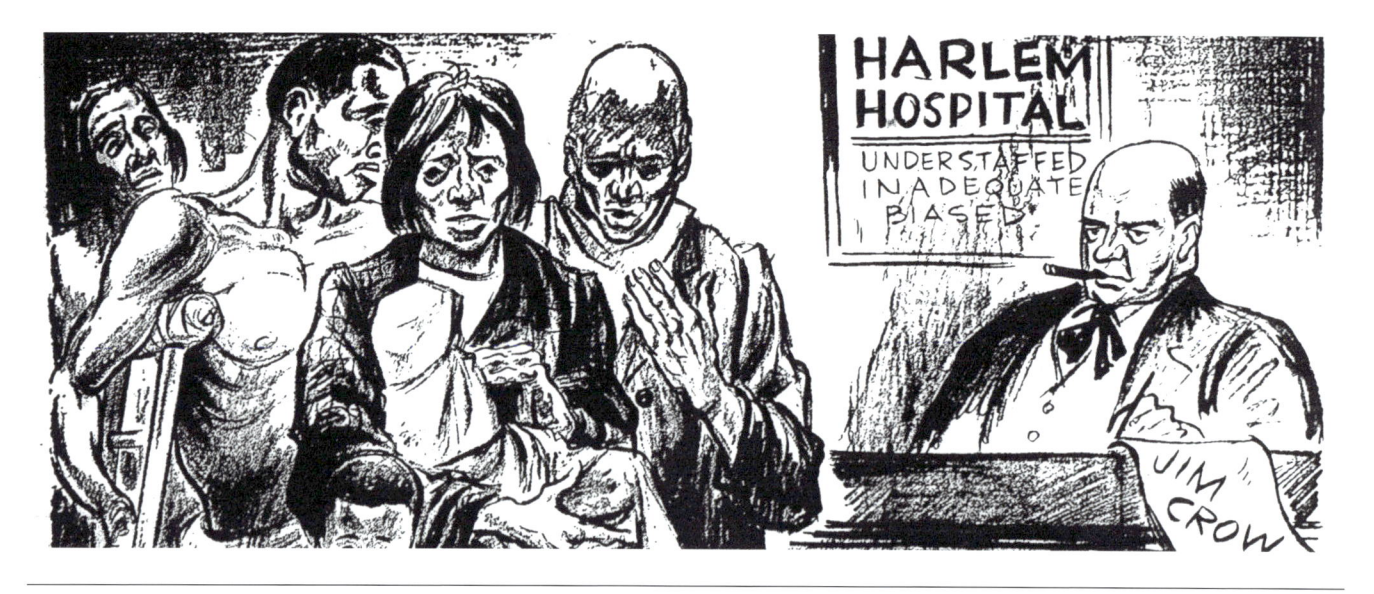

**Adam Clayton Powell Jr.**
(1908–1972)
Leader and Lawmaker

Adam Clayton Powell Jr. was one of the most powerful civil rights leaders of his day, agitating for employment, healthcare, housing, and other issues from his pulpit at the Abyssinian Baptist Church and as a congressman for 26 years.

His activism was spurred by the disproportionate suffering in his neighborhood during the Depression. In his words: "As I walk the streets of the Harlems of the world, the black Harlems, the white Harlems, people are depressed. They are frustrated. They are downtrodden. They see no hope. They see no tomorrow. And I say to them always, keep the faith baby."

Although the end of his career was tarnished by charges of corruption and arrogance, his memory still looms large, especially in upper Manhattan, where his statue graces a plaza on 125th Street and Seventh Avenue is called Adam Clayton Powell Jr. Boulevard.

**Adam Clayton Powell Jr.** c. 1945
Photograph by William C. Shrout

ABOVE
**"Harlem Hospital Must Undergo a Thorough House Cleaning,"** from *The People's Voice*, Adam Clayton Powell's weekly newspaper 1944

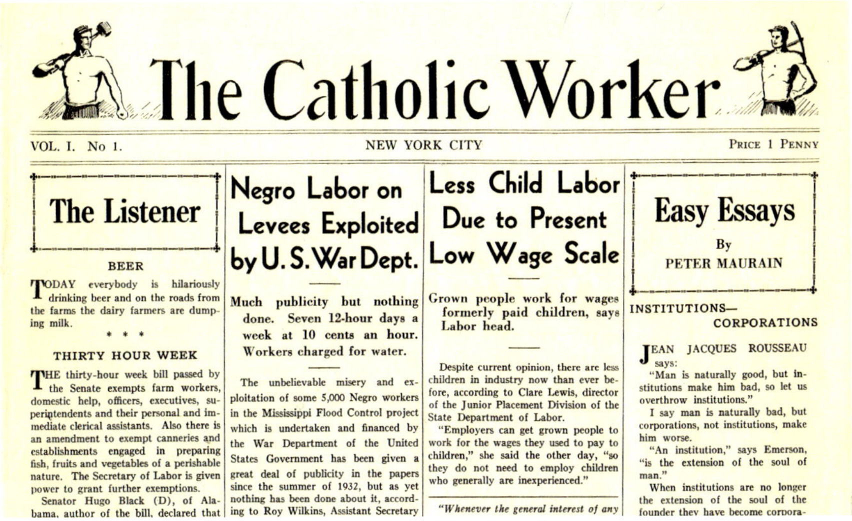

## Dutch Schultz
### (1902–1935)
### Public Enemy No. 1

**Dutch Schultz** c. 1935

ABOVE
***Hello Sam, I Hear Business Is Bad*** (detail) c. 1931
Pencil on illustration board by Rollin Kirby

Born Arthur Simon Flegenheimer in Manhattan's Yorkville neighborhood to German-Jewish immigrants, Dutch Schultz exploited Prohibition's black market in beer and speakeasies to become the FBI's "Public Enemy #1," making money in a multi-ethnic New York underworld of Jewish, Italian, and Irish bootleggers that included Arnold "The Brain" Rothstein, Charles "Lucky" Luciano, and Meyer Lansky.

On January 1, 1920, the 18th Amendment outlawed the manufacture and sale of alcohol. But New York City remained "wet" as bootleggers seized the production and sale of liquor. Seasoned criminals like Schultz supplied drinks through elaborate crime networks and amassed wealth unimagined by their immigrant parents—though many came to a sorry end. Schultz himself was gunned down by rivals in Newark, New Jersey, in 1935.

## Dorothy Day
### (1897–1980)
### Finding a Radical Faith

**Dorothy Day** 1934

ABOVE
***The Catholic Worker***, Vol. 1, No. 1, published and edited by Dorothy Day 1933

Dorothy Day, founder of the Catholic Workers Movement in 1933, promoted the rights of the poor and working class through non-violent direct action, charity, and her prolific writing.

The growing radicalism of the city and its workers during the Depression marked an important turning point for Day. Long frustrated with conflicts between her loyalty to socialism and to Christianity, she built a movement that embraced both, believing that activism and faith were required to truly help people.

Her radicalism carried over into post-World War II New York, as she championed civil and workers' rights and opposed war and militarism until her death in 1980.

CLUB
SAMOA
Club CAROUSEL
3 DEUCES
FAMOUS
DOOR
B.S. PULLY
J.C.
HEARD
OSCAR
PETTIFORD
THREE DEUCES
CLUB CAROUSEL
HARRY the HIPSTER
THREE DEUCES
Presents
ALL STAR QUARTET
J.C. HEARD

# 1941–1960

## Capital of the World

World War II finally broke the hold of the Depression on New York. As the economy boomed after the war, newly powerful unions protected the security of many of the city's blue-collar workers, promoting an expansion of New York's social benefits and securing a middle-class life for many people across the five boroughs.

The postwar era's ambitions also took physical form. City officials modernized the metropolis, tearing down acres of aging buildings, constructing massive apartment complexes for middle- and working-class New Yorkers, and expanding a sprawling highway system. The transformation was profound, erasing much of the 19th-century city, disrupting entire neighborhoods, and inspiring new ideas about how the density of the city could be shaped and managed.

Riding the wave of newfound prosperity, and with Europe's capital cities exhausted, postwar New York became, in the words of writer E.B. White, "the capital of the world," a global leader in finance, advertising, media, and fashion, as well as diplomacy, as the United Nations established its global headquarters on the east side of Manhattan. From Broadway stages to Rockefeller Center's broadcasting studios, money and influence fueled and followed the city's dominance of the nation's arts, entertainment, and information industries. New York City had become not only the world's largest and richest city, but its most influential.

## 1941–1960

# Race and Place

Wartime jobs drew growing numbers of African Americans and Puerto Ricans seeking work and a better life, and the movement continued after the war: from 1940 to 1960, the number of black and Puerto Rican New Yorkers tripled, from 510,000 to 1.6 million. Their experience in the city proved complex. Many found upward mobility, even as discrimination in credit and employment hurt their ability to accumulate wealth to the same extent as their white counterparts.

The new arrivals established vibrant neighborhoods: hundreds of thousands settled in Harlem and East Harlem or put down roots in central Brooklyn, the South Bronx, and Queens. Middle-class and well-to-do black families created their own neighborhoods, such as the Addisleigh Park section of St. Albans, Queens and Corona, Queens, home to Louis Armstrong.

But discrimination also limited housing options. As in other cities, New York realtors and lenders continued federal policies from the 1930s, denying loans in minority neighborhoods and discouraging integration. The resulting racial geography would shape New York for decades to come.

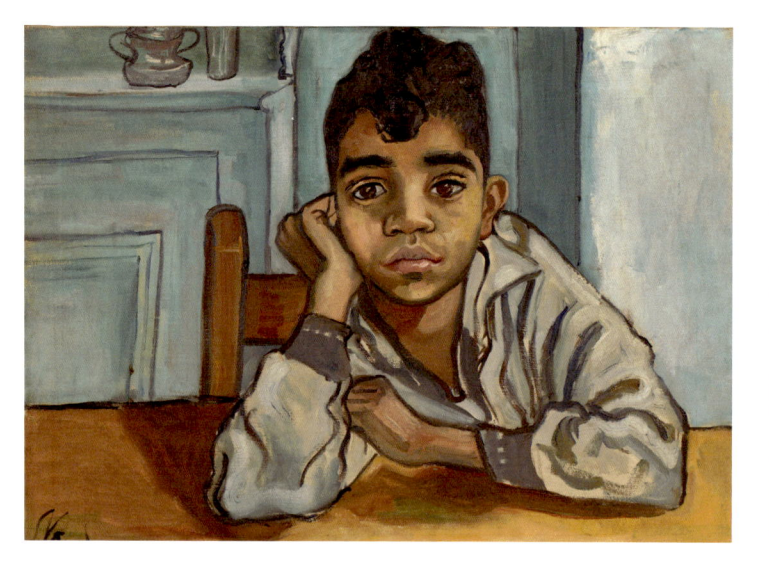

CLOCKWISE FROM TOP LEFT
**A Spanish Boy** 1955
Oil on canvas by Alice Neel

Alice Neel, a longtime resident of East Harlem, painted this portrait of her young neighbor George Arce, a recurring subject of her work during the 1950s.

**"Have you found a mortgage hard to obtain, especially in Harlem" flyer** 1951
Created by Harlem Mortgage and Improvement Council

**Baseball signed by Jackie Robinson and Tom Brown** c. 1947

The growth of black New York during and after World War II coincided with the Brooklyn Dodgers' decision to integrate Major League Baseball by hiring Jackie Robinson to break the color barrier in 1947.

**Holiday dinner at the home of Louis and Lucille Armstrong in Corona, Queens** early 1950s

**Set of keys belonging to Louis and Lucille Armstrong for their house in Corona, Queens** 1950–80

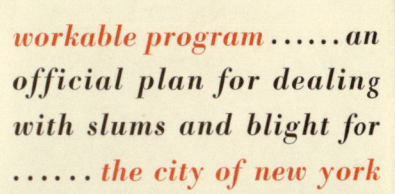

## 1941–1960
# Urban Renewal

A housing shortage, competition from the suburbs, and availability of new government funds drove a massive overhaul of New York's built environment in the years after World War II. Nineteenth-century infrastructure now appeared to be an obstacle to creating a modern, competitive, 20th-century city. Under Title I of the American Housing Act of 1949, Robert Moses partnered with private developers, razing "blighted" areas to make way for subsidized high-rise apartments and other projects, including Manhattan's Lincoln Center.

Urban renewal programs had lofty ambitions to improve housing options for all New Yorkers, and they did provide an affordable alternative to the suburbs for hundreds of thousands. But in practice, "slum clearance" often displaced those most in need—disproportionately in minority areas—prompting writer James Baldwin to charge that "urban renewal means Negro removal." Many also found the bulldozing of countless neighborhoods to be a profound, unsettling change in the life of the city.

CLOCKWISE FROM TOP LEFT
**97th Street and Columbus Avenue, showing the demolition of acres of 19th-century tenements and row houses** 1959
Photograph by Frank Paulin

**"Workable program..." brochure** 1955

**"Relocation Key for Residential Tenants"** c. 1955

Under the city's postwar "tenant relocation" program, residents whose apartments were in the path of urban renewal projects received this brochure in English or Spanish.

**"Culture City," with photograph by Arnold Newman, in LOOK** January 19, 1960

LOOK photographer Arnold Newman posed choreographer Martha Graham, opera impresario Rudolph Bing, conductor-composer Leonard Bernstein, and other future Lincoln Center stars for this photo shoot. Behind them loom 16 acres of tenements slated for demolition.

## 1941–1960
# Ab Ex

At the close of World War II New York emerged as the undisputed international capital of the art world. Emigrés from Europe, like Piet Mondrian and Hans Hofmann, influenced an emerging generation of artists. Among them were founders of the "New York School" of Abstract Expressionism (Ab Ex), including Jackson Pollock, Lee Krasner, and Mark Rothko.

Working in Manhattan and then in his Long Island studio, Pollock created his "action paintings" by dripping paint on canvas. His work was particularly celebrated in New York's galleries and press for putting the city's new generation of painters at the cutting edge of modern art. Mixing art, high fashion, and journalism, Cecil Beaton's photographs of models in front of Pollock's paintings at the Betty Parsons Gallery for *Vogue* magazine encapsulate New York's role as cultural trendsetter after World War II.

ABOVE
**A model poses in front of Jackson Pollock's *Lavendar Mist*, published in the article "Spring Ball Gowns" in *Vogue*** March 1, 1951
Photograph by Cecil Beaton

LEFT
***Free Form*** **1946**
Oil on canvas by Jackson Pollock

OPPOSITE
**Paint can and brush used by Jackson Pollock for "drip" painting** 1950s

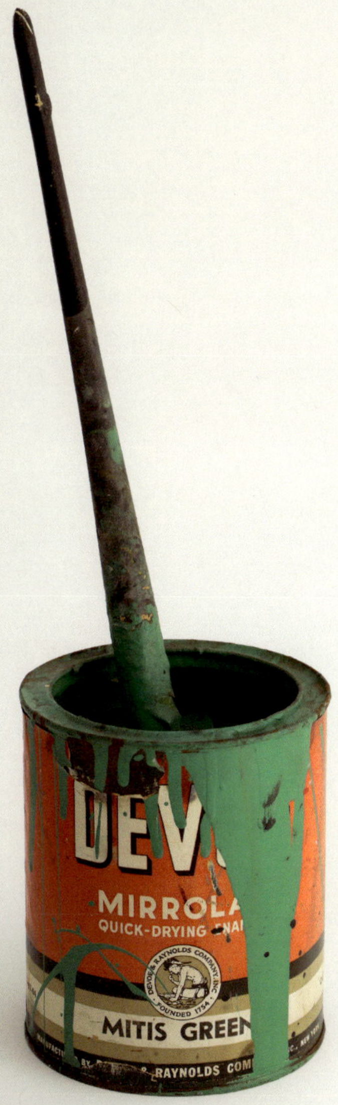
DEV
MIRROLA
QUICK-DRYING
MITIS GREEN
RAYNOLDS COM

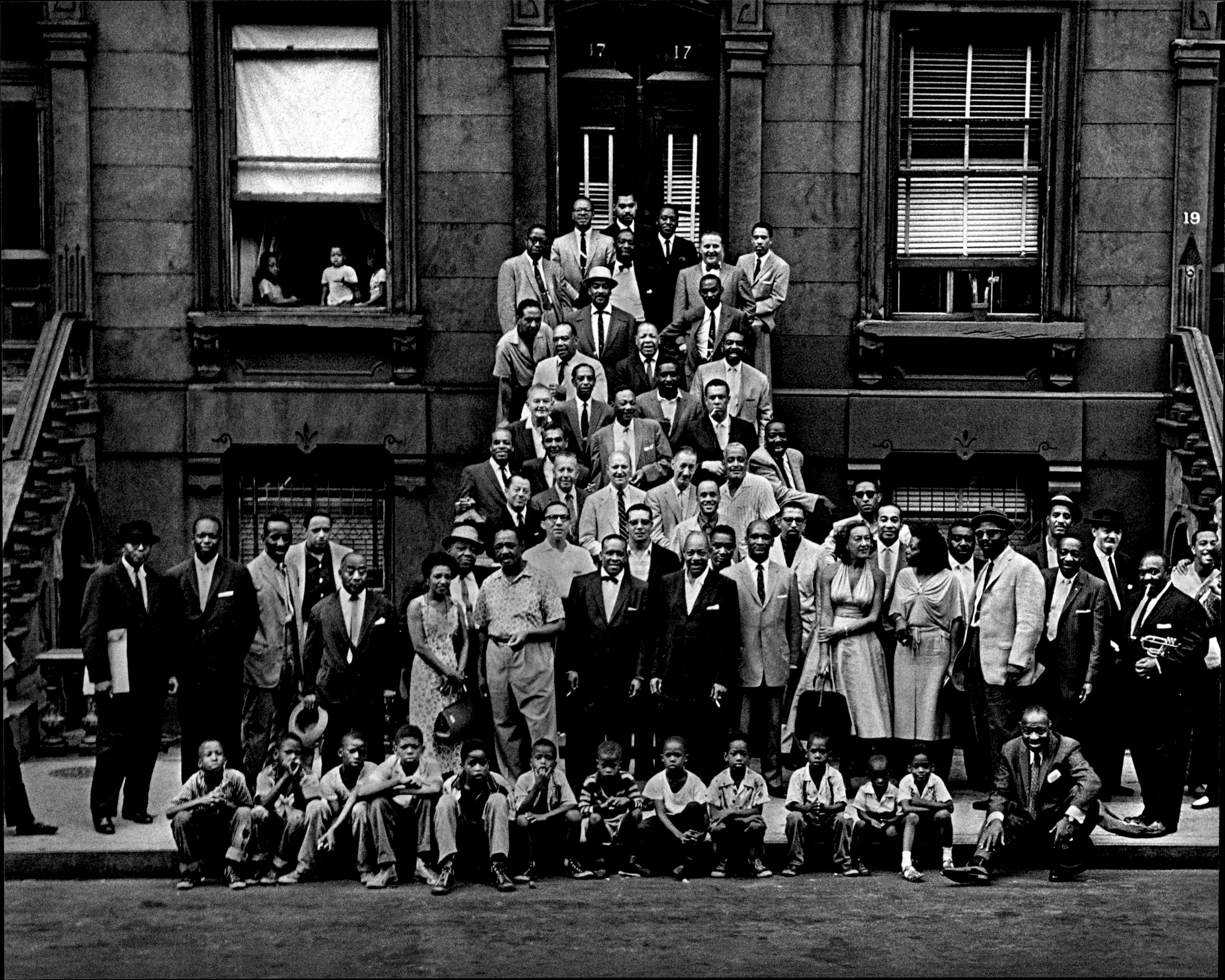
17
17
19

RIGHT
**Dizzy Gillespie and Chano Pozo** 1948
Photograph by Allan Grant

BELOW
**Trumpet owned by Roy Eldridge** 1960–80

The stylistic innovations of jazz trumpeter Roy Eldridge, a major influence on Dizzy Gillespie and other New Yorkers, paved the way for the transition from swing to bebop during the 1940s.

OPPOSITE
**Harlem** 1958
Photograph by Art Kane

## 1941-1960

# Jazz

Musical seeds planted during the 1920s bore fruit in the 1940s and '50s with an explosion of creativity in Harlem and West 52nd Street nightclubs, where artists like Dizzy Gillespie and Charlie Parker crafted "bebop"—a new form of jazz that was soon heard around the world. New York's role as an incubator for generations of jazz innovators was captured by Art Kane in his photograph of 57 musicians on the stoop of 17 East 126th Street for *Esquire* magazine.

New York's community of Afro-Cuban musicians such as Machito and Chano Pozo inspired the rise of Latin jazz or "Cubop," a fusion of African-American and Caribbean musical forms. Along with "Beat" writers, modern dancers, experimental filmmakers, and others, they helped establish New York's reputation as the world's most exciting laboratory of artistic invention.

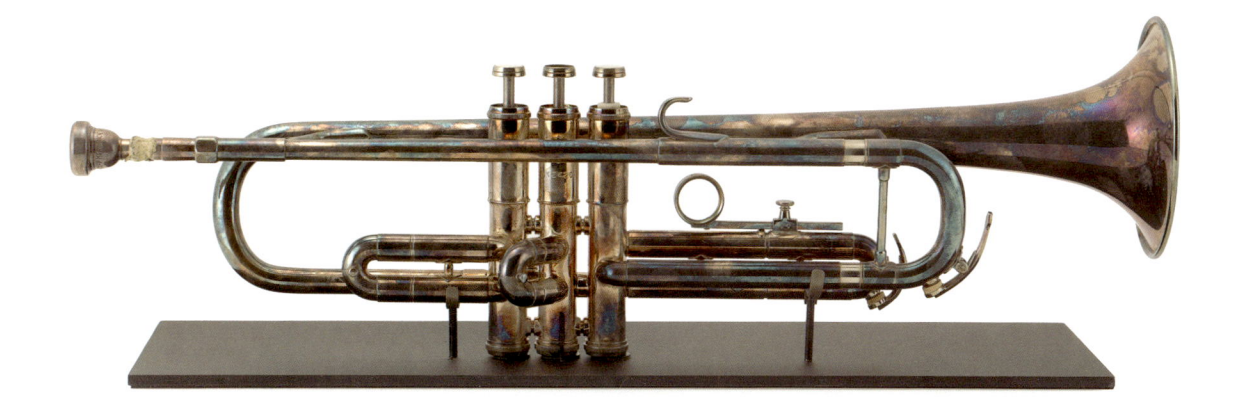

### 1941–1960
# Capital of Fashion

After generations of being overshadowed by Paris, New York fashion moved towards independence as Parisian ateliers shut down during World War II. In the postwar era, the new popularity of American-designed clothing by celebrated Seventh Avenue designers like Anne Klein, Claire McCardell, and Norman Norell, and the look of New York-based films like *Breakfast at Tiffany's* (1961), drove New York's largest industry—garment manufacturing—to new heights.

The city's fashions attained a global audience in the pages of New York-based magazines such as *Vogue* and *Glamour*. Led by Lord & Taylor, New York's department stores for the first time wholeheartedly embraced the creativity of American design, with its emphasis on practicality and sportiness.

CLOCKWISE FROM ABOVE
**Glass chandelier used in Tiffany & Company window dressing** 1961

**Wool gabardine suit** 1951
Designed by Irene

**Wool ensemble** 1956
Designed by Norman Norell for Traina-Norell

OPPOSITE
**Audrey Hepburn as Holly Golightly, film still from *Breakfast at Tiffany's*** 1961

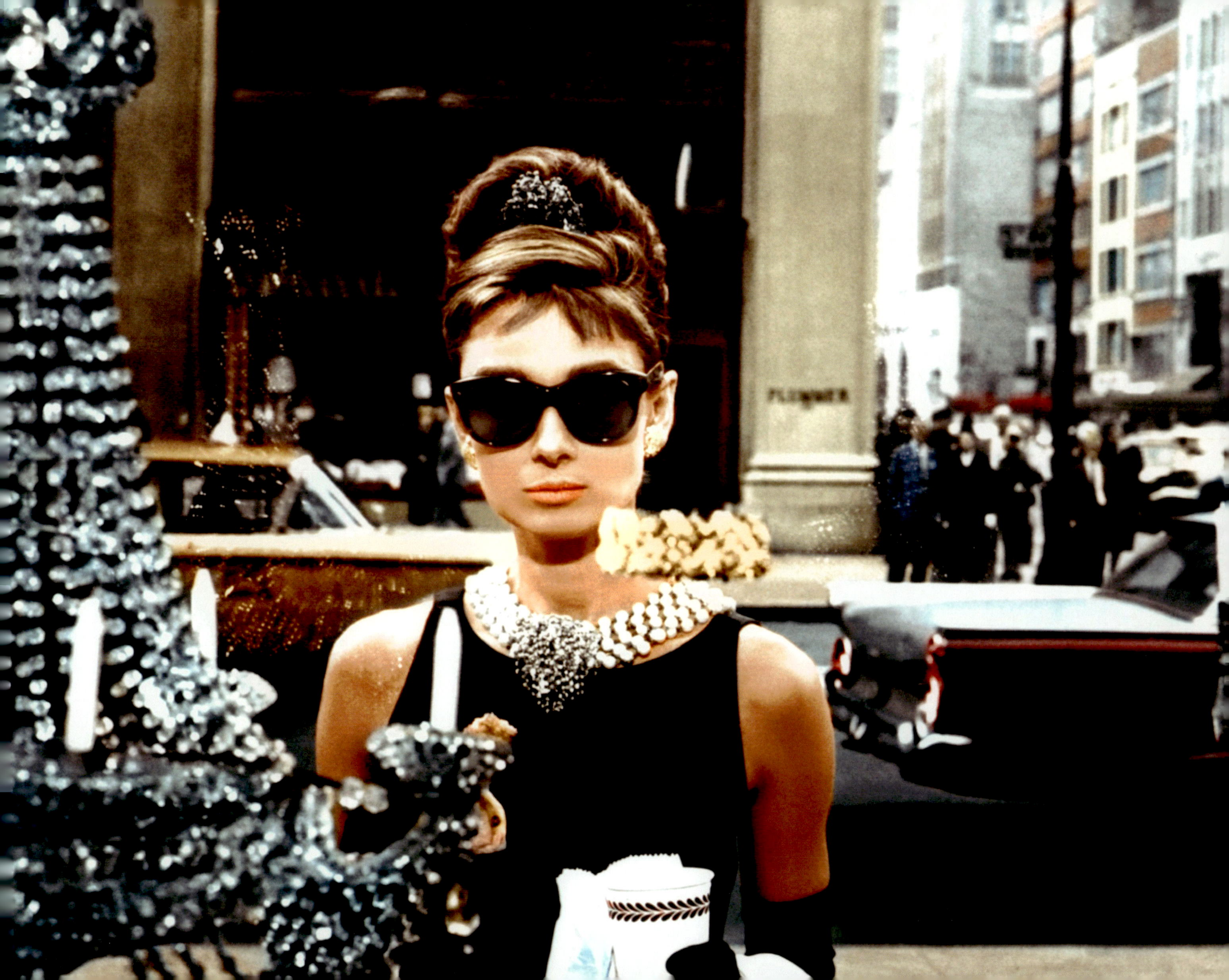

# New Yorkers
## 1941–1960

**David Rockefeller** 1967

### David Rockefeller
### (1915–2017)
### Reclaiming Downtown

By the 1950s, at a time when the aging streets of Lower Manhattan had not seen a new skyscraper for decades, banker David Rockefeller launched an ambitious project to redefine New York's oldest neighborhood and original financial center: he planned and built a stunning glass and aluminum tower to house a new Chase Manhattan bank headquarters. One Chase Manhattan Plaza, designed by Skidmore, Owings & Merrill (SOM), opened in 1961.

Rockefeller later pushed for a downtown center for world trade—a vision realized with the help of his brother, Governor Nelson Rockefeller, when the Twin Towers were completed in 1973. He celebrated the success of his vision of a 24-hour downtown community in 2002: "By almost any measure… our efforts to breathe new life into a moribund downtown community had succeeded beyond our wildest expectations."

ABOVE
**Mayor Robert Wagner Jr. (third from left) and David Rockefeller (second from right) with model of One Chase Manhattan Plaza**

## Antonia Pantoja
(1922–2002)
### Fighting for Puerto Rican New York

Between 1940 and 1960, more than 800,000 Puerto Ricans moved to the U.S. mainland—about 85 percent of them to New York City. They transformed a small community into a city within a city, but they often faced discrimination, poverty, and a declining industrial job market.

Antonia Pantoja, a schoolteacher from San Juan, became one of this community's important leaders. In 1957 she joined a new agency, the Commission on Intergroup Relations, and created the Puerto Rican Forum to "fight to eliminate the problems that were making our community weak, poor, silenced, submissive." Pantoja went on to found ASPIRA, Inc. in 1961, which trained politicians, activists, and reformers to lead New York's growing Puerto Rican community in the following decades.

**Antonia Pantoja**

ABOVE
**Patch for the ASPIRA leadership program**

## Dorothy Shaver
(1893–1959)
### First Lady of American Fashion

The first woman to head a major department store, Lord & Taylor, Dorothy Shaver helped secure New York's place as a global fashion center by promoting American designers and American style during the Depression, when the more popular French fashion was hard to come by, and later after WWII when she promoted shopping for "The American Look" as a patriotic act.

Shaver also revolutionized the shopping experience through what was called "The Shaver Touch," made up of comfortable seats, morning coffee, and personal shoppers. As she said, "Nobody knows fashion better than we do; we sell fashion, buy fashion, live fashion."

**Dorothy Shaver** 1955

ABOVE
**Lord & Taylor window display featuring American designers**
1933
Photograph by Worsinger

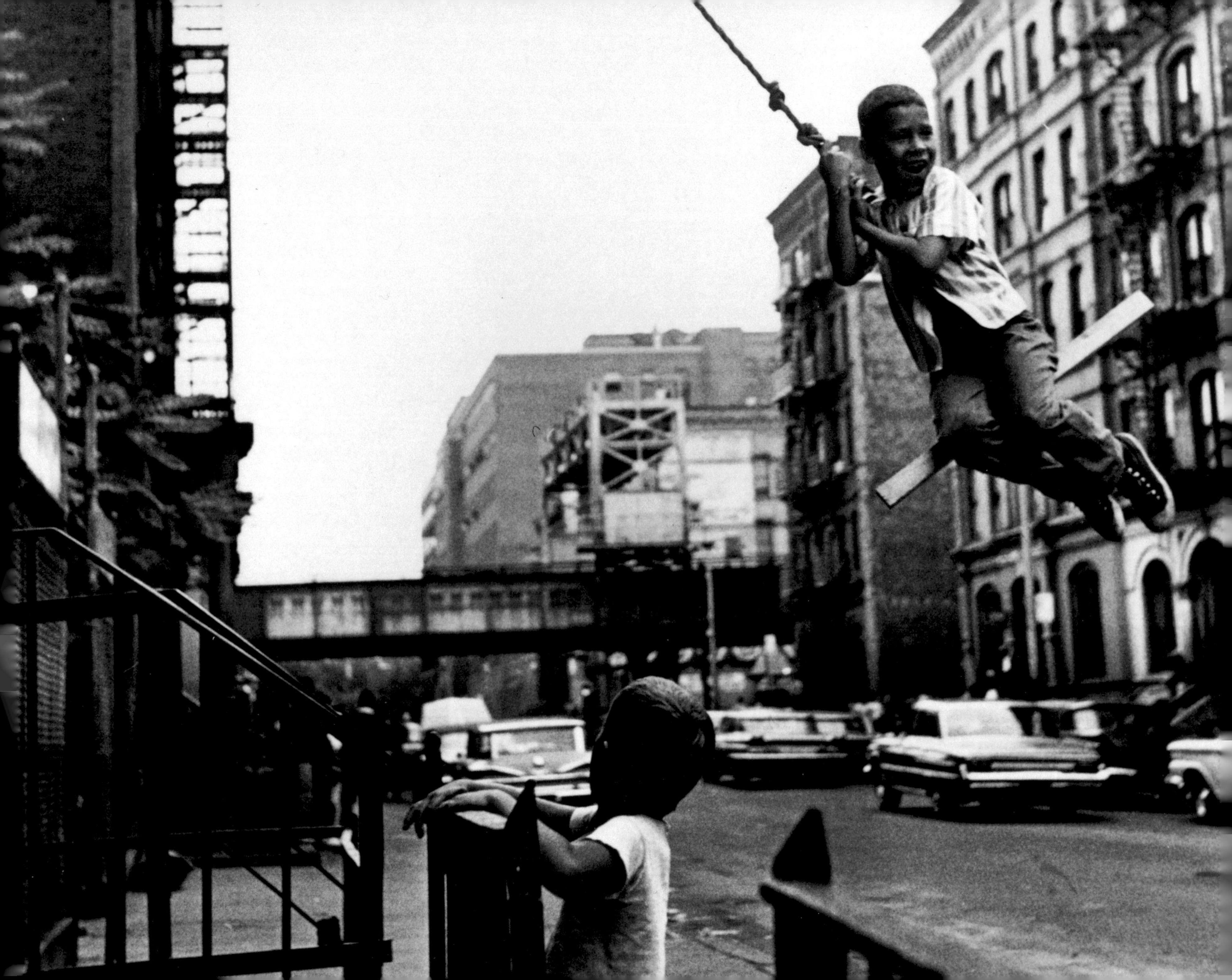

# 1960–1970

## What Is the City For?

By the 1960s New York was feeling the effects of a nationwide economic shift driven by deindustrialization and suburbanization. Century-old factories, warehouses, and piers sat empty, and the supply of well-paying blue-collar jobs dwindled. The decline hit the growing African-American and Puerto Rican communities especially hard, as the ladder to middle-class success wobbled. Many New Yorkers faced growing poverty, often sharpened by racism that limited where they lived and worked.

These changes spurred a variety of responses. Artists reoccupied former industrial spaces as lofts and studios; activists rescued and repurposed historic sites; business leaders reimagined downtown as a center for maintaining New York's hold on world trade, embodied in the world's tallest skyscrapers. And some wondered whether the city needed a human-scale alternative to the vision of postwar development, with its massive new office and apartment complexes.

Protest came from many corners, as the city became one of the era's most important incubators of political ferment. Uprisings against the Vietnam War and for civil rights; for black, Latino, and student power; and for women's and gay liberation galvanized many New Yorkers. With them came new tensions that challenged the coalition that had sustained the city's liberal politics since the New Deal.

OPPOSITE
*Freedom and Order: Children Playing, East 116th Street* (detail) 1968
Photograph by David M. Bernstein

## 1960–1970

# Business Exodus

In the 1960s and '70s, industrial and maritime firms seeking lower costs and more space began to leave the city, taking jobs and tax revenues with them. The results were sobering: in 1950, 917,000 New Yorkers had worked in manufacturing; by 1980, that number had dropped to 507,000. During the 1960s alone the city lost one-fifth of its factory jobs, as entire districts were emptied of their plants, stores, and warehouse businesses.

In the once-vibrant port, more than the 430,000 jobs disappeared in the same period. And, after businessman Malcom McLean Jr. launched a vessel from New York harbor in 1956 filled with 35-foot-long storage containers (which could be unloaded by cranes rather than by hand), the number of longshoremen plummeted: from 48,000 in the mid-1950s to just 12,000 in the 1980s.

As manufacturing, warehousing, and other businesses left the city, industrial districts fell empty. In lower Manhattan, many 19th-century commercial buildings were razed to make way for new high-rise office towers, further transforming the geography of the city.

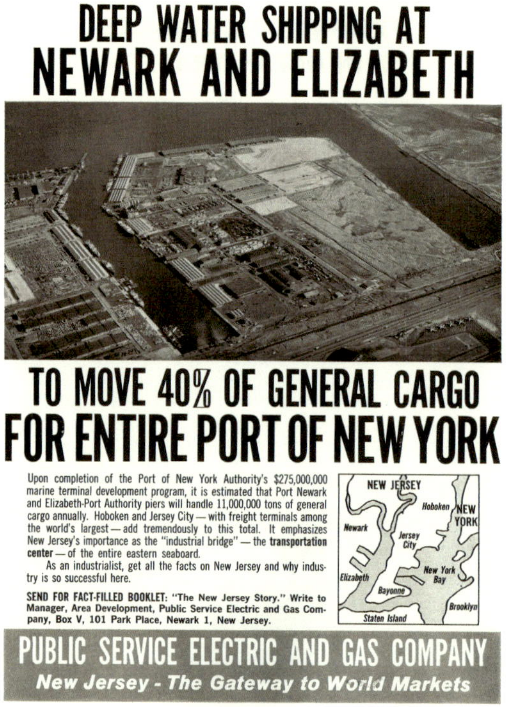

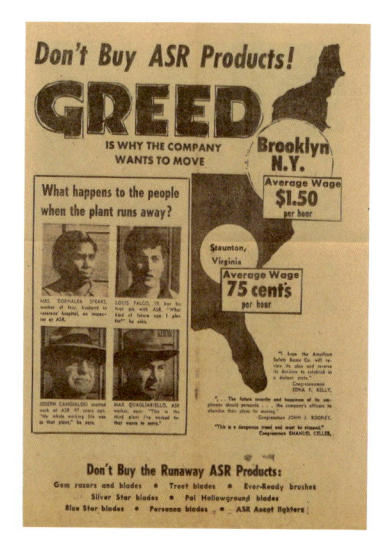

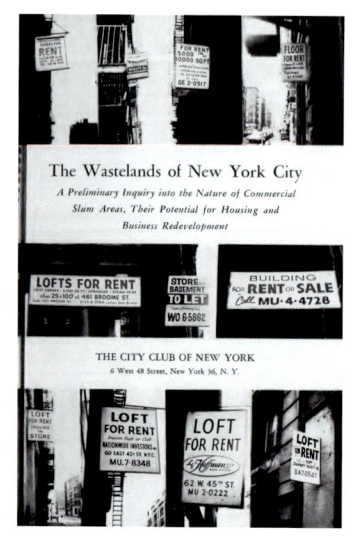

CLOCKWISE FROM TOP LEFT

**Advertisement for deep water shipping at the New Jersey ports of Newark and Elizabeth, from *New York Port Handbook*** 1961

New technologies (and increasing air traffic) profoundly affected the port—another pillar of employment—by eliminating thousands of jobs, a shift confirmed when the city's shipping operations moved across the harbor to more spacious quarters in New Jersey.

**"Don't Buy ASR Products!" flyer protesting the American Safety Razor Company** 1955

The American Safety Razor Company's 1955 move from downtown Brooklyn to Virginia was typical of New York firms moving south to take advantage of a "more favorable business climate."

***The Wastelands of New York City*, published by City Club of New York** 1962

By the early 1960s the "commercial slum district" of SoHo (South of Houston St.) in lower Manhattan was a symbol of New York's deindustrialization—a desert of abandoned garment lofts.

OPPOSITE

***West Street Between Jay and Duane Streets* (detail)** 1966–67
Photograph by Danny Lyon

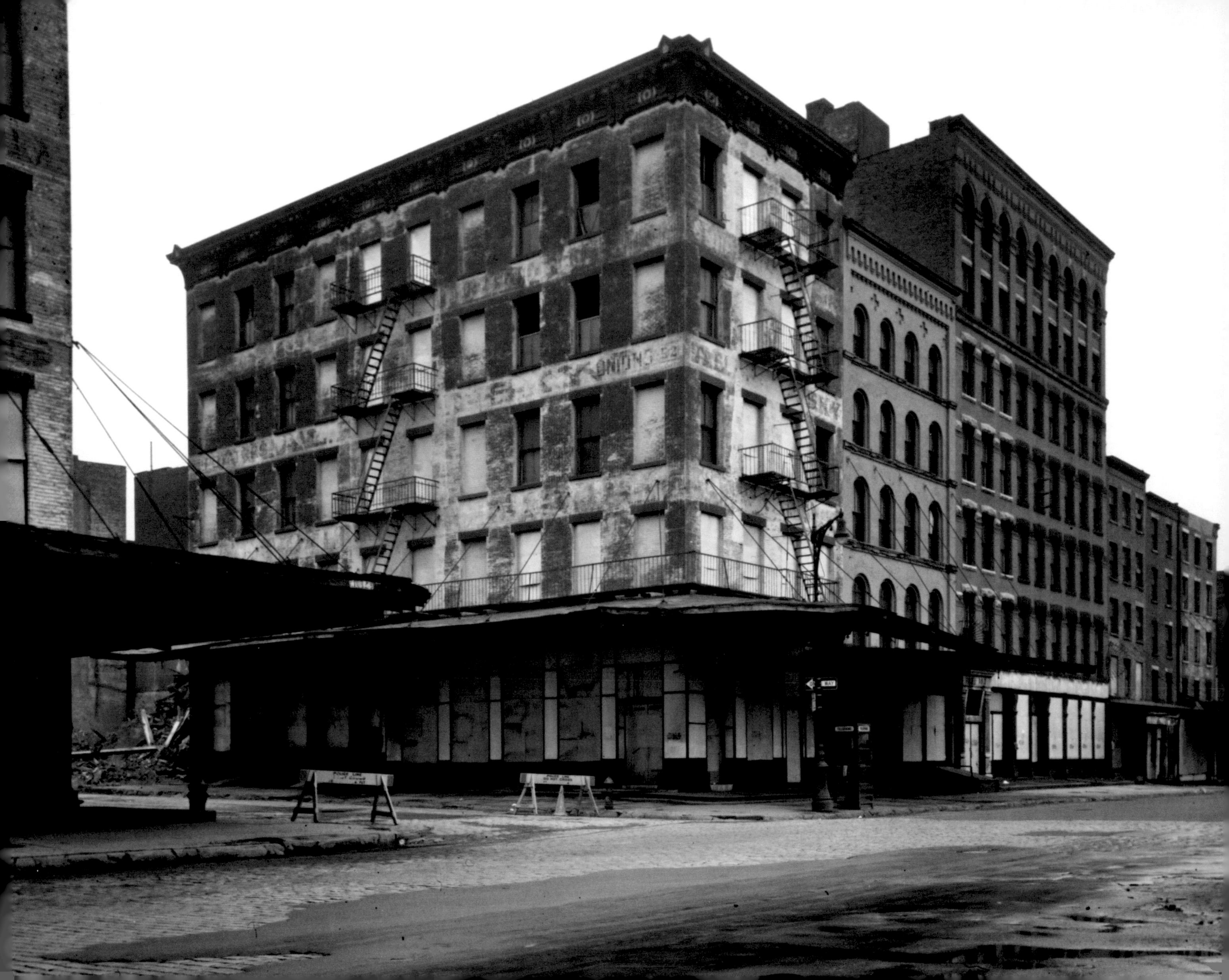

## 1960–1970

# New Visions

What to do with the deindustrializing landscape? One solution was to reinvent the port. In the 1960s the Port Authority tore down a district of electronics shops to build a grand new office complex: the World Trade Center. Occupying 16 acres, with workspace for 50,000 people, the buildings were promoted as home to global maritime trade, but they soon became a symbol of the city's white-collar future, occupied by government and financial offices.

As skyscrapers replaced older buildings, some New Yorkers pushed back, asserting the value of low-rise urban density. In the waterfront neighborhood around Coenties Slip, artists like Robert Indiana, Ellsworth Kelly, and Agnes Martin were attracted by abundant space and cheap rents. Artists also joined preservationists in the fight to save abandoned commercial lofts in districts like SoHo (South of Houston Street). The changing cityscape became both the setting and the inspiration for the Pop Art and Minimalist movements that extended New York's global avant-garde artistic influence.

FAR LEFT
**Orb** conceived 1960, executed 1991
Painted bronze by Robert Indiana

Inspired by the landscape, Indiana incorporated materials, including wooden beams and rusted wheels, that he found along the waterfront into his sculptural assemblages.

CLOCKWISE FROM TOP LEFT
**World Trade Center under construction** 1972
Photograph by T. Sheehan

**"Cross Manhattan Arterials and Related Improvements" brochure** 1959

A landmark in the reinvention of SoHo came when activists defeated the Lower Manhattan Expressway, which would have demolished 19th-century cast-iron lofts to run a highway from the Holland Tunnel to the Manhattan Bridge.

**Architect Philip Johnson (left) and author Jane Jacobs (center) protest the demolition of Pennsylvania Station** 1963
Photograph by Walter Daran

**Hard hat worn by ironworker David Rice during the construction of the World Trade Center** c. 1970

David Rice was one of 10,000 workers who built the World Trade Center and a member of the Kahnawake Mohawk people, many of whom built New York skyscrapers.

## 1960–1970

# Crisis and Confrontation

In 1964 a riot swept through Harlem and Bedford-Stuyvesant, Brooklyn after a policeman shot and fatally wounded a black teenager. The riot revealed the frustrations and anger of many in the city's African-American community, and the conditions that they faced in a deteriorating city. The "urban crisis" quickly became a focus for journalists, politicians, and neighborhood residents.

Activists fought back. Rent strikes targeted slumlords and picket lines protested racist hiring. Wearied by decades of efforts to integrate the city's public schools, housing, and job market, some called for racial self-determination: in 1968 local black activists won control of the public schools in Ocean Hill-Brownsville, Brooklyn. A resulting series of teachers' strikes—pitting the heavily white and Jewish teachers' union against "community control" advocates—inflamed already tense race and ethnic relations.

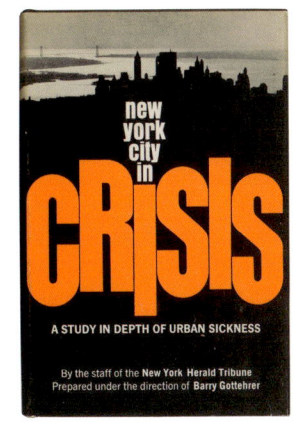

CLOCKWISE FROM ABOVE

**Rent strike** 1963

Jesse Gray (at left) and other Harlem activists used tactics calculated to gain media attention—like bringing rats to public rallies to protest vermin-infested apartments.

**Riot in Harlem** 1964

***New York City in Crisis* by Barry Gottehrer, published by David McKay, Philadelphia** 1965

According to the author, "New York is the greatest city in the world—and everything is wrong with it."

**Brooklyn CORE garrison cap** 1960s

The Brooklyn chapter of CORE (Congress of Racial Equality) organized vigorous protests against discrimination in hiring, housing, and schools.

141

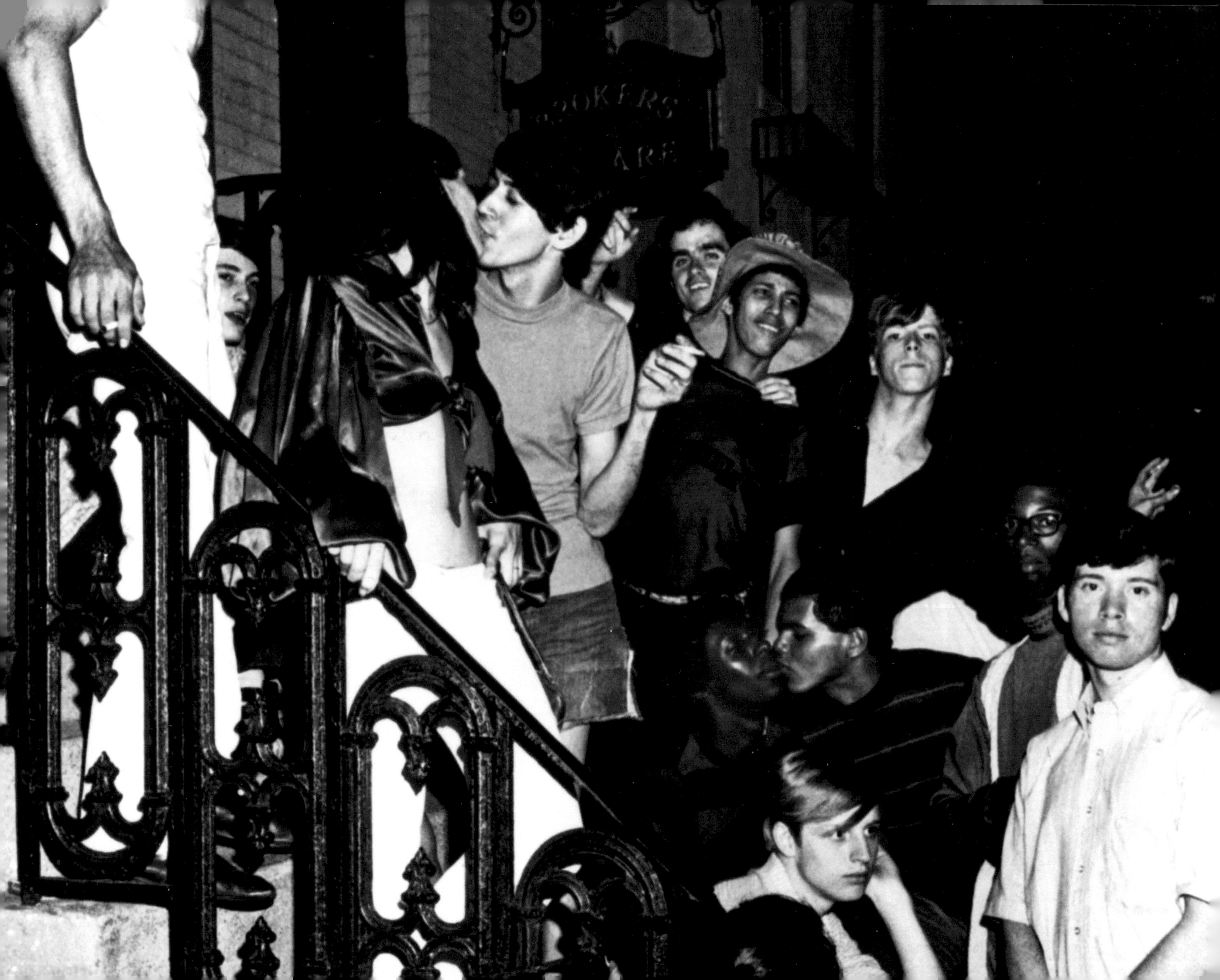

## 1960-1970

# Power and Pride

The 1960s saw a wide range of self-help initiatives to address neighborhoods struggling with declining physical and social conditions, as black, Puerto Rican, and Asian-American activists took their communities' future into their own hands by organizing local garbage cleanups and medical testing, building low-income housing, and reclaiming abandoned lots for gardens and playgrounds.

Local politics fused with national issues, as the Vietnam War and anger over racism, poverty, and inequality spurred crusades for power and liberation in the late 1960s. The Black Panthers, anti-war protesters, feminists, gay militants, and the Puerto Rican activists in the Young Lords all proved willing to challenge officials, police, business leaders, and the press to fight for change. They also partnered with neighbors, clergy, students, and each other to lobby for government funds on behalf of their neighborhoods. Racial and cultural pride infused the work of young intellectuals, artists, writers, and performers.

CLOCKWISE FROM ABOVE

**Doll with striped caftan jumpsuit** c. 1965
Made by Ruby Bailey

Harlem dressmaker Ruby Bailey, an immigrant from Bermuda, designed dolls to display her increasingly Afrocentric creations, embodying the Black Pride movement.

**Children outside the Bedford-Stuyvesant Neighborhood Restoration Center** 1973

The Bedford-Stuyvesant Restoration Corporation sought to improve housing and promote economic development in one of the city's poorest neighborhoods.

**Young Lords storefront** 1969
Photograph by Fred W. McDarrah

The Young Lords cleaned streets, organized health screenings, occupied churches and hospitals to demand better services, and advocated for improved living conditions in predominantly Puerto Rican neighborhoods like East Harlem, the South Bronx, and the Lower East Side.

OPPOSITE

**Stonewall celebrations (detail)** 1969
Photograph by Fred W. McDarrah

The Stonewall Uprising of June 1969 began when gay, lesbian, and transgendered New Yorkers fought back against police raiding their Greenwich Village club.

## New Yorkers 1960–1970

ABOVE
***Ms.* magazine staff meeting** 1975

**Gloria Steinem** 1975

### Gloria Steinem
(b. 1934)
A Revolution from Within

A staunch advocate for women's rights—supporting causes from access to contraception to equal employment opportunities to the Equal Rights Amendment—Gloria Steinem got her start as part of the long-form "New Journalism" movement, writing for New York-based magazines *Esquire*, *New York*, and *Show* (where she went undercover to write about the experience of working for New York's Playboy Club).

In 1971 Steinem cofounded *Ms.* magazine, written by women for women and headquartered in New York City. The magazine tackled issues ignored by the popular press from the unpaid labor of housework to the repeal of laws criminalizing abortion. She continues to advocate for women's rights globally, proclaiming that her work "is really no simple reform. It really is a revolution."

**Elsie Richardson**
**Fulton Street, Brooklyn, before (left) and after the completion of Fulton Street South, a housing project of the Bedford Stuyvesant Restoration Corporation** c. 1985

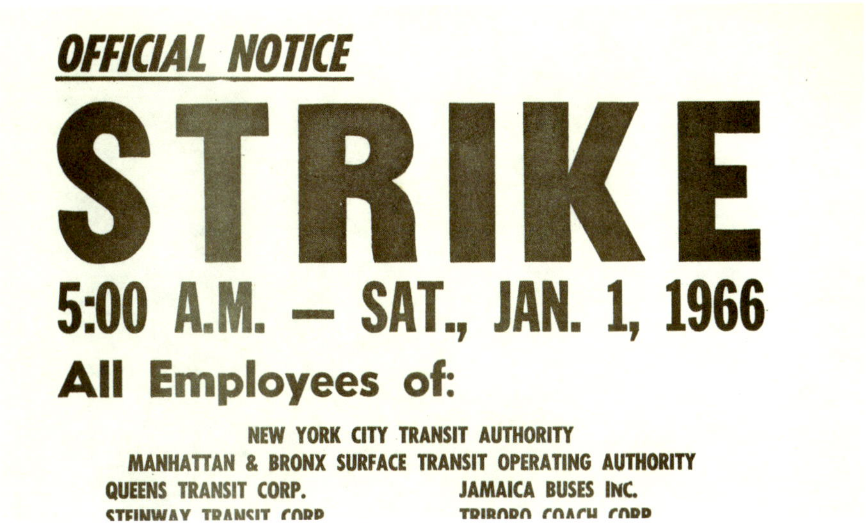

### Elsie Richardson
### (1922–2012)
### Investing in Bed-Stuy

In the mid-1950s Elsie Richardson moved to Brooklyn's Bedford-Stuyvesant neighborhood, then a mixed-income neighborhood of European immigrants, African Americans, and a growing number of new arrivals from the West Indies. Over the next decade, as Bed-Stuy turned into one of the city's poorest neighborhoods, Richardson fought back.

In 1967 Richardson founded the Bedford-Stuyvesant Restoration Corporation to address the problems of the community. A model for other neighborhood organizations and community development corporations, the Corporation built or renovated 2,200 units of housing, provided $60 million in mortgage financing, and brought $500 million in investments to central Brooklyn.

**Mike Quill** 1946

ABOVE
**Flyer calling on employees of the New York City Transit Authority to strike** 1966

### Mike Quill
### (1905–1966)
### Facing Down City Hall

Mike Quill led the Transport Workers Union (TWU) for three decades, from the 1930s to the 1960s, building its membership to 32,600. During a period when unions in private industry took advantage of New Deal protections and a strong economy to win better pay, shorter hours, and reliable contacts, Quill navigated transit workers' complex relationship with the city government.

In 1966 Quill's TWU became the first major public union to go on strike for higher wages. His audacious action inspired a wave of strikes by other city employees throughout the late 1960s, almost all of which resulted in better contracts for city workers, while also costing the city increasingly scarce tax dollars.

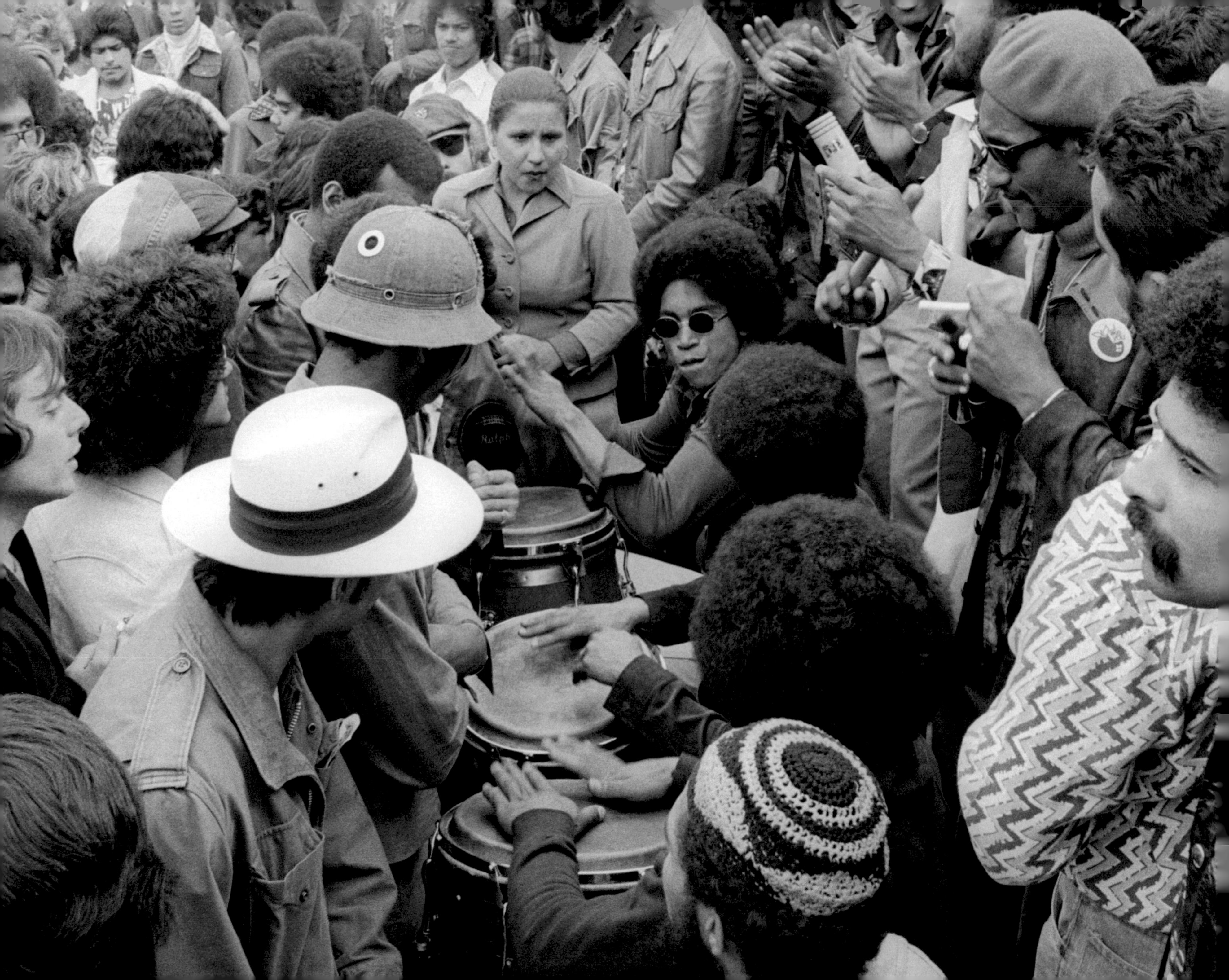

# 1970–1980

## On the Brink

By the 1970s New York City was running out of money. Vietnam-era inflation and the rising cost of city services had more than doubled the budget. As migration to the suburbs accelerated, New York's population shrank significantly for the first time. Together with the departure of many businesses, a national recession, and a shift of federal and state priorities away from cities, this meant that New York had shrinking resources to cover escalating costs.

As the city teetered on the edge of default, the sense of urban deterioration spread well beyond the "inner city." Crime, garbage, and real estate abandonment contributed to fears that New York was on the brink of collapse. As budget cuts reduced public services, the city seemed to be on a downward spiral. Its survival became a test of the very idea of the livable modern city.

Yet, millions of New Yorkers refused to give up on urban life. Seizing upon the relatively affordable space and the freedom that New York offered, they created new opportunities, from urban homesteading to community gardens to new arts organizations. Some embraced the city's gritty reputation itself as an opportunity, inventing new art forms and projecting New York's image across the globe through productions as diverse as *Saturday Night Live* and *Sesame Street*.

OPPOSITE
*Latinos play conga drums around Bethesda Fountain on a Central Park Sunday* 1974
Photograph by Allan Tannenbaum

## 1970–1980
# Budget Woes

To keep the city afloat, Mayors John V. Lindsay and Abraham Beame turned to the problematic strategies of short-term borrowing and using the capital budget to pay operating costs, putting the city's credit in jeopardy. In 1975, when banks would no longer buy or sell the city's bonds, President Gerald Ford initially refused to provide loans to bail out the city. The fiscal crisis threatened institutions and contributed to a sense of a city exhausted by urban blight and decay.

Working with bankers, labor leaders, and officials, New York Governor Hugh Carey, himself a Brooklyn native, forged a pact under which municipal labor unions used their pension funds to loan the city money. New York avoided default, but the liberal city of expansive public services and big spending—the New York of the New Deal generation—seemed to be a thing of the past.

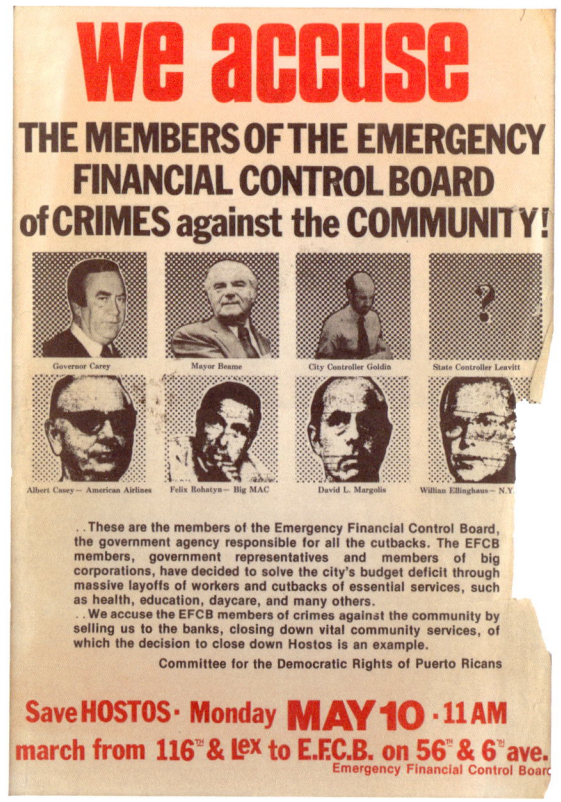

ABOVE
**Flyer protesting the possible closure of Hostos Community College** 1976

Activists charged that officials were willing to sacrifice the South Bronx's Eugenio Maria de Hostos Community College because it served a largely poor, Hispanic population.

LEFT
**Mayor Abraham Beame with a copy of the *Daily News*** 1975

Mayor Beame ripped his copy of the paper in half shortly after this photo was taken. Two months later President Ford signed legislation providing short-term loans.

OPPOSITE
***Subway #1*** 1984–85
Terracotta and glass by Bruno Lucchesi

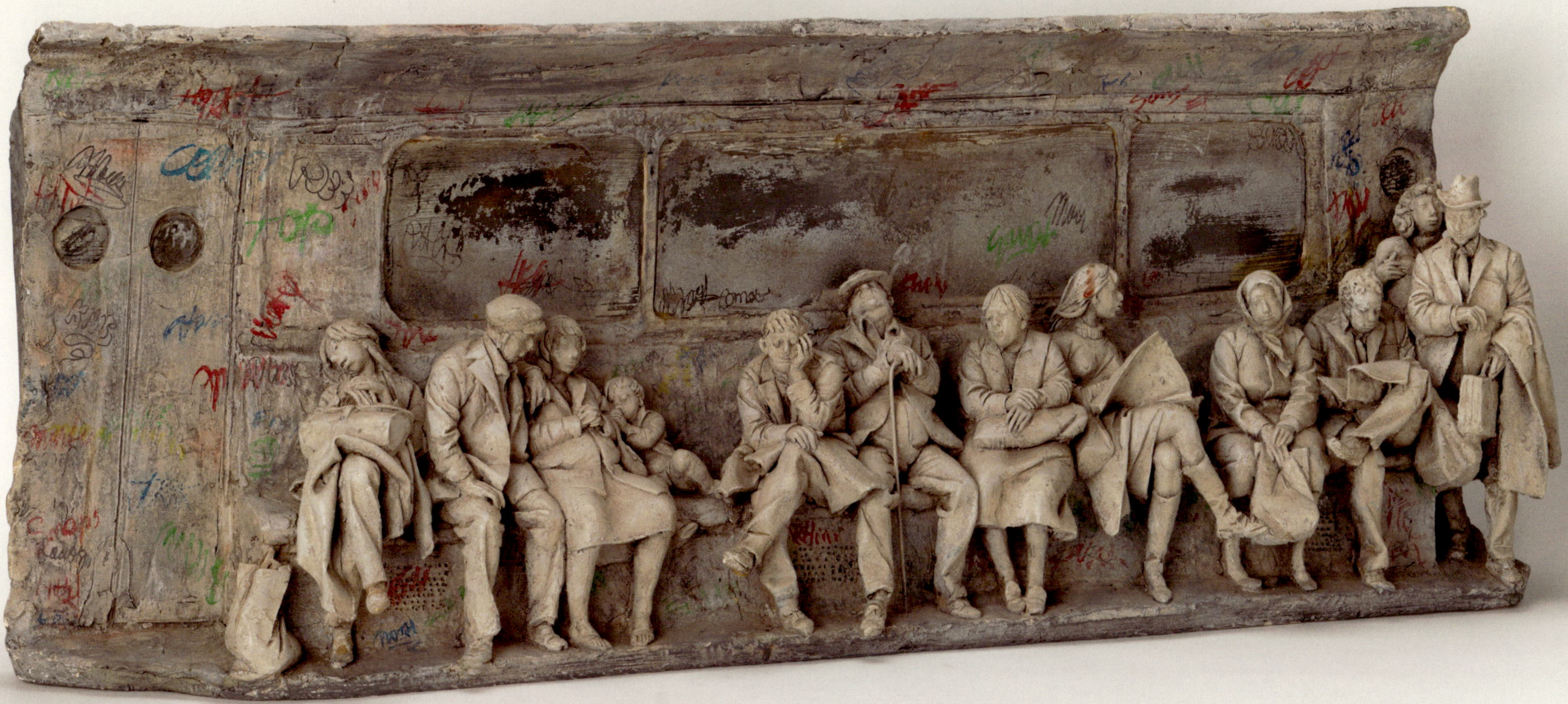

## 1970–1980

# City on Fire

Budget cuts meant slashed services, as the city laid off 25,000 employees and closed firehouses. Landlords and lenders wrote off whole neighborhoods, and fires swept through central Brooklyn, southern Queens, and the South Bronx—where Charlotte Street became a national symbol of urban decay. Vandals set some fires in abandoned buildings, while others were set by landlords seeking insurance payouts. Even the tenants themselves were reportedly responsible for some of the arson, in the desperate hope that being burned out of their homes could make them eligible for better housing. In 1975 alone almost 400,000 fires were called in to the FDNY.

Some officials called for "planned shrinkage"—cutting off services to "dying" neighborhoods to save money and to accelerate the abandonment of these poor, largely minority communities. Meanwhile, residents of nearby areas, especially in the central and north Bronx, wondered if "urban blight" would soon engulf their own communities. When shots of a burning South Bronx building were televised from a helicopter during the 1977 World Series at Yankee Stadium, the image of a seemingly unraveling city reached viewers from coast to coast.

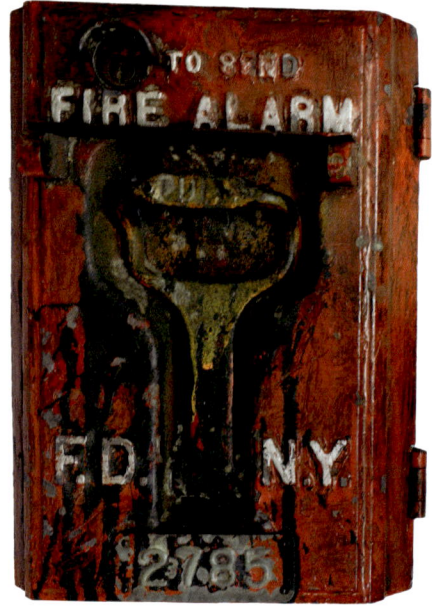

ABOVE

**Fire Department call box 2785 from Crotona Park East and Charlotte Street, Bronx**

So many false alarms were called in from this box that firefighters, overwhelmed by the frequency of real fires in the area, tied it shut and covered it with dog feces to deter false calls.

LEFT

**"¡Fuego! [Fire!]"** c. 1975

This Spanish-language poster, created by the Fire Department's Community Relations Bureau, instructs tenants how to escape a burning building.

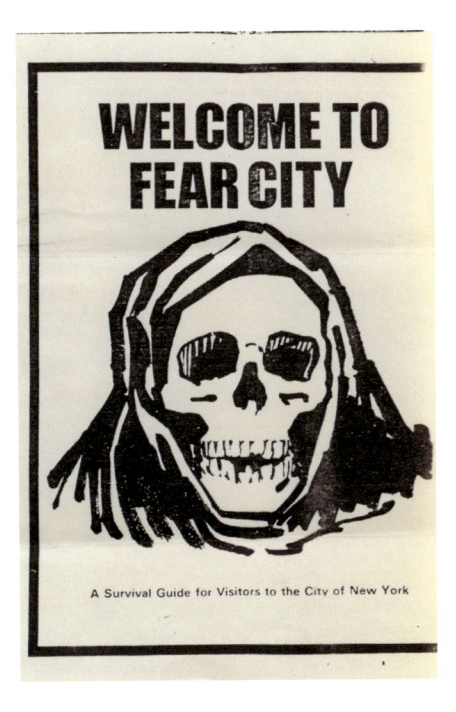

## 1970–1980

# "Fear City"

Reports of crime soared in the 1970s, hitting all-time highs at the same time that the city's police force was reduced by a third. By 1975, 275 gangs with 11,000 total members roamed the city. The annual number of murders spiked, rising from 435 homicides citywide in 1960 to 1,201 in 1970 and 1,812 in 1980. Heroin addiction, muggings, and arson became part of the city's image in the global media, posing a major public relations crisis for officials who sought to attract new businesses and tourists (and to slow the middle-class exodus out of the city) in order to rebuild New York's economy.

Fear accelerated in the summer of 1977 as David Berkowitz, a serial killer who called himself the "Son of Sam," was caught after shooting 13 New Yorkers in nighttime attacks. On the night of July 13 during that same summer, a citywide power failure led residents of some of the poorest neighborhoods to loot stores, fight police, and set fires.

CLOCKWISE FROM ABOVE

**"Welcome to Fear City: A Survival Guide for Visitors to the City of New York"** c. 1975

The Council for Public Safety, a coalition of city unions, published this booklet as a protest against layoffs due to the fiscal cuts and distributed it to tourists.

**"The Lights Go Back On,"** *Daily News*
July 15, 1977

**Courtroom sketch of the sentencing of David Berkowitz, "Son of Sam," in Brooklyn Supreme Court** 1978
Watercolor by Anthony Accurso

## 1970–1980

# Hip Hop

Hip hop was born in the South Bronx and spread to Brooklyn and Queens during the 1970s, as budget cuts to public school music programs drove young musicians to DJing instead of performing live music, and a new generation of African-American, Caribbean, and Hispanic New Yorkers shared musical styles.

Teenagers—many too young to get into dance clubs—staged hip-hop shows, rap, DJ, MC, and B-Boy (breakdance) contests in public housing recreation rooms, high schools, and parks, where they plugged their sound systems into lampposts. The birth of hip hop, in some of the city's hardest-hit neighborhoods, planted the seeds of one of America's most important cultural exports and demonstrated the ability of diverse New Yorkers to create something new in the city's streets.

The rise of hip hop and graffiti art went hand-in-hand. With art programs also cut back, young "taggers" took to decorating subway cars and neighborhood walls. While some New Yorkers, including writer Norman Mailer, championed graffiti as a fresh and democratic art form, others blasted it as an ugly symptom of the city's inability to maintain its public realm.

CLOCKWISE FROM TOP LEFT
**Flyer for a hip-hop party called "Funk in Heaven in '77"** 1977

**Untitled drawing** 1983–84
Ink on paper by Keith Haring and LAII

Keith Haring was inspired to become a street artist by the graffiti he saw on the city's walls and subway cars when he came to New York to attend art school. He often collaborated with Angel Ortiz, a graffiti artist who was known by the tag "LAII".

**CYA by 2 MAD–CYA** c. 1980
Photograph by Henry Chalfant

OPPOSITE
**Cold Crush Brothers including Grandmaster Caz (at right)** 1982
Photograph by Joe Conzo Jr.

Grandmaster Caz (Curtis Brown), who became a pioneer of hip hop in the Bronx, reported that he developed his art using the mixing equipment he stole from an electronics store during New York's July 1977 blackout.

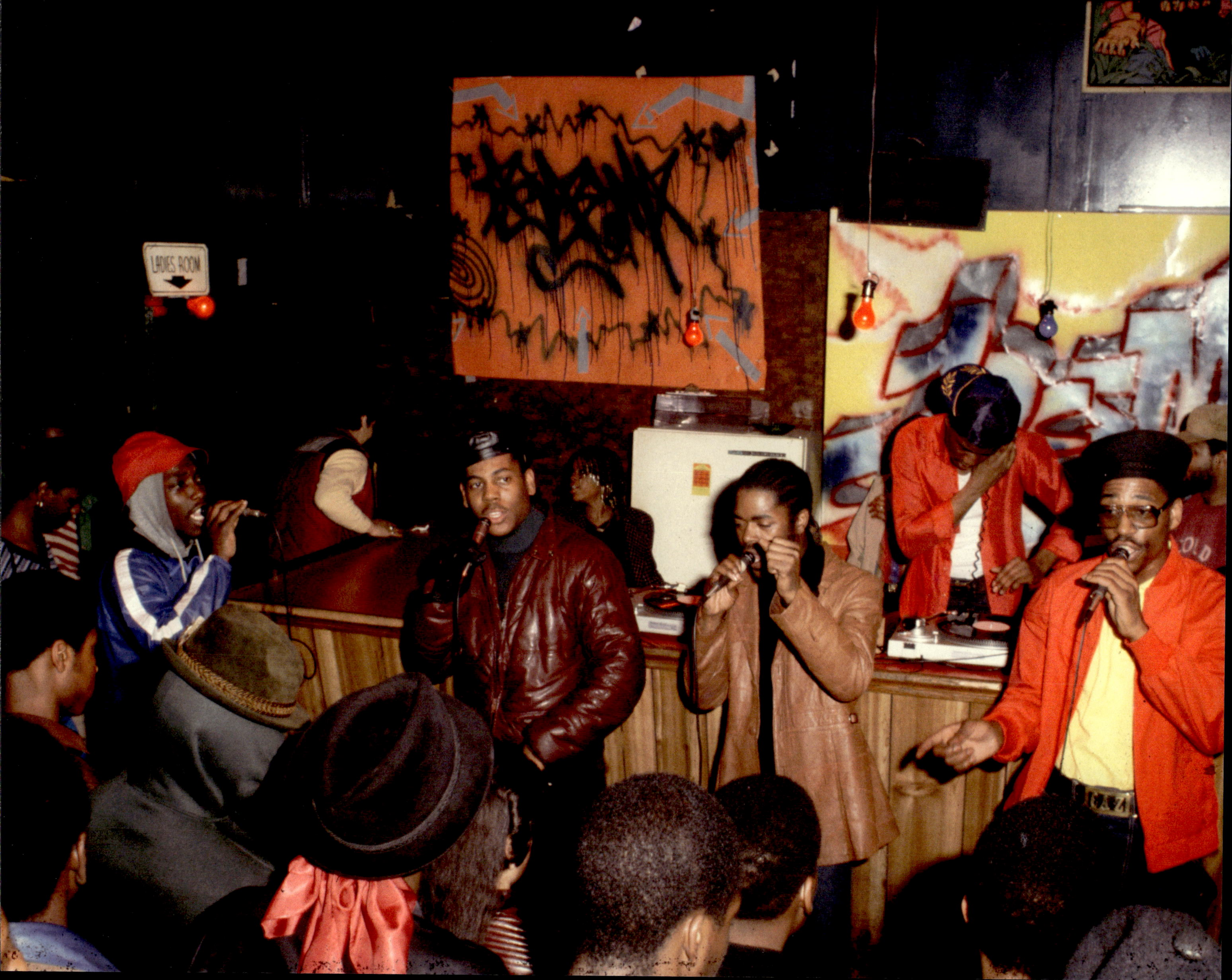
LADIES ROOM

## 1970–1980

# Resilience

Despite widespread laments about the decline of New York in the 1970s, many New Yorkers expressed their faith in the city. They invented a host of new institutions and movements—block associations, neighborhood gardens, environmental programs, a defiantly open gay subculture—that sustained and enlivened New York. "Urban homesteading" suggested confidence in the future of the city, as middle-class families chose older neighborhoods rather than a move to the suburbs. Meanwhile, residents of "blighted" areas formed nonprofits to revive their neighborhoods and planted gardens across the city in abandoned lots.

Increasingly visible gay communities fostered a new social and creative culture. Following the Stonewall Uprising of 1969, LGBT life in New York became far more open. Gay New Yorkers created new social spaces on abandoned piers, in bathhouses and dance clubs, and in a host of new organizations.

CLOCKWISE FROM TOP LEFT
**Community garden in the South Bronx** c. 1980

In 1978 the city officially encouraged community gardens by offering leases to neighborhood groups.

**"Clinton Hill, Brooklyn 'The Sane Alternative,'" flyer promoting Brooklyn as an alternative to the suburbs, published by the Society for Clinton Hill** 1976

**South Bronx Banana Kelly** c. 1978
Photograph by Allan Tannenbaum

Named for a section of the South Bronx's Kelly Street, the Banana Kelly Community Improvement Association was founded in 1978 to reclaim abandoned Bronx buildings slated for demolition.

**Marchers in the first Gay Pride parade held on the anniversary of the Stonewall Uprising (then called Gay Liberation Day)** 1970
Photograph by Fred W. McDarrah

CLOCKWISE FROM ABOVE
**Towel from Continental Baths in the Ansonia Hotel** c. 1970

**Light towers at Studio 54** 1978
Photograph by Allan Tannenbaum

**Studio 54 guest list including musicians Ringo Starr, Peter Frampton, David Bowie, and Liberace along with television and media executives** 1978

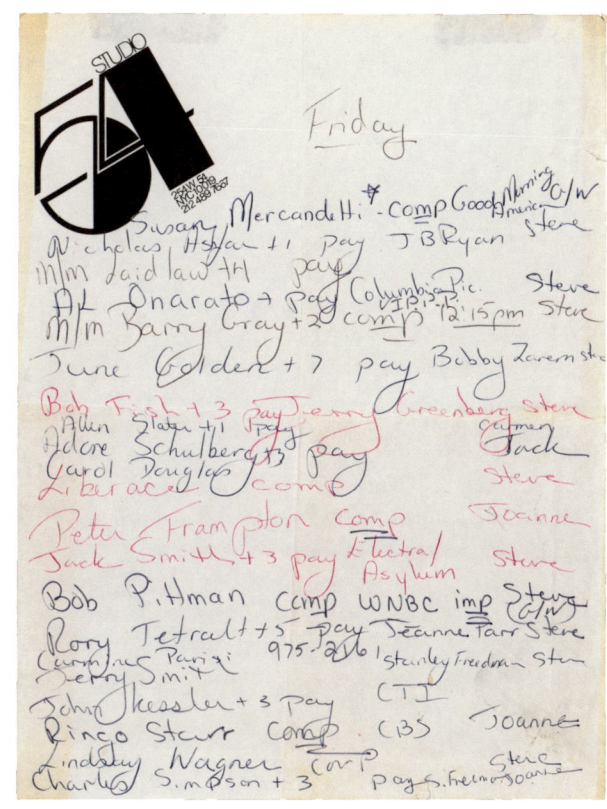

## 1970–1980

# Nightlife

The city's creativity was expressed in its nightlife, which generated business and new cultural forms in the 1970s, from disco at Studio 54 to punk rock at CBGB on the Bowery to experimental theater at La Ma Ma in the East Village.

New York became the main incubator for disco and the rise of a new kind of dance club. With roots in the city's gay clubs and loft dance parties, by 1977 disco moved into the mainstream with the popularity of the movie *Saturday Night Fever* (set in Brooklyn) and the opening of Studio 54 in midtown. The club drew would-be patrons from around the region, who crowded at the door because they were not on the club's legendary guest list.

Social spaces catering primarily to gay men added to the air of cultural experimentation. They included the Continental Baths in the Ansonia Hotel, which boasted of being able to serve 1,000 men 24 hours a day with private rooms, a disco, and a cabaret where Bette Midler, Andy Kaufman, and the New York Dolls performed.

155

# New Yorkers 1970–1980

**Stephen Burrows** 1970
Photograph by Charles Tracy

### Stephen Burrows
(b. 1943)
Dressing Up for Fun City

With unconventional materials, bold colors, and fluid cuts, fashion designer Stephen Burrows created clothes that were at the epicenter of an era of fun and liberation. Called "the brightest star in American fashion" by *The New York Times* in 1977, Burrows helped define the look of 1960s and '70s New York and placed the New York fashion scene in a new position on the global stage.

Burrows designed his unisex, colorful, body-conscious looks for a group of friends he called "the commune" and for the patrons of the nightlife hotspot Max's Kansas City. In 1973 he joined Bill Blass, Halston, Anne Klein, and Oscar de la Renta as the first American designers to show in Paris, creating a splash with their spirit of energy and freedom.

ABOVE
**Fashion illustration** 1972
Ink and colored pencil on paper by Stephen Burrows

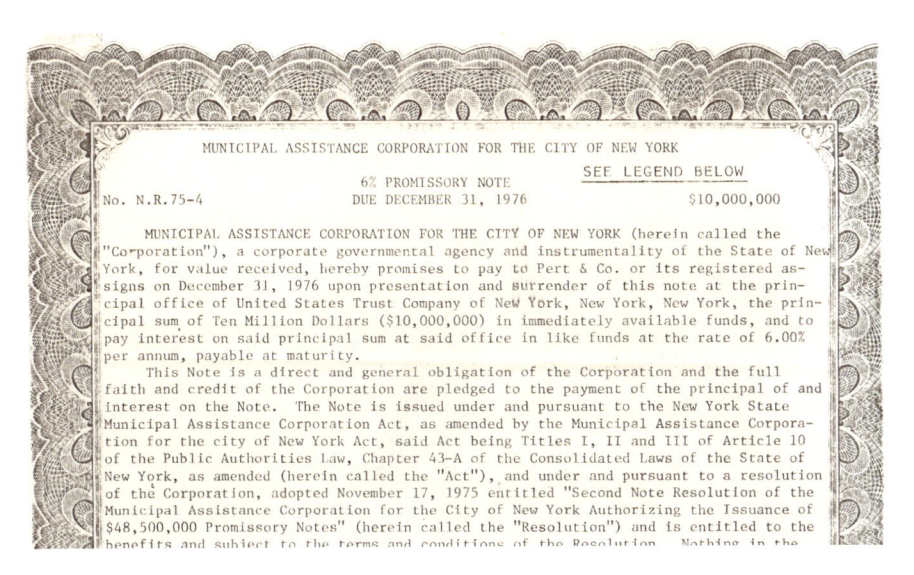

**Felix Rohatyn**
(b. 1928)
Fending Off Default

Investment banker Felix Rohatyn found himself thrust into civic leadership when, in June of 1975, New York Governor Hugh Carey confided to him that New York City was unable to pay its debts.

Rohatyn helped create a new state agency, the Municipal Assistance Corporation (MAC), to restore the city's credit. Soon the city cut services, laid off employees, raised subway fares and taxes, and cut its capital budget, all in an effort to show fiscal responsibility, angering city residents and activists along the way. Rohatyn and his colleagues also persuaded the city's municipal unions and banks to purchase MAC bonds. By December of 1975 President Ford authorized short-term loans to the city, resolving the immediate crisis.

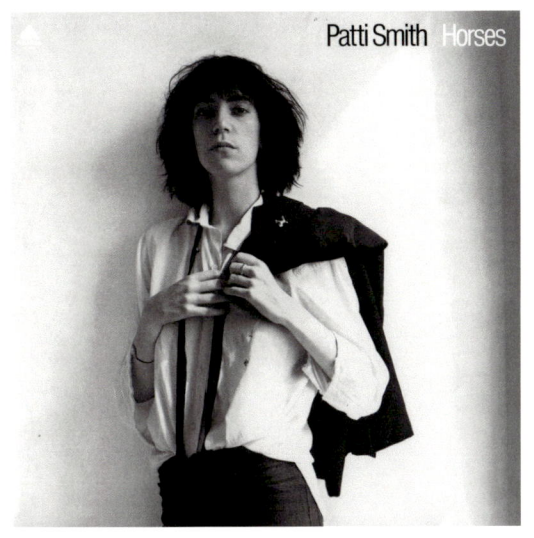

**Felix Rohatyn** 1979
Photograph by Fred W. McDarrah

ABOVE
**MAC Promissory Note (detail)**
1976

**Patti Smith**
(b. 1946)
Godmother of Punk

Musician Patti Smith arrived in New York City in 1967 with $32, a plaid suitcase, and a passion for poetry, art, and music. She found a city where 50 cents could buy a hot meal, and the apartment in Fort Greene that she shared with artist and photographer Robert Mapplethorpe was only $80 a month.

Shifting from poetry to punk rock in 1971, Smith and her band performed at key New York rock venues from Max's Kansas City to CBGBs. Merging punk and spoken word, her work captured the essence of the edgy, creative artistic ferment of the downtown scene of the 1970s. Her legendary 1975 album *Horses* epitomizes the moment; the album's cover image, shot by Mapplethorpe, remains one of the most iconic rock and roll portraits of all time.

**Patti Smith** 1976

ABOVE
***Horses*, record cover** 1975

ONE WAY
紐約第一駕駛學
MARKET ST
市場街
三樓
MANHATTAN BR
福州小食
東
長春花舖
麗琪
ROYCE
天天
男女
豬肉乾

# 1980–2001

## New York Comes Back

As the city recovered from the fiscal crisis in the closing decades of the 20th century, it underwent a remarkable turnaround. In the space of less than a generation, New York went from being a place whose very existence was uncertain, to a city characterized by overwhelming success and popularity. But the soaring economy had its winners and losers, and extremes of wealth and poverty, of inclusion and exclusion, became conspicuous in the city's public image in a way that had not been seen in decades.

The changes were felt throughout New York's economy, population, and physical environment. By 1981 the city's financial house was returning to order and white-collar businesses streamed in, as concentrated flows of computerized information, credit, and investment money made New York a global financial center in new ways. The city's density rebounded as newcomers arrived, especially immigrants who were welcomed by new federal laws, and their labor and entrepreneurial energy in turn drove the recovery of the city's economy and neighborhoods. And the cleanup of icons like Times Square and Central Park, along with a remarkable drop in crime, made many people feel that the city was safer and more well cared-for than it had been in generations.

OPPOSITE
**New York City** 1996
Photograph by Chien-Chi Chang

## 1980–2001

# A New Gilded Age

Wall Street produced jobs, revenue, and prestige for the city in the 1980s as white-collar employment surged. Along with national and global financial trends, Mayor Edward I. Koch's pro-business strategies helped spark the rapid revival. This was especially notable in the growth industries of finance, insurance, and real estate, as jobs in banking increased from 97,000 in 1969 to 171,000 in 1986. By 1995, financial companies and related services made up 15 percent of the city's workforce and almost 30 percent of its gross economic output.

New wealth made Wall Street moguls powerful and glamorous. It also invented an alluring array of new financial products and strategies that attracted global investors and traders, from "junk bonds" and leveraged buyouts to mortgage-backed securities. As the world's resurgent money capital, New York was the setting for the consolidation of dozens of banks into a smaller number of mega-banks, including Citigroup and JPMorgan Chase, which changed the way the world did business.

CLOCKWISE FROM TOP LEFT
**Production storyboard for *Wall Street*** 1987
Ink on paper

"Greed is good," the mantra of Oliver Stone's villainous corporate raider in his 1987 film *Wall Street*, was inspired by a statement by notorious New York financier Ivan Boesky.

**Donna Karan Barbie** 1995

New York designer Donna Karan's mid-1980s "Seven Easy Pieces" wardrobe epitomized the style of businesswomen working in the new economy.

**Bloomberg keyboard** c. 1989

Bloomberg L.P. was founded by Michael R. Bloomberg and three partners in 1982. By 1992, 20,000 "Bloomberg Terminals" transformed businesses by offering financial firms worldwide a continuous stream of data, analytics, and news.

OPPOSITE
**I (Heart) New York concept sketch** 1976
Ink and tape on paper envelope by Milton Glaser

By the early 1980s New York had begun to repackage its mean streets for tourists and entrepreneurs. Designer and *New York* magazine co-founder Milton Glaser, working for the New York State Department of Commerce, created the "I (Heart) New York" logo as part of a public relations campaign to lure tourism and new businesses.

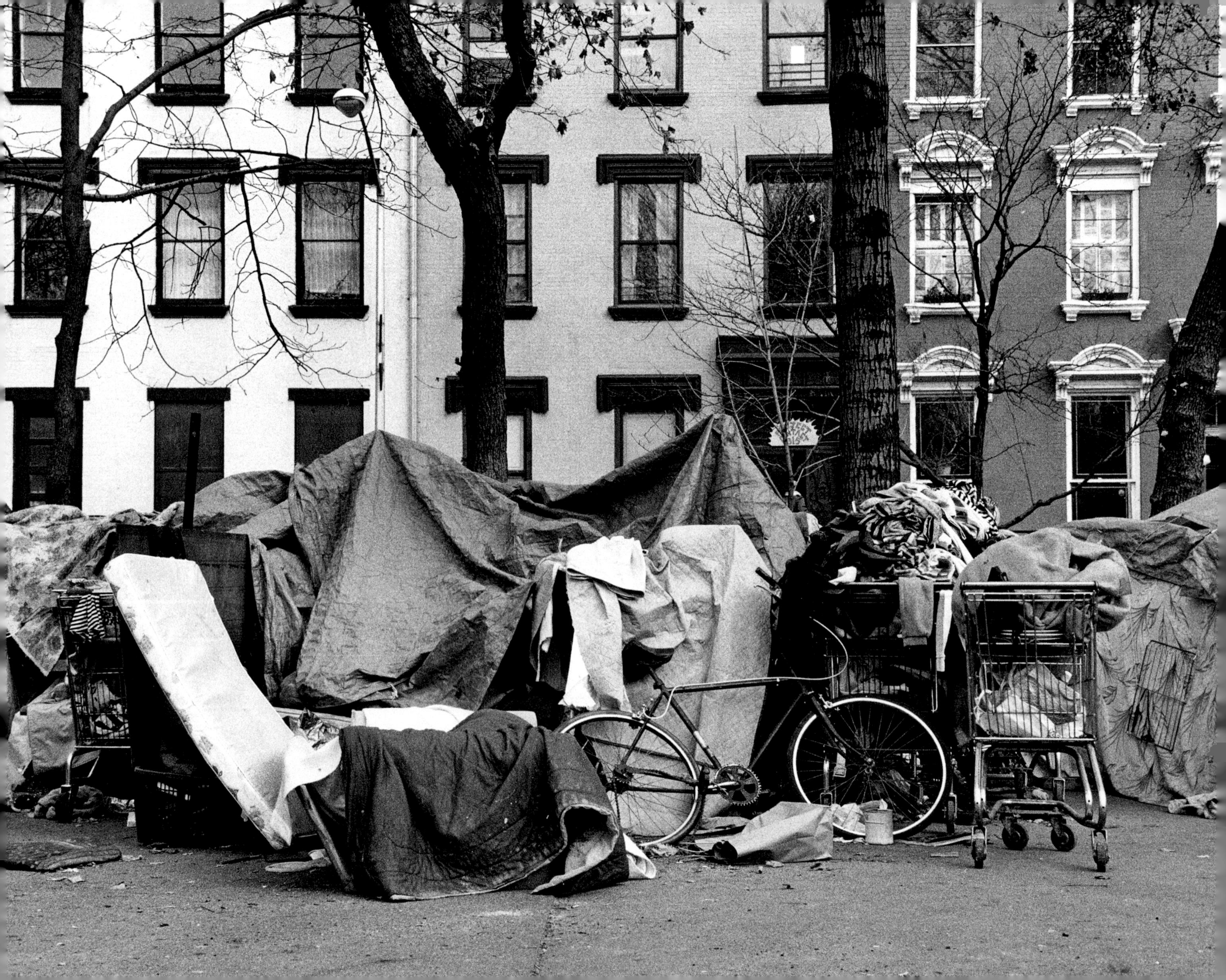

CLOCKWISE FROM ABOVE
**Collection of heroin "brand" bags** 1990s

A crack cocaine epidemic swept through many of the city's poorest neighborhoods in the 1980s and early '90s, while heroin addiction and related crime remained a major problem.

**Gay Men's Health Crisis dance-a-thon fundraising letter** 1991
Featuring the artwork of Keith Haring

**Bear dressed as "The Angel" from *Angels in America*** 1998
Fabricated by Lynn Carroll and Karein Weston

Broadway Cares/Equity Fights AIDS raised more than $2 million between 1998 and 2012 by auctioning teddy bears representing characters from Broadway shows like Tony Kushner's *Angels in America*, a play centered on the lives of gay men and the impact of the AIDS epidemic.

OPPOSITE
**Homeless Structures, Tompkins Square Park**
1989
Photograph by Margaret Morton

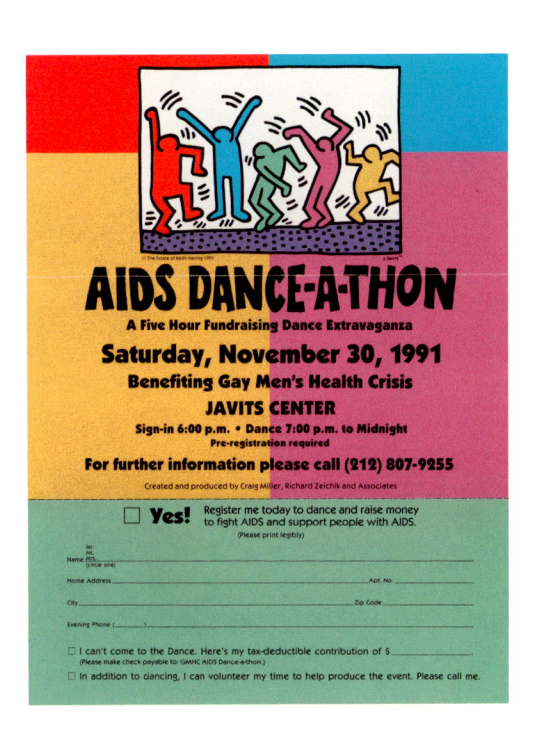

## 1980–2001
# A Tale of Two Cities

In many ways, New York remained a middle-class city in the post-fiscal crisis era. Yet as manufacturing (and its unionized jobs) continued to decline in importance, many New Yorkers felt priced out of the new economy, with their incomes failing to keep up with the rising cost of living in the city. And, as many of New York's poorest faced homelessness or addiction, the sense of two New Yorks—one of "haves" and one of "have-nots"—resonated in ways not felt since Jacob Riis's day a century earlier.

New York's homeless population swelled as poverty, the discharge of mentally ill patients from state facilities, addiction, and lack of funding for housing alternatives drove thousands into the streets. By 1987, 27,000 New Yorkers were sleeping in public shelters, and makeshift dwellings became a common sight across the city. The city, home to the nation's largest gay population, was also deeply affected by the HIV-AIDS crisis after the disease was identified in 1981. All of this, along with tensions around gentrification, sharpened the sense of a city divided between the privileged and the needy.

## 1980–2001

# A New Immigrant Economy

The energies of immigrants from around the world also spurred New York's turnaround in the last decades of the 20th century. By the 1980s, the effects of more open immigration laws were felt in full force, as newcomers helped to reverse the city's population decline, sending the number of New Yorkers surging from seven million to just over eight million in only 20 years.

These newest New Yorkers came from across North and South America, the Caribbean, Asia, Africa, and the Pacific, as well as Europe. They helped transform neighborhoods throughout the five boroughs, injecting fresh ambition and cultural variety into the fabric of the city, and restoring the population density that had been diminished in the preceding decades.

By the century's end New York was one of the world's most ethnically diverse cities, with 36 percent of its population born overseas. The four largest immigrant groups were from the Dominican Republic, China, the former Soviet Union, and Jamaica, but no one group dominated. New York absorbed and incorporated the new arrivals, although demographic change, economic competition, and cultural differences sometimes sparked tensions that tested the famed tolerance of the city.

TOP LEFT
**37–66 103rd Street, Queens** 1983–88

TOP RIGHT
**37–66 103rd Street, Queens** 2016
Photograph by Joshua Simpson

As suggested by these "before" and "after" photographs of a block in North Corona, Queens, that neighborhood was one of many reinvigorated by the entrepreneurial energy of arrivals from around the world.

CLOCKWISE FROM LEFT
**Lowell Hawthorne in the production facility for Golden Krust Caribbean Bakery, Bronx** 2012

The Hawthorne family started Golden Krust Caribbean Bakery in 1989 to sell Jamaican foods, catering to a growing West Indian population.

**Dominican merengue group La Banda Gorda performing in Hamilton Heights, Manhattan** 2009

The largest immigration of the late 20th century came from the Dominican Republic.

**Russian Banya, Brighton Beach, Brooklyn** 2016
Photograph by Joshua Simpson

The relaxation of Soviet immigration policy during the 1970s, followed by the USSR's collapse in 1991, transformed neighborhoods as Ukrainian Jews and Muslims from Central Asia arrived. Israel Odessky from Ukraine opened Brooklyn's first Russian baths in 1980.

**Youth group at Transfiguration Church** 1975

In the late 20th century the first large numbers of Chinese women arrived in New York, leading to a growing population of families. The Lower East Side's Church of the Transfiguration was just one organization to run a Saturday school for children to learn Chinese language and culture, as well as a youth group.

## 1980–2001
# A Safer City

The New York Police Department (NYPD) was rebuilt in the 1990s under Mayors David N. Dinkins and Rudy Giuliani. More officers were hired, police now walked neighborhood "beats," and in 1993 Commissioner William Bratton began a crackdown on low-level "quality-of-life" offenses. In 1994 the city introduced COMPSTAT (Computer Comparison Statistics), enabling the NYPD to monitor crimes across the city's precincts.

Crime rates fell in New York for the first time in decades, with the murder rate alone down more than 65%. Many credited the increase in police officers and more coordinated policing. Others linked the drop to broader shifts, including an aging population and the decline of the crack epidemic.

But the transformation of New York into the safest large city in the nation came with tensions of its own. Critics pointed to high incarceration rates, stop-and-frisk, and the nation's strictest drug laws, and especially to their impacts on black and Hispanic New Yorkers. High-profile incidents such as the 1997 police abuse of Abner Louima in Brooklyn and the 1999 police shooting of Amadou Diallo, an unarmed immigrant from Guinea, highlighted ongoing questions about policing in the city's minority communities.

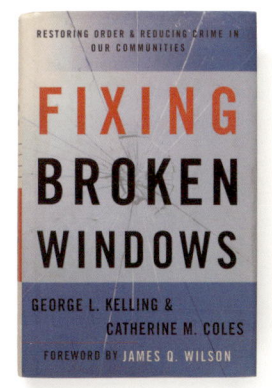

CLOCKWISE FROM ABOVE
**"The Beat Cop Is Back"** c. 1990
Subway poster by New York's Finest Foundation

**Prayer vigil held by Al Sharpton to protest the acquittal of four police officers in the shooting death of Amadou Diallo** 2000
Photograph by Spencer Platt

***Fixing Broken Windows: Restoring Order and Reducing Crime in Our Communities* by George L. Kellings and Catherine M. Coles, published by Free Press** 1996

Theorists George L. Kelling and James Q. Wilson argued in a 1982 article (later a book co-authored by Kelling and Catherine M. Coles) that small offenses created an environment that encouraged more serious crimes.

## 1980–2001

# Cleaning Up

Nothing symbolized the revival of New York more than its physical transformation. By the 1990s New York was cleaner and more orderly than it had been in decades. Developers transformed Times Square from a maze of X-rated theaters into a gleaming family entertainment district; Central Park received a major physical restoration; and neighborhoods of formerly abandoned buildings were repopulated.

In the wake of fiscal crisis cutbacks, the city mobilized private dollars to maintain its public spaces. Public-private partnerships took the form of nonprofit conservancies like the Central Park Conservancy (1980) and business improvement districts (BIDs), that cleaned up neighborhoods and parks from Times Square to Fordham Road in the Bronx, Forest Avenue in Staten Island, Brooklyn's Prospect Park, and downtown Flushing, Queens.

While some lamented that government was not taking the lead on these urban problems, others praised BIDs and conservancies for leveraging the energy, private money, and expertise of the city's business community.

CLOCKWISE FROM ABOVE
**West 42nd St.** 1984
Photograph by Andreas Feininger

**Harlem Meer, Central Park** c. 1979
Photograph by Sara Cedar Miller

**Harlem Meer, Central Park** 2008

**Boots worn by "Mrs. Potts" character in Disney's Broadway production** *Beauty and the Beast* 1993–94

OPPOSITE
**Disney Store and** *Lion King* **marquee in Times Square** 1998
Photograph by Scott J. Ferrell

The Times Square BID (1992) helped drive a sweeping reinvention of Times Square, as family-friendly attractions replaced X-rated theaters.

BRITISH AIRWAYS
DIGGETTY
DISNEY
DAM
DISNEY
THE NEW TIMES SQUARE
RED ZONE
BUSES ONLY
STORE
DISNEY PRESENTS
THE LION KING
THE BROADWAY MUSICAL
"IT'S LIKE BEING IN A DREAM AWAKE!"

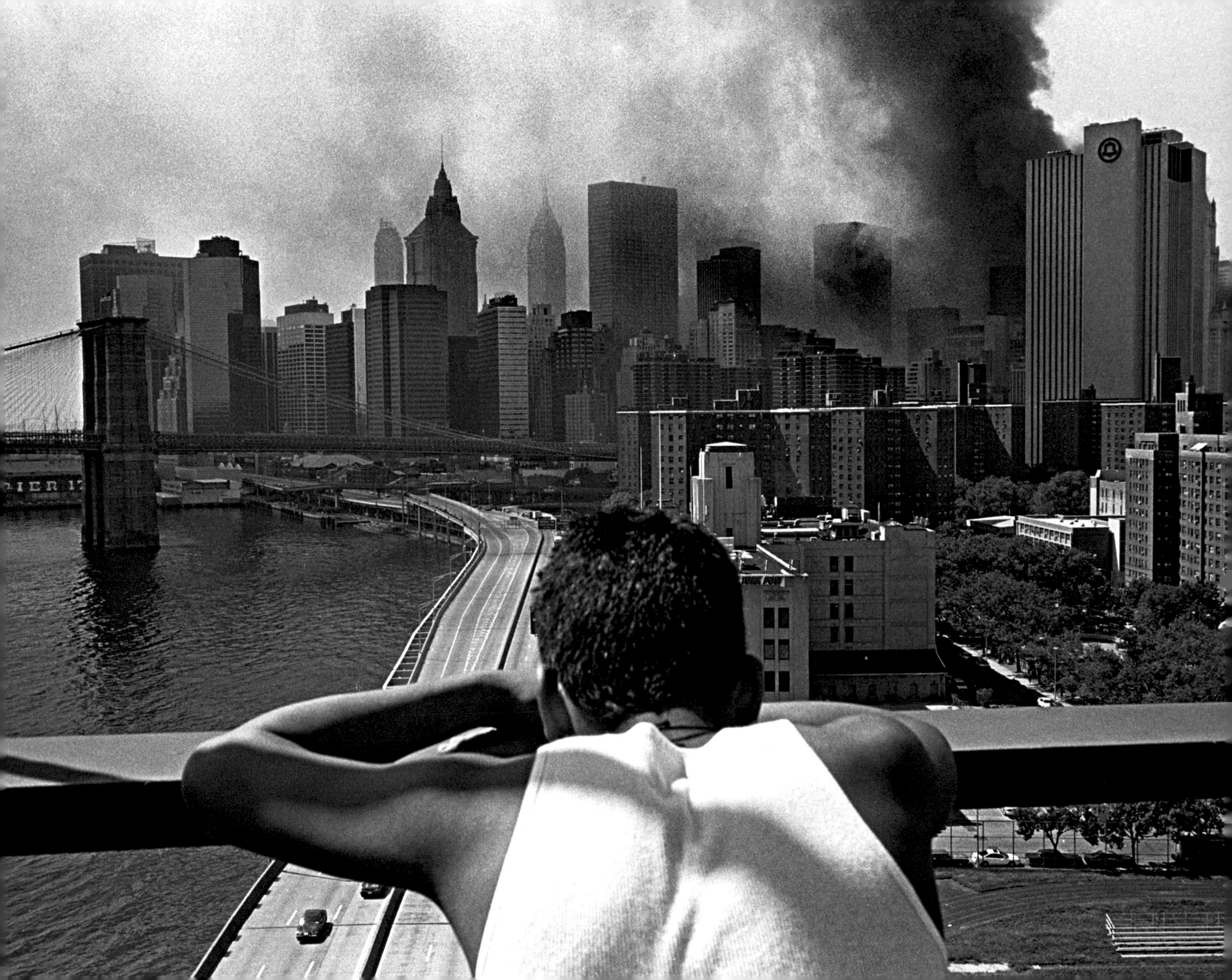

## 1980–2001

# September 11

On September 11, 2001, arguments over the city's character were abruptly silenced—and the city's sense of invulnerability shattered—when terrorists piloted two airliners into the Twin Towers of the World Trade Center killing 2,753 people, including over 400 first responders: firefighters, police, and paramedics. As New Yorkers grieved, they reconsidered the meanings of urban safety and wondered how the city's spirit—and economy—would recover.

The site at "Ground Zero" became a symbol of the tragedy, but also a beacon of resolve. Volunteers streamed in to aid in rescue and recovery—many of them continue to suffer from health problems long after. Although debates soon emerged over how to rebuild and how to balance public safety and civil rights, the setback to the city as a whole proved less long lasting than feared. Despite dire predictions, lower Manhattan's and the city's rapid rebound signaled New York's continued vitality and global importance.

OPPOSITE
**Man looking out over lower Manhattan**
September 11, 2001
Photograph by Joseph Rodriguez

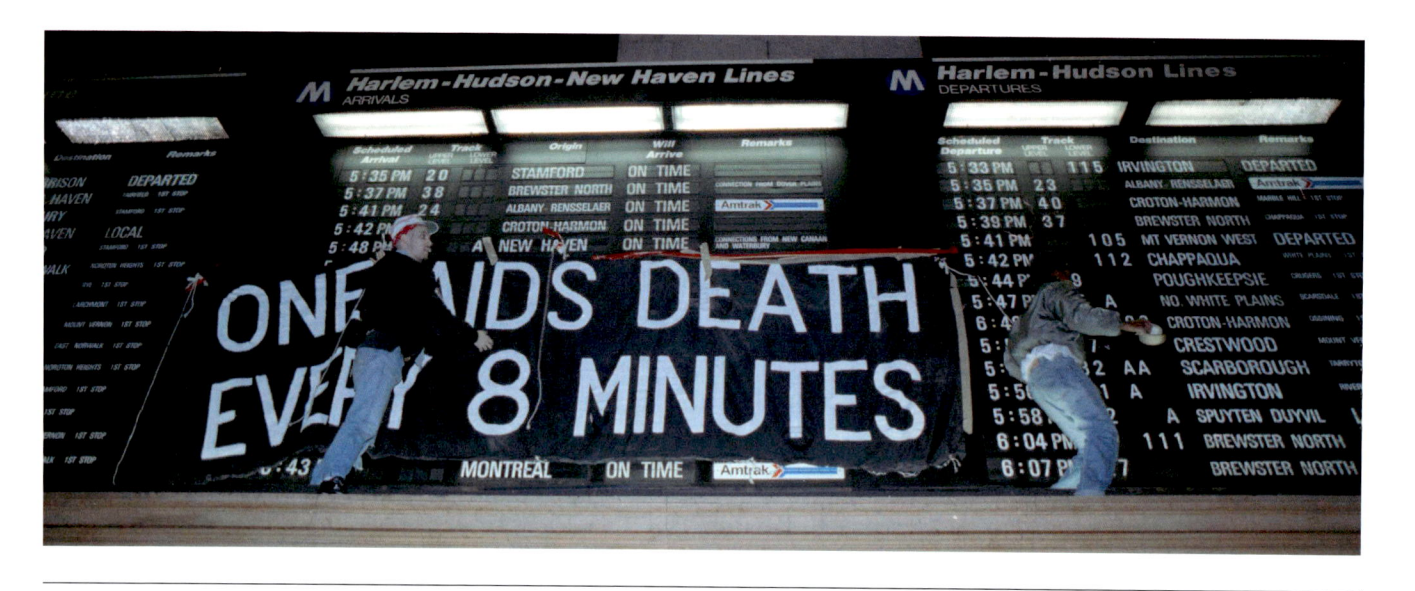

# New Yorkers 1980–2001

*ABOVE*
**ACT UP demonstration in New York's Grand Central Terminal** 1991

**Larry Kramer** 1989
Photograph by Sara Krulwich

## Larry Kramer
(b. 1935)
### Acting Up

In the 1980s, Larry Kramer, already a controversial playwright and novelist, harnessed fiery rhetoric to inspire gay men and lesbians to build new networks of care and activism in response to AIDS and to claim their voice as a distinct minority group in New York politics and culture.

In 1982 Kramer co-founded the Gay Men's Health Crisis, to provide AIDS funding, care, and education. Forced out of the organization in 1983 for writing a scathing critique of the city and his fellow gay men, Kramer wrote *The Normal Heart*, a play about the organization's founding. In 1987 he launched the controversial ACT UP (AIDS Coalition to Unleash Power), which used confrontational and creative protests to demand action.

## Jean-Michel Basquiat
(1960–1988)
### From Brooklyn to SoHo

Brooklyn-born Jean-Michel Basquiat first came to the notice of the art world in 1976 with a graffiti project in SoHo and the East Village. In 1980 he was featured in the legendary "Times Square Show," which merged the downtown art scene with hip hop- and graffiti-influenced artists from the Bronx and Queens.

By 1984 Basquiat had become a sensation. But he struggled with fame and with drug addiction, dying of an overdose at the age of 27. As hip-hop pioneer Fab Five Freddy said, "Jean-Michel lived like a flame. He burned really bright. Then the fire went out. But the embers are still hot."

**Jean-Michel Basquiat** 1985

ABOVE
**Jean-Michel Basquiat with his work** 1988

## Joanna Wan-Ying Chan (陳尹瑩)
(b. 1939)
### Staging Chinese New York

Among the millions who arrived in the wake of the liberalization of immigration laws in 1965 was Sister Joanna Chan, a Catholic missionary nun working at Chinatown's Transfiguration Church, who devoted herself to bridging gaps among people, institutions, and nations, from Asia to New York.

A multidisciplinary artist, she started her work with the children in the growing population of Chinese immigrant families. She went on to found vital cultural institutions like the Four Seas Players, and to write, direct, and produce plays in the common languages of Chinatown (Cantonese, Mandarin, and English) to bring the larger community together.

**Joanna Wan-Ying Chan** 2016
Photograph by Julie Cunnah

ABOVE
**Program cover for *Tai Nui Fa*, the Chinese New Year Celebration pageant performed by the Four Seas Players at Transfiguration** 1970

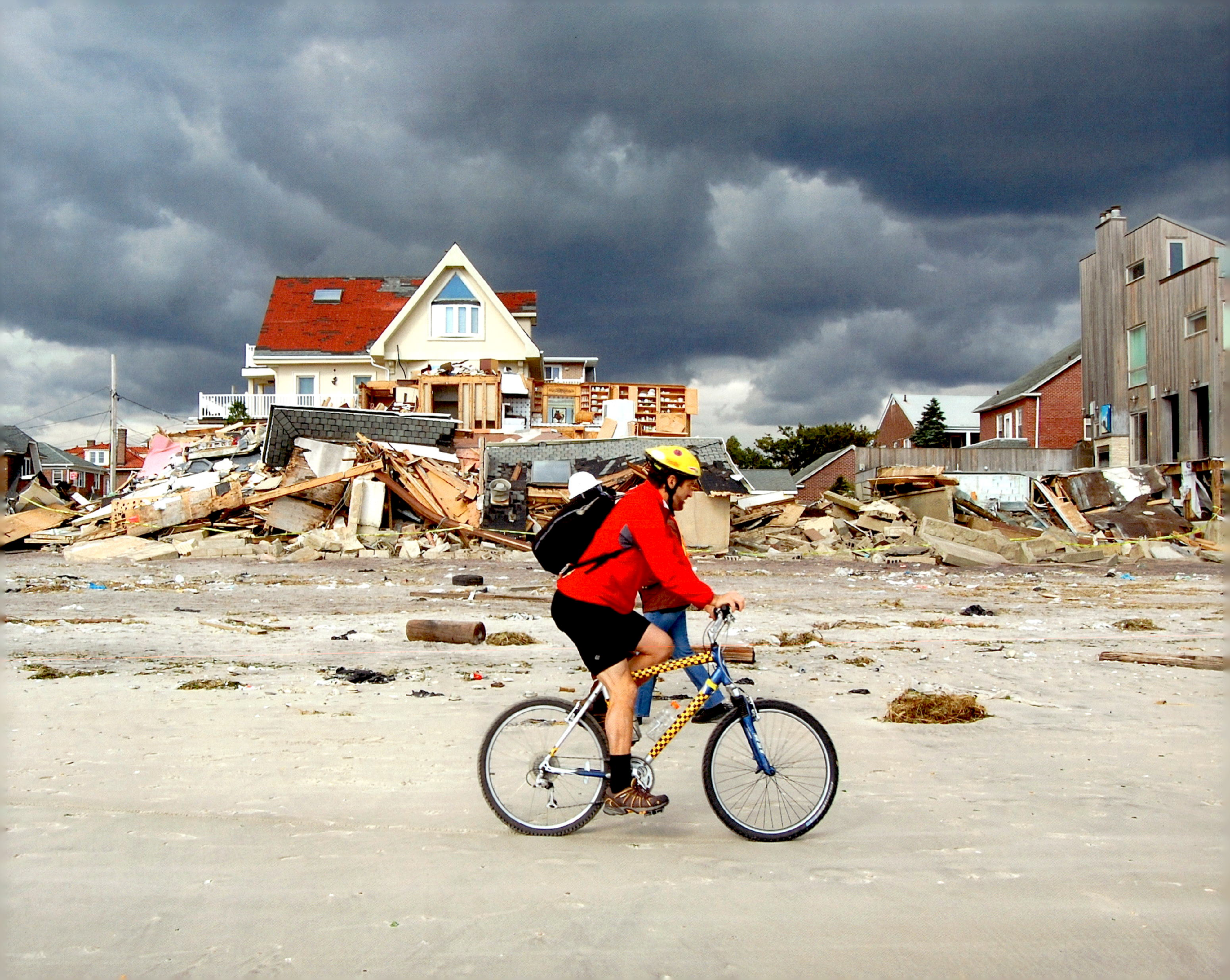

# 2001–2012

## Debating the City

Despite the terrible setback of September 11, 2001, New York City continued to experience dramatic growth in the new millennium, as ambitious new development swept all five boroughs. Signs of change were everywhere throughout the city. New York's density underwent a dramatic alteration, as bicycle lanes and pedestrian plazas transformed the streets; new parks, housing, and businesses reclaimed the waterfront; and property values (and the cost of living) soared in neighborhoods that some had written off just a generation earlier, causing some to wonder whether the city might become a victim of its success.

Money, density, diversity, and creativity remained distinguishing features of life in New York. But pressing questions remained about the city's future: How should money be spent? Who would benefit from new developments? Among the city's diverse communities, who would control the direction of change? Who would be able to afford to live in the city? These questions became even more urgent after October 2012, when a natural disaster of unprecedented proportions—Hurricane Sandy—exposed the city's vulnerability to the very waters that had once made the port so successful.

OPPOSITE
**Aftermath of Hurricane Sandy, Belle Harbor, Queens** 2012
Photograph by Paul Lurrie

## 2001–2012
# New Developments

During Michael R. Bloomberg's administration (2002–13), the post-9/11 city reclaimed its confidence as a center of corporate enterprise, high finance, and real estate development. Rezoning policies encouraged new office and residential construction across the city, along with "greening" of urban spaces. Developments on the waterfront of all five boroughs re-envisioned the shoreline as a mixed zone of public and private activity. And major new projects sprang up, including the Hudson Yards on the far west side of Manhattan, the largest private development in the history of the United States.

The mayor's policies also sparked arguments over the direction of New York's economy, control of the city's streets, and the role of government in regulating the public behavior of individuals. Changes like doubling the city's system of bike lanes from 300 to 750 miles were met with enthusiasm by cyclists and environmentalists, but aroused opposition in neighborhoods where some residents argued that the new lanes reduced parking, slowed car traffic, endangered pedestrians, and hurt businesses.

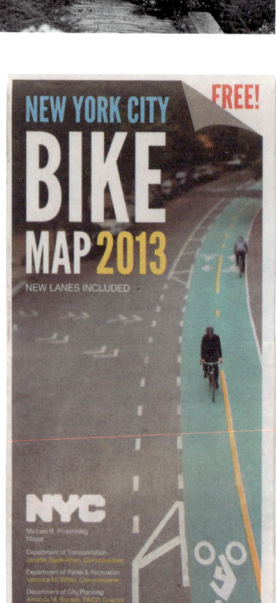

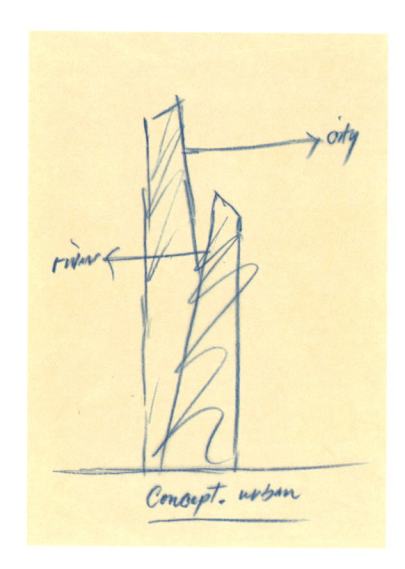

CLOCKWISE FROM TOP LEFT
**Future site of Brooklyn Bridge Park, looking west** c. 1975
Photograph by Edmund Vincent Gillon

**Concept drawing for Hudson Yards** 2012–13
Designed by William Pedersen/Kohn Pedersen Fox Associates

**New York City Bike Map, published by the New York City Department of Transportation** 2013

**"Bikelash," with photograph by Danny Kim,** *New York* March 28, 2011

OPPOSITE
**Brooklyn Bridge Park** 2016
Photograph by Joshua Simpson

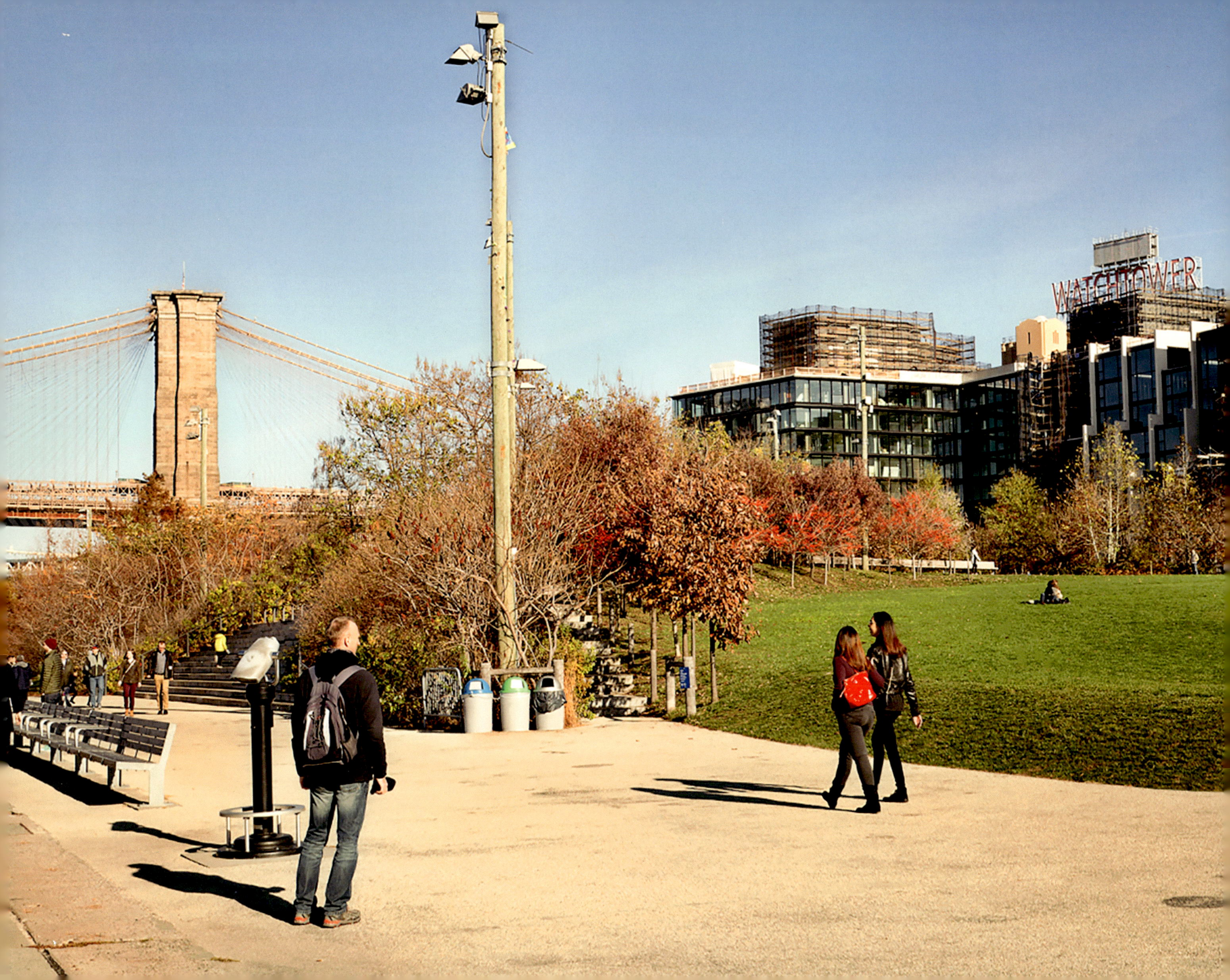
WATCHTOWER

## 2001–2012
# Meltdown

The optimism of the early 21st century was challenged by the financial crisis of 2007–08, when the collapse of the housing market and major financial companies plunged the world economy into recession. The historic New York firms Bear Stearns, Lehman Brothers, and Merrill Lynch imploded, and New York City lost 100,000 private sector jobs in a year, with the jobless rate reaching 9.5 percent by mid-2009.

The crisis was triggered by trading in complex financial instruments, some based on complicated mathematic formulas like the Gaussian Copula Equation, which had been packaged and traded on Wall Street and elsewhere. Three years later, the role of New York banks in the crisis, and the fact that 1.7 million New Yorkers still lived in poverty, fueled thousands of Occupy Wall Street protesters to occupy lower Manhattan's Zuccotti Park for nearly two months, demonstrating against the wealthiest "one percent" and helping to forge a new language for national political debate.

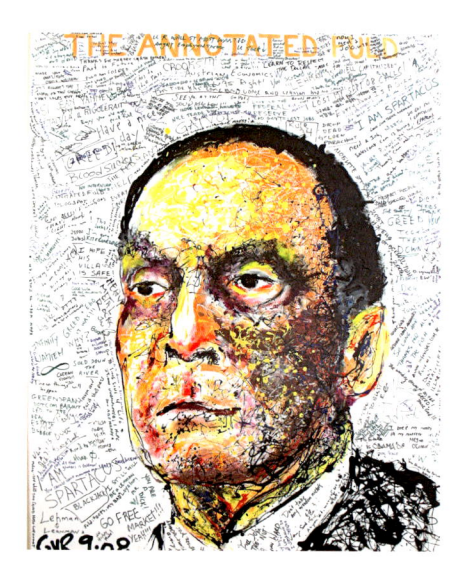

CLOCKWISE FROM TOP
**The Annotated Fuld a portrait of Lehman Brothers CEO Richard Fuld** 2008/2016
Oil on canvas by Geffrey Raymond

**The Occupied Wall Street Journal**
October 8, 2011

**Gaussian Copula Equation**

**Former Lehman employee signs *The Annotated Fuld* outside the firm's headquarters on the day it declared bankruptcy** 2008
Photograph by Keith Bedford

$$Pr[T_A<1, T_B<1] = \Phi_2(\Phi^{-1}(F_A(1)), \Phi^{-1}(F_B(1)), \gamma)$$

RIGHT

**"Tomorrowland," with cover art by John Blackford,** *New York* June 5, 2006

## 2001–2012
# Facing the Future

*New York* magazine was just one of the publications that tried to gaze into the city's future as the new millennium dawned. In 2006 it predicted that by 2016 lower Manhattan would "become a real neighborhood," the Brooklyn and Queens waterfront might become "the ultimate address," a new "it" neighborhood would grow up around the High Line, and Staten Island might become "the California of New York."

# New Yorkers 2001-2012

ABOVE
**Tribeca Film Festival** 2002

**Jane Rosenthal** 2014
Photograph by Eric Ryan Anderson

## Jane Rosenthal
(b. 1956)
Bringing the City Back with Film

Hollywood Producer Jane Rosenthal returned to New York in 1989 to co-found Tribeca Films, a few blocks from the World Trade Center. On September 11, 2001 she saw the devastation of the area firsthand. In a matter of months she, Craig Hatkoff, and Robert De Niro put together the first Tribeca Film Festival, to bring economic and creative life back to downtown.

Although there had been talk of a film festival for years, the idea took on new urgency as a way to revive lower Manhattan. In April 2002, with the help of 1,300 volunteers, more than 150,000 people attended the festival, and contributed to the creative reinvention of New York in the aftermath of tragedy.

## Robert Hammond and Joshua David
### Saving the Highline

In 1999, two Chelsea residents, Joshua David and Robert Hammond, saw an opportunity in an abandoned elevated rail line built in 1934. The two soon founded Friends of the Highline, a non-profit group dedicated to repurposing the remnant of the city's industrial past as a public greenway.

With the 2004 rezoning of the area from light industrial to mixed commercial and residential use, the development of the park triggered a building bonanza and an increase in property values in the surrounding area, while also setting a model for adaptive reuse of the city's industrial infrastructure.

**Robert Hammond and Joshua David** 2012
Photograph by Dimitrios Kambouris

ABOVE
**The highline elevated railway before and after the creation of Highline Park**

## Preet Bharara
### (b. 1968)
### The Sheriff of Wall Street

In the aftermath of the 2008 mortgage crisis and financial meltdown—at a time when the ethics and practices of New York finance had come under scrutiny—U.S. Attorney Preet Bharara waged a war on insider trading and corruption, winning convictions of Wall Street executives and state officials.

Although some criticized the so-called "Sheriff of Wall Street" for focusing on insider trading rather than on the damaging fraud that led to the 2008 meltdown, Bharara argued that the evidence was not there to convict: "When you see a building go up in flames, you have to wonder if there's arson. Now, sometimes it's not arson, it's an accident. Sometimes it is arson, and you can't prove it."

**Preet Bharara** 2010
Photograph by Fred R. Conrad

ABOVE
**Preet Bharara announcing insider trading charges** 2011

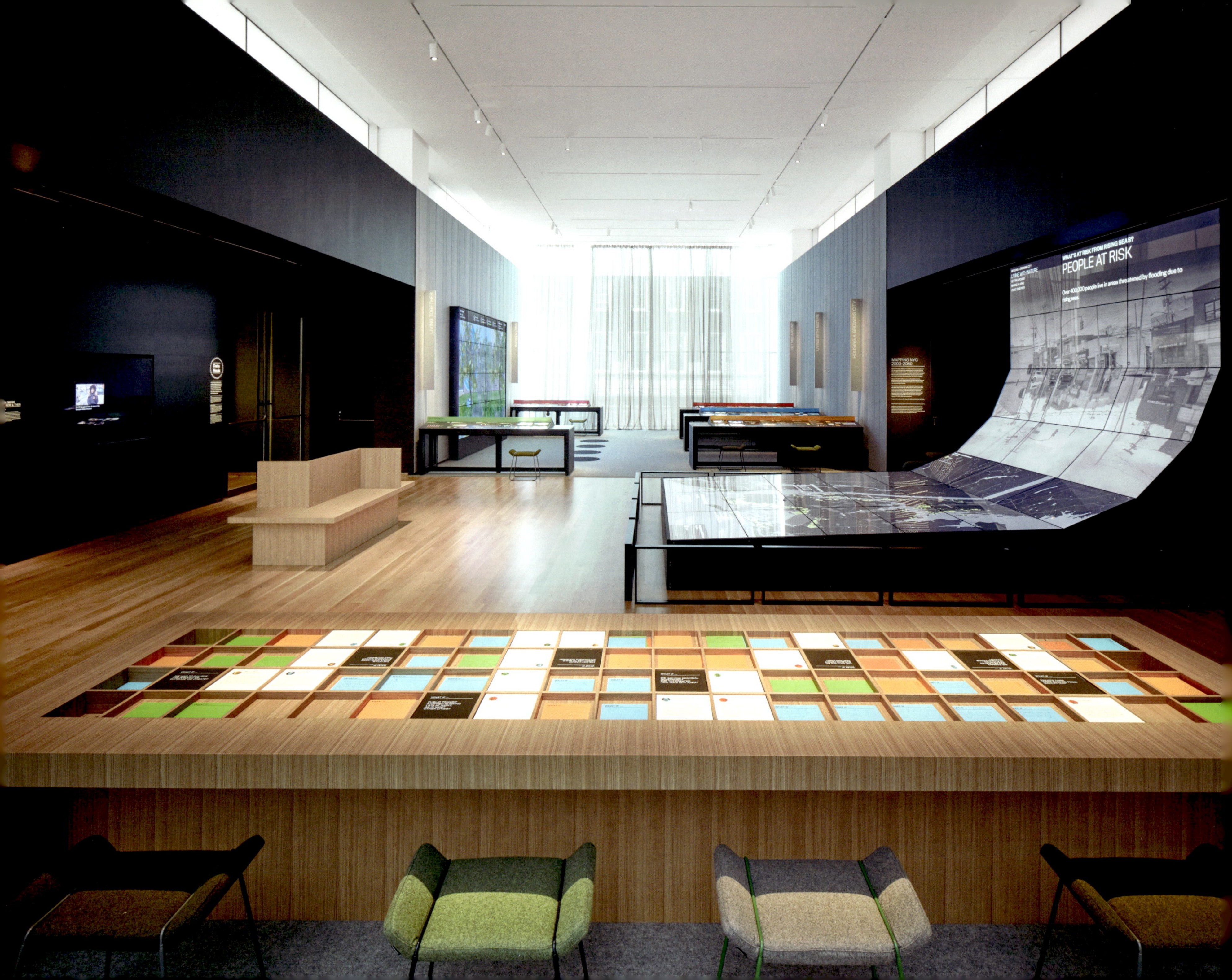

# INTO THE FUTURE...

themes of New York's history—the energy of its people and the creativity of their efforts to make this dense, diverse, intensely competitive place livable—will stretch long into the future. The investigation of the city's living legacy of money, diversity, density, and creativity continues in the Museum's innovative *Future City Lab*, the largest gallery of this three-part exhibition.

The Lab takes on five pressing challenges for New York in the coming generations: Housing a Growing City, Getting Around, Making a Living, Living Together, and Living with Nature. It shows that, as an iconic global city, New York is exceptional in many ways, but it also shares much with other cities as they face the 21st century. As the world becomes more urban and interconnected, the issues of modernizing and maintaining infrastructure, managing population growth, maintaining competitiveness in a global economy, fostering inclusivity, and transitioning to more sustainable and resilient systems are matters of deep importance for metropolitan life throughout the globe.

and visualizations of the most up-to-data about the city, the Lab features a wealth of information on the city and where it may be headed. But, true to its name, it is through participation that the Lab comes fully alive, as visitors pose their own provocative questions about the future and try their hands at interactive design challenges to address the challenges facing individual New York neighborhoods.

The Lab must therefore be experienced to be fully understood. But on the pages that follow, you can get a taste of the Lab by learning about the five challenges and hearing from some of the New Yorkers whose voices help to introduce the New York of today and tomorrow, drawn from video artist Neil Goldberg's commissioned piece for the Lab: *Then & Now & Then*.

OPPOSITE
**Installation views of the**
***Future City Lab***

Now Playing
Budget Impact
Environmental Benefit
Mobility
Safety
STAND HERE
to see yourself
in the future

WHAT IF ...

HOUSING A GROWING CITY
WHERE DO NEW YORKERS LIVE NOW?
MOSTLY LOW-RISE
While high-rise living is an iconic part of New York, most of the city is covered by single-family houses and walk-up apartment buildings. Only Manhattan is dominated by tall, elevator buildings.

# Where Does New York Go From Here?

These five challenges, explored in the *Future City Lab*, will impact how people will live and work in New York over the next 20 years.

## Housing a Growing City
How can we meet the housing needs of New Yorkers?

New York City's population is growing. It is already the largest U.S. city, with 8.5 million people in 2014, and the population is expected to pass 9 million by 2040. Growth is a sign of health, and as the population grows, areas of the city will become denser. How can we manage greater density and protect the quality of urban life? In a city with rising housing costs, how can we provide for this growing population and keep the city affordable for low- and moderate-income New Yorkers?

## Living with Nature
How can New York City enhance its natural environment and cope with climate change?

New York is more than its built environment: it is a complex set of ecosystems. A healthy environment and access to nature are critical to New Yorkers' quality of life. While there have been remarkable improvements in the city's ecology in recent decades, we face multiple threats from climate change, and as a water-bound city New York is especially vulnerable to rising sea levels. What can we do to protect and strengthen our city's relationship to nature?

## Getting Around
How can we make it easier for people to get into and around the city?

New York City is unique in the U.S. because most people do not use a car to get around. Its vast transit system is the lifeblood of the city. Public transit supports the city's density and reduces New Yorkers' carbon footprint. But the system is also challenged: it is aging, overcrowded, and costly to maintain and expand. Meanwhile, new ideas about transportation are changing the ways New Yorkers get around and the ways streets are used. What could the transit and streets of the future be like?

## Making a Living
What can we do to provide economic opportunities for the next generation?

People come to New York in search of jobs and opportunities to improve their lives and support their families. The city's economy is thriving, but many New Yorkers are left out. And the high cost of living in the city increases the need for new opportunities to give all New Yorkers the chance to prosper. How can we promote economic growth and mobility?

## Living Together
How can we foster a more inclusive city?

New York City is a microcosm of the world. It is the most diverse city in the U.S., and it has no majority group; its residents come from everywhere. New Yorkers mix every day in the city's streets, subways, and parks, but by many measures their lives remain separate, divided by income, race, and ethnicity. What can we do to dissolve lines that divide us while supporting the expression of diverse identities?

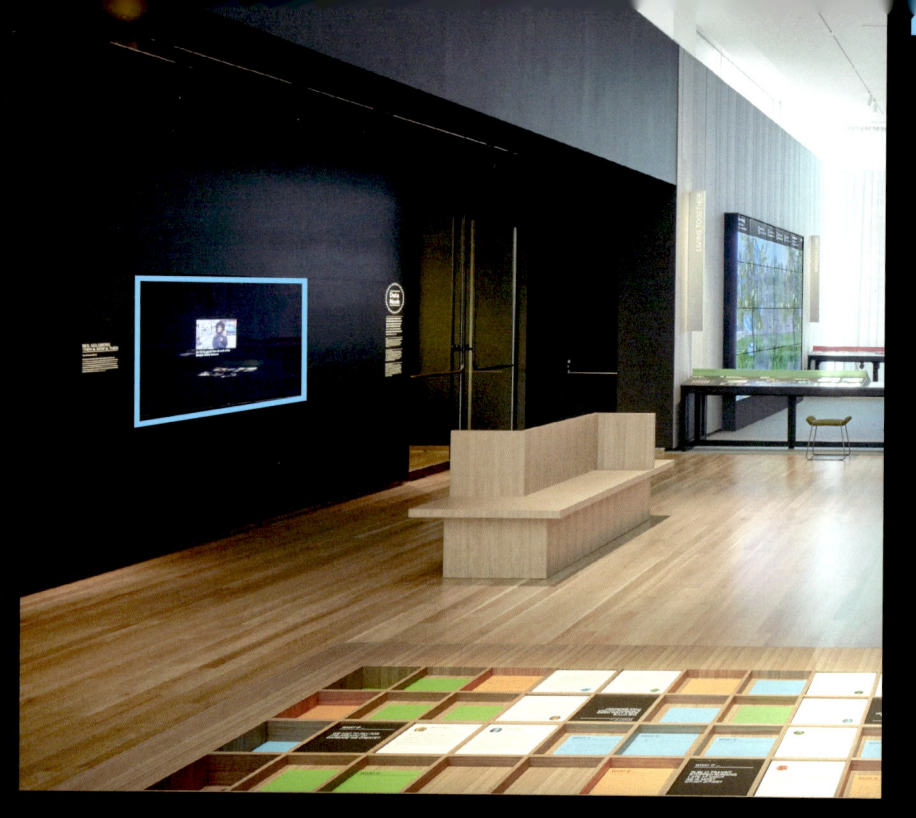

"It feels like one of the rights you have here as a citizen of New York is the phenomenon of friction and entanglement with people that are strangers to you." **Miguel**

### *Then & Now & Then* (2015–16)
Video by Neil Goldberg

*Then & Now & Then* is an artwork by the video artist Neil Goldberg commissioned for the *Future City Lab*. This 25-minute video explores how a variety of New Yorkers think about their city and their hopes and fears about its future. Goldberg interviewed more than 50 people living across the five boroughs to produce this polyphonic conversation; a selection of their thoughts are collected here.

"I think that energy of the margins and the center—that tension—is something that is really part of the core of what New York is about. Great artistic energy comes from that."

**John**

"I don't think I'm ever in as much of a hurry as I am when I'm in New York City. Because New York City has a way of making me late to everything. I've made rushing a part of who I am. I'm one of the fastest disabled people you'll ever chase down a crosswalk."

**Maysoon**

"New York City isn't passive-aggressive, like the West Coast is. It's aggressive-aggressive."

**Hari**

"The city is the continuum. We are not the continuum. We come and go, in this glorious, beautiful city that has been alive for a lot longer than we have, and that will continue to be alive after we're gone. … I'm really sorry that I didn't get to see the beautiful, wonderful things that were here in 1840. But you know what? I didn't. I got my things instead."

# Acknowledgments

Over 250 people participated in the creation of the exhibition *New York at Its Core* under the Museum directorships of Susan Henshaw Jones and Whitney Donhauser. I had the distinct honor of leading the project team alongside Project Director Susan Gail Johnson. Lead members were the late Hilary Ballon, the curator of the *Future City Lab*, along with Kubi Ackerman, Steven H. Jaffe, and Lilly Tuttle.

In addition to the advisory committees listed here and the many additional scholars who were generous with their time and expertise, we could not have completed this immense project without the invaluable assistance of Amelia Brackett, Camille Czerkowicz, Jessica Lautin, B.J. Lillis, Charlie Morgan, Brett Palfreman, and Shraddha Ramani. Key curatorial support came from our colleagues Donald Albrecht, Emily Chapin, Sean Corcoran, Phyllis Magidson, Sarah Seidman, Morgen Stevens-Garmon, Lindsay Turley, and many others, including all of the Museum's collections, exhibitions, and digital staff, with leadership from Todd Ludlam, Julius Quito, and Patricia Zedalis. We were aided by an army of talented scholarly content developers, interactive content assistants, and interns, who made possible the research that is reflected in the gallery and in these pages. The design teams of Studio Joseph, Local Projects, and Pentagram were true partners throughout the project.

The creation of this beautiful book was spearheaded by Susan Gail Johnson, with design by Pentagram. Special thanks goes to Michael Bierut, Britt Cobb and Katie Rominger of Pentagram for their creative work and to Miranda Hambro and Victoria Martens and the Museum's collections team for making the photography of the exhibition objects possible. Countless lenders and artists made their objects and images available and helped to bring the story of New York City's 400 years to life in these pages. They, along with the generous funders listed on the facing page, and the dedicated staff of the Museum, too many to name here, have my deepest thanks.

**Sarah M. Henry**
Deputy Director and Chief Curator

## Historical Advisors

Thomas Bender, NYU
Elizabeth S. Blackmar, Columbia University
Peter Derrick
Hasia R. Diner, NYU
Joshua Freeman, City University of New York
Evelyn Gonzalez, William Paterson University
Owen Gutfreund, City University of New York
Kenneth T. Jackson, Columbia University
Lisa Keller, SUNY-Purchase College
Thomas Kessner, City University of New York
Julia Ott, The New School
Carla Peterson, University of Maryland
Lynne Sagalyn, Columbia University
John Kuo Wei Tchen, NYU
Mike Wallace, City University of New York
Craig S. Wilder, MIT
Sean Wilentz, Rutgers University

## Advisors for *Future City Lab*

Gail Benjamin, Urban Land Use Institute
Vishaan Chakrabarti, Columbia University, Practice for Architecture and Urbanism
Owen Gutfreund, City University of New York
Jill Lerner, Kohn Pedersen Fox
Mitchell Moss, NYU
Charles J. O'Byrne, Related Companies
Jerilyn Perine, Citizens Housing and Planning Council
Lynne Sagalyn, Columbia University
Joseph J. Salvo, NYC Department of City Planning
Van C. Tran, Columbia University

# Funders

**New York at Its Core
is made possible by**

James G. Dinan and Elizabeth R. Miller
Pierre DeMenasce
The Thompson Family Foundation
Jerome L. Greene Foundation in honor of Susan Henshaw Jones
Heather and Bill Vrattos

Charina Endowment Fund
National Endowment for the Humanities
Citi
Zegar Family Foundation
Tracey and Kenneth A. Pontarelli
Hilary Ballon and Orin Kramer
Jill and John Chalsty
Dyson Foundation
The Robert A. and Elizabeth R. Jeffe Foundation
Valerie and Jack Rowe
Mary Ann and Bruno A. Quinson

Carnegie Corporation of New York
Booth Ferris Foundation
Institute of Museum and Library Services
The David Berg Foundation
The Joelson Foundation
The Hearst Foundations
Stephen and Stephanie Hessler
William and Elizabeth Kahane
James A. Lebenthal
John Strang Trust
An Anonymous Donor

Newton P. S. and Polly Merrill
Laura Lofaro Freeman and James L. Freeman
Cynthia Foster Curry
Stephen and Cynthia Ketchum
Robert and Carola Jain
Anna-Maria and Stephen Kellen Foundation
Todd DeGarmo/STUDIOS Architecture
Jim and Diane Quinn
Mitchell S. Steir/Savills Studley
Netherland-America Foundation
American Express Foundation
The Barker Welfare Foundation
Con Edison
Dutch Culture USA/Consulate General of the Netherlands in New York
Leslie and Mark Godridge
Lorna and Edwin Goodman
Kathy and Othon Prounis
Daryl Brown Uber/William E. Weiss Foundation

Ann and Adam Spence
The Ambrose Monell Foundation
Atran Foundation
Nancy and James Druckman
Tom and Deban Flexner
Budd and Jane Goldman
Jim Hanley/Taconic Builders Inc.
Sylvia Hemingway
Susan Jang and Kenneth E. Lee

Gurudatta and Margaret Nadkarni
Nixon Peabody LLP
Mr. and Mrs. Stanley DeForest Scott
Elizabeth Farran and W. James Tozer Jr.
John and Barbara Vogelstein Foundation

Greater Hudson Heritage Network
New York State Council on the Arts with the support of Governor Andrew M. Cuomo and the New York State Legislature
Melissa Mark-Viverito, Speaker, New York City Council
EvensonBest
Daniel R. Garodnick, New York City Council
Elizabeth Graziolo
David Guin and Kym McClain
Stanford and Sandra Ladner
Lucius N. Littauer Foundation
Mary Ann and Martin J. McLaughlin
Museum Association of New York
New Netherland Institute
Jane B. and Ralph A. O'Connell
Constance and Arthur Rosner
Sandy and Larry Simon
Taconic Charitable Foundation
New York Council for the Humanities
Benjamin J. Kallos, New York City Council
The Longhill Charitable Foundation

The Vidda Foundation
Kathleen S. Brooks Family Foundation
Whitney and Peter Donhauser
Ferris Foundation/ Susan Henshaw Jones
Jeffrey Tabak/ Miller Tabak + Co. LLC
The Trafelet Foundation
Mark Forrest Gilbertson

# Image Credits

Pages **6**: Dutch National Archives; **8**: Courtesy Jeff Chien-Hsing Liao; **12** (29.100.709), **18** (top, 29.100.792), **19** (top left, 29.100.2206), **32** (top, 29.100.3289B), **40** (29.100.1344), **47** (29.100.2302), **82** (29.100.2359): Museum of the City of New York, gift of J. Clarence Davies; **14** (top left): Skokloster Castle; **14** (middle left, 65.49.10), **14** (bottom left, 65.49.11), **14** (bottom right, 65.49.31): Museum of the City of New York, gift of Museum of the American Indian, Heye Foundation; **14** (top right), **18** (bottom): Metropolitan Museum of Art; **15** (top left): Museum of the City of New York, gift of Norton Merriman, Theodore Roosevelt Pelt, Rodney W. Williams, L. Gordon Hammersley, Herbert L. Satterlee and the Ship Model Society, M34.63; **15** (top right), **78** (top left), **117** (bottom left), **118** (bottom right), **127** (bottom), **164** (top left): New York City Municipal Archives; **15** (bottom): Collections of the Rock Foundation on loan to the Rochester Museum & Science Center, Rochester, NY; **16** (left), **16** (top center), **16** (center): New York State Museum, Albany, NY; **16** (top right), **46** (middle right): NYC Archaeological Repository: The Nan A. Rothschild Research Center / New York City Department of Parks and Recreation; **16** (middle right): Museum of the City of New York, Furniture and Decorative Arts Collection, F2012.64.383; **16** (bottom, with mat: 14 x 18 in., object #1885.5), **17** (bottom, 30 1/2 x 27 1/4 x 1 in., object #1951.414c), **27** (top left, image #26276g), **28** (43 x 65 x 2 in., object #1907.32), **39** (top right, image #92473d), **81** (top left, image #89193d): New-York Historical Society; **17** (top): Museum of the City of New York, gift of Mrs. Newbold Morris, 34.86.1; **19** (top right): Collegiate Church Corporation; **19** (bottom left): Museum of the City of New York, Postcard Collection, F2011.33.2123A; **19** (bottom right): The Rijksmuseum; **20**: Museum of the City of New York, bequest of Mrs. J. Insley Blair in memory of Mr. and Mrs. J. Insley Blair, 52.100.30; **22** (top): Museum of the City of New York, on Loan from the United States District Court for the Southern District of New York, L2966A-C; **22** (left): Bibliotheque Nationale, Paris, France / Archvies Charmet / Bridgeman Images; **22** (right): Museum of the City of New York, gift of Mrs. Andrew G. Carey, 56.267; **23** (top left): Museum of the City of New York, gift of Walter B. Cowperthwaite, 38.230.1; **23** (right), **26** (bottom): Columbia University, Rare Book and Manuscript Library; **23** (center): New York City Department of Parks & Recreation / Hendrick I. Lott House Preservation Association; **23** (bottom): Museum of the City of New York, gift of William Asadorian, 82.181.9; **24** (top, X2011.5.229), **49** (top left, X2010.11.14495), **60** (49.14), **68** (bottom, 75.50), **70** (top), **70** (bottom), **85** (X2010.11.8463), **89** (top, X2010.11.6513), **94** (center, X2010.11.13698), **110** (top left, 51.298), **135** (top right, X2010.11.4557), **140** (top center, X2010.11.4103), **154** (top left, X2010.11.6488), **171** (bottom right): Museum of the City of New York; **24** (middle left, 76.79), **58** (top, 95.54.15), **58** (bottom, 95.54.13), **91** (bottom right, 2011.5.3), **117** (bottom right, 85.138.4): Museum of the City of New York, museum purchase; **24** (center): Museum of the City of New York, gift of Mr. Lewis Gouverneur Morris, 58.30.1; **24** (bottom left): Museum of the City of New York, gift of Mrs. Lavinia Davis Downs, Edward Davis, Freda Davis, Campbell Davis, and Wendell Davis Jr., 76.107; **24** (bottom center, 49.82.28), **24** (middle right, 34.265), **25** (top right, 39.249): Museum of the City of New York, anonymous gift; **24** (bottom right): Museum of the City of New York, gift of Mr. and Mrs. George F. Baker, Jr., 49.22; **25** (top left): Museum of the City of New York, bequest of Mrs. Henry de Bevoise Schenck, 43.91.73; **25** (bottom): Museum of the City of New York, gift of the Brooklyn Volunteer Firemen's Association, 34.419.33; **26** (top): Library of Congress; **27** (top right), **97** (top right): American Jewish Historical Society, New York, NY and Boston, MA; **27** (bottom left): Museum of the City of New York, gift of William Hamilton Russell, 50.215.4; **27** (bottom right): Crystal Bridges Museum of American Art, Bentonville, Arkansas, 2005.8; **30** (top left): Museum of the City of New York, gift in memory of Justina de Peyster Martin, by her sister Estelle de Peyster Hosmer, 41.133.1; **30** (top right): Museum of the City of New York, gift of Mrs. Gordon Cadwalader, Mrs. John Wightman, and Mr. William L. Nicoll, 48.250.2; **30** (bottom left): Museum of the City of New York, gift of F.I. Hauptman, 37.352; **30** (bottom right): Museum of the City of New York, gift of Mr. Charles A. Dana, Jr., 82.13; **31**: Museum of the City of New York, gift of Mrs. Henry Wheeler de Forest in memory of her husband, Henry Wheeler de Forest, 54.209C-D; **32** (bottom left), **38** (bottom): Museum of the City of New York, gift of Mrs. Alexander Hamilton and General Pierpont Morgan Hamilton, 71.31.3; **32** (bottom right): Museum of the City of New York, gift of Colonel Le Roy Barton, 52.67.2; **33** (top): Museum of the City of New York, gift of the Avalon Foundation, 53.2; **33** (bottom left): Museum of the City of New York, gift of Miss Annie Doughty, 32.392.6; **33** (center), **33** (bottom), **154** (top right): Brooklyn Historical Society; **34**: Museum of the City of New York, gift of Mrs. Arthur H. Hall, 32.271.9; **35** (top left, 55.6.12), **53** (bottom right, 55.6.2): Museum of the City of New York, gift of Mrs. Francis P. Garvan; **35** (top right): Museum of the City of New York, gift of David M. Neuberger, 37.259.1; **35** (bottom): Museum of the City of New York, gift of Edward W.C. Arnold, 51.218; **36** (left, 59.117.1AB), **36** (right, 59.117.11AB): Museum of the City of New York, gift of the estate of Miss Mabel Choate; **37**: Image copyright © The Metropolitan Museum of Art, Image source: Art Resource, NY; **38** (top), **80** (top): Art and Picture Collection, The New York Public Library, Astor, Lenox and Tilden Foundations; **39** (top left), **39** (bottom left), **59** (bottom right), **71** (top left), **71** (bottom right), **75**, **78** (bottom), **80** (bottom), **91** (bottom left), **92**, **97** (top left), **99** (right), **103** (top left), **120** (top right), **123** (bottom right): Library of Congress, Prints and Photographs Division; **42**: Museum of the City of New York, gift of A. C. Delacroix, X2011.40.2; **43**: Office of the Manhattan Borough President Gale A. Brewer; **44** (left): Museum of the City of New York, gift of Cornelius von Erden Mitchell, Esq., 38.261.1; **44** (right): Museum of the City of New York, bequest of Gherardi Davis in memory of his wife Alice Davis, 41.304.4A-B; **45** (top): Museum of the City of New York, gift of Helen Tower Wilson, 2002.35.11; **45** (bottom left): Museum of the City of New York, gift of James Speyer, 38.88; **45** (bottom right): Museum of the City of New York, gift of U.S. General Services Administration, 2007.11.10; **46** (top left and right): Museum of the City of New York, gift of Mr. Leonard S. Grime, 74.145A-D; **46** (middle left), **117** (top right): Rare Book Division, The New York Public Library, Astor, Lenox and Tilden Foundations; **46** (bottom), **113** (top right): Lionel Pincus and Princess Firyal Map Division, The New York Public Library, Astor, Lenox and Tilden Foundations; **48** (top), **49** (bottom right), **91** (top right): Miriam and Ira D. Wallach Division of Art, Prints and Photographs, Print Collection, The New York Public Library, Astor, Lenox and Tilden Foundations; **48** (bottom): Courtesy of the Kansas State Historical Society; **49** (top right): Historic Map Works LLC / Getty Images; **49** (bottom left), **52** (bottom), **71** (top right), **81** (top right), **81** (bottom right), **108** (top right), **138** (bottom): The Internet Archive; **50**: Museum of the City of New York, gift of Mrs. Robert M. Littlejohn, 33.169.1; **52** (top left): Museum of the City of New York, gift of William Mcfee, M38.7; **52** (top right): New-York Historical Society Library; **53** (top): Museum of the City of New York, gift of Carl F. Grieshaber, 32.483; **53** (bottom left): Harvard Theater Collection, Houghton Library, Harvard University; **54** (top left, 2007.11.4-8), **54** (top right, 2007.11.3), **54** (middle left, 2007.11.1), **54** (middle right, 2007.11.13), **54** (bottom, 2007.11.14): Museum of the City of New York, gift of U.S. General Services Administration; **54** (top center): Museum of the City of New York, gift of Miss Cora B. Rugg, 32.288; **55**: Museum of the City of New York, gift of Lou Sepersky and Leida Snow, 97.227.3; **56**, **67** (top left), **79** (top right), **79** (bottom left and right), **96**, **99** (left), **108** (bottom), **110** (top right), **113** (top left), **126** (top right), **127** (center), **138** (top left), **141** (center), **157** (top right), **165** (top), **165** (bottom), **174** (bottom right): private collection; **57** (top left): Museum of the City of New York, gift of Bryman Ridges, 50.81.1; **57** (top right): Museum of the City of New York, gift of Roosevelt Memorial Association, 41.366.30; **57** (bottom left, 49.66.20AB), **57** (bottom right, 49.66.2): Museum of the City of New York, gift of Colonel and Mrs. LeRoy Barton; **59** (top left): The New-York Historical Society / Getty Images; **59** (top right): Library of Congress, Rare Book and Special Collections Division; **59** (bottom left): Amistad Research Center, New Orleans; **62** (top): Used with permission of NYSE Group, Inc. Courtesy New York Stock Exchange Archives; **62** (bottom): Museum of the City of New York, gift of Mrs. George W. Wardner, 81.58.1; **63**: Museum of the City of New York, gift of Henry Fendall, 43.420A-C; **64**: Museum of the City of New York, gift of Mrs. Rosemary Haywood, 69.126.2AB; **65** (93.1.1.18072), **66** (top, 93.1.1.17313), **79** (top left, 93.1.1.18325), **88** (top left, 93.1.1.17115), **103** (top right,

93.1.3.32): Museum of the City of New York, gift of Percy Byron; **66** (bottom): Museum of the City of New York, gift of Union Theological Seminary, 53.296AB; **67** (top right): Museum of the City of New York, gift of Jacob A. Voice, 35.30.4; **67** (bottom left, 90.13.1.149), **68** (top left, 90.13.1.158), **68** (center, 90.13.1.151), **69** (90.13.1.126), **90** (top left, 90.13.2.139), **90** (top right, 90.13.2.138), **98** (right, 90.13.3.122): Museum of the City of New York, gift of Roger William Riis; **67** (bottom right): Museum of the City of New York, gift of the Estate of Mrs. Pauline Stein, 48.108.14AB; **68** (top right, F2012.58.1059), **71** (bottom left, F2012.58.1269), **103** (bottom left, F2012.58.216), **118** (bottom left, F2012.58.1454): Museum of the City of New York, Portrait Archives; **72**: Museum of the City of New York, gift of Mrs. William B. Miles, 32.275.2; **74** (top left): Museum of the City of New York, gift of the Dacotah Prairie Museum, X2011.34.2160; **74** (top right): Museum of the City of New York, gift of Miss Isabel Johnson, X2011.34.2164; **74** (bottom left): Collection of Yeshiva University Museum; **74** (bottom right): Museum of the City of New York, Collection on Yiddish Theater, F2012.63.524; **76**: Shorpy; **77** (top left): Museum of the City of New York, gift of the collection of Robert R. Preato, 91.76.23; **77** (top right): Division of Home and Community Life, National Museum of American History, Smithsonian Institution; **77** (bottom): Museum of the City of New York, gift of William J. Hanley, 34.404.27; **78** (top right): From the Collections of The Henry Ford, gift of the Edison Pioneers; **81** (bottom left): National Portrait Gallery, Smithsonian Institution; **84** (top): Museum of the City of New York, gift of Mr. Shirley C. Burden, 57.15.10; **84** (bottom left): Museum of the City of New York, gift of The Pierrepont Family of Brooklyn, 41.35.133; **84** (center. 85.83.9), **84** (bottom center, 85.83.14), 84 (bottom right, 85.83.8): Museum of the City of New York, gift of City of New York Department of Transportation; **86**: Museum of the City of New York, gift of Sonia and Alexander Alland Jr., 93.91.437; **87** (top left): Museum of the City of New York, gift of the Estate of Townsend Morgan, 41.111.3; **87** (top center): Museum of the City of New York, gift of Estella Cameron Silo in memory of her husband, James Patrick Silo, 33.386A-B; **87** (top right): Museum of the City of New York, gift of Samuel T. Staines, 42.421; **87** (bottom): Museum of the City of New York, gift of George S. Hellman, 36.319; **88** (top right): Museum of the City of New York, gift of Dr. Ann W. Shyne, 67.17.1A-B; **88** (bottom left): Museum of the City of New York, gift of Henry A. Ahrens, Esq., 42.288; **88** (middle right): Museum of the City of New York, gift of Mrs. J. Clyne, 62.51.3; **89** (bottom left), **106** (bottom): Music Division, The New York Public Library, Astor, Lenox and Tilden Foundations; **89** (bottom right): Museum of the City of New York, gift of John Leibowitz, 34.106; **91** (top right): Museum of the City of New York, gift of Mr. Shirley C. Burden, 57.15.17; **94** (top left, X2011.34.324), **94** (top right, X2011.34.311): Museum of the City of New York, gift of Mr. Donald Beggs; **94** (bottom): © The Morgan Library & Museum, AZ148, photography by Graham S. Haber, 2016; **95**: The Philadelphia Museum of Art / Art Resource, NY /

© Aperture Foundation Inc., Paul Strand Archive; **97** (bottom): Collection of Russ & Daughters; **98** (top left): General Records of the Department of Labor, National Archives; **98** (bottom): Museum of the City of Naew York, gift of Mr. John Gregg, 73.215.2; **100** (top left): Museum of the City of New York, gift of Lt. George Eysser, 76.102.3; **100** (top right, 45.117.33), **101** (45.117.260): Museum of the City of New York, gift of The Family of Governor Alfred E. Smith; **100** (bottom), **119** (bottom), **145** (top right): The La Guardia and Wagner Archives, La Guardia Community College / The City University of New York; **102** (top): Museum of the City of New York, gift of Louis J. Arata, X2010.11.5023; **102** (bottom): Linda Lear Center for Special Collections and Archives, Connecticut College; **103** (bottom right): Schomburg Center for Research in Black Culture, Jean Blackwell Hutson Research and Reference Division, The New York Public Library, Astor, Lenox and Tilden Foundations; **104, 108** (center): Schomburg Center for Research in Black Culture, Photographs and Prints Division, The New York Public Library, Astor, Lenox and Tilden Foundations; **106** (left): Museum of the City of New York, gift of Mrs. William Van Wyck, 54.373; **106** (right): Museum of the City of New York, gift of Mrs. Rudolph Weld, 35.51.1; **107** (top left): Museum of the City of New York, gift of Mrs. W.G. Hassler, 2001.35.1.120; **107** (bottom left): The Miriam and Ira D. Wallach Division of Art, Prints and Photographs, Photography Collection, The New York Public Library, Astor, Lenox and Tilden Foundations; **107** (right): Museum of the City of New York, gift of Shreve, Lamb & Harmon, 38.407; **108** (top left): Museum of the City of New York, gift of Mrs. Lucy B. L'Engle, 71.25.10; **109**: Museum of the City of New York, gift of Ms. Barbara S. Doty, 2002.108.16; **110** (bottom): Museum of the City of New York, gift of Carl Van Vechten, 42.316.393 / © The Van Vechten Trust; **111** (left): Museum of the City of New York, gift of Mr. Elisha Dyer, 53.25.2; **111** (center): Museum of the City of New York, gift of Miss Adele Spaulding, 46.393.6; **111** (top and middle right): Museum of the City of New York, gift of Mrs. William B. Remington, 56.71.73; **111** (bottom): Museum of the City of New York, gift of Ms. Claire Lewis, 91.102.2A-C; **112** (top), **113** (bottom left), **141** (top left): Bettmann / Getty Images; **112** (bottom): Hulton Archive / Getty Images; **113** (bottom right): Museum of the City of New York, gift of J. Clarence Davies, Inc., 89.56; **114**: Museum of the City of New York, gift of the Metropolitan Museum of Art, 49.282.22; **116** (top left): Museum of the City of New York, gift of Federal Works Agency, Work Projects Administration, Federal Art Project, 43.131.1.40; **116** (top right), **123** (bottom left): GRANGER - All Rights Reserved; **116** (bottom): Museum of American Finance, NYC; **117** (top left): Tamiment Library and Robert F. Wagner Labor Archives; **118** (top left): Associated Press; **118** (top right): Museum of the City of New York, gift of Mary and Helen O'Sullivan In Memory of Robert Moses, 94.64.7A-D; **119** (top left), **119** (top right), **127** (top right), **140** (top right): MTA Bridges and Tunnels Special Archive; **120** (top left): Museum of the City of New York, gift of

Samuel H. Gottscho, 88.1.1.4653; **120** (bottom left): New York City Department of Parks & Recreation; **120** (bottom right): Museum of the City of New York, Manuscripts and Ephemera Collection, F2012.18.240; **121**: New York City Parks Photo Archive; **122** (top): General Research Division, The New York Public Library, Astor, Lenox and Tilden Foundations; **122** (bottom): William C. Shrout / Getty Images; **123** (top left): Museum of the City of New York, gift of Mr. Rollin Kirby, 43.366.268; **123** (top right): Department of Special Collections and University Archives, Marquette University Libraries; **124**: Library of Congress, William P. Gottlieb Collection, Prints and Photographs Division; **126** (top left): Museum of the City of New York, gift of Thelma Hall and Lisa Dawn Simmons, 98.46.5 (20 1/2 x 27 in., 52.1 x 68.6 cm) / © The Estate of Alice Neel / Courtesy David Zwirner, New York / London; **126** (middle left), **126** (bottom): Louis Armstrong House Museum; **126** (middle right): Courtesy Jerry Stern; **127** (top left): Museum of the City of New York, gift of Frank Paulin, 93.80.18; **128** (left): Digital Image © The Museum of Modern Art / Licensed by SCALA / Art Resource, NY / © 2017 The Pollock-Krasner Foundation / Artists Rights Society (ARS), New York; **128** (right): Cecil Beaton / Vogue / Conde Nast / © 2017 The Pollock-Krasner Foundation / Artists Rights Society (ARS), New York; **129**: Pollock Krasner House and Study Center, East Hampton, New York; **130**: Courtesy Art Kane Archive, NYC; **131** (top): Allan Grant / Getty Images; **131** (bottom): Institute of Jazz Studies, Rutgers University-Newark, gift of Roy Eldridge, Roy Eldridge Collection; **132** (left): Museum of the City of New York, gift of Mrs. Peter Baumberger, 84.14.23AB; **132** (top right): Museum of the City of New York, gift of Mr. Gene Moore, 97.125.2; **132** (bottom): Museum of the City of New York, gift of Mrs. Betty Eastham, 99.37.1; **133**: Courtesy Everett Collection / © Paramount Pictures Corp.; **134** (top): Rockefeller Archive Center; **134** (bottom): Bernard Gotfryd / Getty Images; **135** (top left), **135** (bottom left): The Antonia Pantoja Papers, Archives of the Puerto Rican Diaspora, Centro de Estudios Puertorriqueños, Hunter College, CUNY; **135** (bottom right): Lord & Taylor; **136**: Museum of the City of New York, gift of David M. Bernstein, 2001.51.5; **138** (top right): George Kirschner Collection on the American Safety Razor Corporation Strike of 1954, Archives Service Center, University of Pittsburgh; **139**: Museum of the City of New York, gift of Ms. Soraya Betterton, 2014.88.5 / © Danny Lyon / Magnum Photos; **140** (left): © 2017 Morgan Art Foundation / Artists Rights Society (ARS), New York; **140** (center): Collection 9/11 Memorial Museum, gift of Joseph David Kentarontie Rice, Kahnawake Mohawk Native Ironworker; **140** (bottom center): Walter Daran / Getty Images; **141** (top right): Buyenlarge / Getty Images; **141** (bottom): Brooklyn Public Library – Brooklyn Collection; **142, 143** (bottom), **154** (bottom), **157** (bottom left): Fred W. McDarrah / Getty Images; **142** (top left): Museum of the City of New York, gift of the Estate of Ruby Bailey, 2004.41.30; **143** (top right), **145** (top left): Bedford-Stuyvesant Restoration Corporation; **144** (top): Jill Freedman / Getty Images; **144** (bottom): Jack Mitchell / Getty Images; **145** (bottom left): Courtesy Celeste Lumpkins-Moses, Granddaughter of Elsie

191

Richardson & Family; **145** (bottom right), **148** (left), **151** (top right), **164** (center): New York Daily News Archive / Getty Images; **146**, **154** (middle right): Courtesy Allan Tannenbaum; **148** (right): Hostos Community College Archives and Special Collections / The City University of New York; **149**: Museum of the City of New York, gift of Mr. Bruno Lucchesi, 94.80.1 / Courtesy Bruno Lucchesi; **150** (left), **150** (right): Collection of the New York City Fire Museum; **151** (top left): The Jack Bigel Collection, Newman Library, Baruch College; **151** (bottom): Museum of the City of New York, bequest of Anthony Accurso, 90.41.20; **153**: Courtesy Joe Conzo Jr.; **152** (top left): Cornell Hip Hop Collection, Cornell University Library; **152** (top right): Museum of the City of New York, gift of Martin Wong, 94.114.333 / Keith Haring artwork © Keith Haring Foundation; **152** (bottom): Courtesy Henry Chalfant; **155** (top left): Museum of the City of New York, gift of Mr. Coy L. Ludwig & H. Daniel Smith, 97.121.1; **155** (top right): Allan Tannenbaum / Getty Images; **155** (bottom): Museum of the City of New York, gift of Stephen Desroches, 2015.7.2; **156** (top): Courtesy Stephen Burrows; **156** (bottom): Charles Tracy Estate; **157** (top left): Baruch College Archives; **157** (bottom right): Michael Ochs Archive / Getty Images; **158**: © Chien-Chi Chang / Magnum Photos; **160** (top left): Courtesy Oliver Stone; **160** (top right): Museum of the City of New York, gift of Bloomingdale's, 96.128.1; **160** (bottom): Bloomberg, L.P.; **161**: Digital Image © The Museum of Modern Art / Licensed by SCALA / Art Resource, NY / Courtesy Milton Glaser; **162**: Museum of the City of New York, 91.14.6 / Courtesy Margaret Morton; **163** (top left): Clayton Patterson – Clayton Archive; **163** (top right): Museum of the City of New York, gift of Mark Ouderkirk, X2011.12.133 / Keith Haring artwork © Keith Haring Foundation; **163** (bottom): Museum of the City of New York, gift of Leon Constantiner, 98.38.2; **164** (top right), **164** (bottom right), **175**: Courtesy Joshua Simpson; **164** (middle right): Angela Jimenez / The New York Times / Redux; **164** (bottom left), **171** (top right): Courtesy Joanna Chan; **165** (center): Spencer Platt / Getty Images; **166** (center): Andria Patino / Alamy Stock Photo; **166** (top right): Museum of the City of New York, gift of Andreas Feininger, 90.40.25; **166** (bottom): Central Park Conservancy and Sara Cedar Miller; **166** (top left): Museum of The City of New York, gift of the Buena Vista Theatrical Group, Ltd., 2004.1.1; **167**: Scott J. Ferrell / Congressional Quarterly / Alamy Stock Photo; **168**: © Joseph Rodriguez; **170** (top): Ron Frehm / Associated Press: **170** (bottom): Sarah Krulwich / The New York Times / Redux; **171** (top left): Julio Donoso / Getty Images; **171** (bottom left): Richard Drew / Associated Press; **172**: Courtesy Paul Lurrie; **174** (top left): Museum of the City of New York, gift of Blair Davis, 2013.3.2.1753; **174** (top right): William Pedersen / Kohn Pedersen Fox Associates; **174** (bottom left), **177**: *New York Magazine* / New York Media; **176** (top left): Courtesy Geoffrey Raymond; **176** (right): Museum of the City of New York, gift of Andrea Renner, 2016.21.4; **176** (bottom left): Keith Bedford / The New York Times / Redux; **178** (top): Tribeca Film Festival; **178** (bottom): Eric Ryan Anderson / Getty Images; **179** (top left): Stacy Walsh Rosentock / Alamy Stock Photo; **179** (top left): Maremagnum / Getty Images; **179** (top right): Bloomberg / Getty Images; **179** (bottom left): Dimitrios Kambouris / Getty Images; **179** (bottom right): Fred R. Conrad / The New York Times / Redux; **180**, **186**: Thomas Loof / Museum of the City of New York; **183** (all): Christiane Patic / Local Projects; **184** (left), **185** (center): Shutterstock; **184** (right): Courtesy Keith Michael; **185** (left): Courtesy Matt Saacke; **185** (right): Courtesy P. Lem; **187** (all): Courtesy Neil Goldberg